CRAFT DESIGN AND TECHNOLOGY

A COMPLETE COURSE FOR GCSE

STEWART DUNN

UNWIN HYMAN

Preface

Craft, Design and Technology: a Complete Course for GCSE follows on from the book **An Introduction to Craft, Design and Technology** by the same author. It provides all the information needed to meet the CDT GCSE requirements of all the examination boards. The book is an 'in depth' core text for GCSE that can be used for courses in CDT: Design and Realisation, CDT: Technology, and CDT: Design and Communication.

The book is user friendly for teacher and student alike, providing the following features: back cover thumb index for quick access; use of two colours throughout to clarify and simplify explanations, with full colour in the Appearance and the Graphical Communication sections; an Examination Guide and Model Marking Scheme to help candidates prepare for examinations.

Activities and revision questions suitable for class work or homework appear on each page, and there are examination-type questions at the end of each section. Throughout, the approach is a visual one, and a systems approach is used where possible, for example in the Electronics section. Hundreds of ideas are given for project work, and mini courses within the main text are identified by colour boxes.

The content of the book has been determined by the Examination Board syllabuses, but the amount of space given to each topic was influenced by what pupils actually need when carrying out projects and homework.

I hope your enjoyment in using this book is as great as mine has been in testing the circuits, the programs, and in developing the EZI-DUN system, intended to make life easier for the hard-pressed teacher and student alike.

Stewart Dunn

The author is at the forefront of technology teaching and has taught and examined all the main subject areas of Craft, Design and Technology to examination level. He has been on numerous advisory panels and has run in-service courses. He is presently involved in the development of the new technology teaching system called EZI-DUN Construction System that is illustrated in this book on pages 11, 12, 15, 31, 34, 92, 93, 103 and 130. Mr Dunn would like to hear from anybody interested in helping develop this system via the publishers Unwin Hyman Limited.

Acknowledgements

I would like to thank all those who have helped in any way with the production of this book. Thanks go in particular to Maja Dunn, Mark Dunn, Alan Dunn, Jennifer Dunn, Stanley Green, Jan Shimmin, Graham Keyworth and Geoff Bobb, who have helped with checking text and giving all sorts of help and advice too numerous to mention. Thanks also to CDT advisers, headteachers, teachers and friends who have helped.

I would particularly like to acknowledge the following firms that have helped either by providing photographs or equipment to photograph.

Stewart Dunn

Commotion and Vento Solenoids Ltd, from which EZI-DUN Construction System is available

Page iv, picture of Elektron For more details of electric vehicles and race meetings etc, contact:
The Battery Vehicle Society,
13 Golden Sq,
London W1R 3A6

Pages iv and 92
Trekker from:
Clwyd Technics,
Antelope Industrial Estate,
Rhydymwyn,
nr. Mold,
Clwyd CH7 5JH

Pages 15, 31 40 and 134
LEGO® UK Ltd,
Education Division,
Ruthin Rd,
Wrexham,
Clwyd LL13 7TQ

Pages 31, 93, 130
Commotion,
241 Green St,
Enfield,
London EN3 7TD
(technology supplies)

Pages 31 and 103
Most of the parts used in the two photographs are available from:
Vento Solenoids Ltd,
Kiln Farm,
Milton Keynes MK11 3HA

Page 33
C R Clarke & Co (UK) Ltd,
Unit 3,
Betws Industrial Park,
Foundary Rd,
Ammanford,
Dyfed SA18 2LS
(plastics equipment)

Page 34
CNC milling machine and training lathe from:
Boxford Ltd,
Wheatley,
nr. Halifax
Yorkshire HX3 5AF

Page 54
Staedtler drawing equipment from:
Staedtler (UK) Ltd,
Pontyclun,
Mid Glamorgan CF7 8YJ

Page 97
Photoelastic stress photo from:
Sharples Stress Engineers Ltd,
Unit 331,
Walton Summit Centre,
Bamber Bridge,
Preston,
Lancs PR5 8AR

Page 130
Denford Machine Tools Ltd,
Birds Royd,
Brighouse,
Yorkshire HD6 1NB

Most of the models were made and photographed by the author.

Published in 1989 by
UNWIN HYMAN LIMITED
15/17 Broadwick Street
London W1V 1FP

Illustrated by RDL Artset Ltd
Front cover design by Colin Lewis
Typeset by MS Filmsetting Limited, Frome, Somerset
Produced in Hong Kong by Colorcraft Ltd.

British Library Cataloguing in Publication Data

Dunn, Stewart, *1947–*
    Craft, design and technology:
    a complete course for GCSE.
    1. Design – For schools
    I. Title
    745.4

ISBN 0-7135-2802-8

CONTENTS

An electric racing car - the body was vacuum formed and then the details added.

Perran Newman of the Battery Vehicle Society racing 'Elektron' at Duxford Airfield.

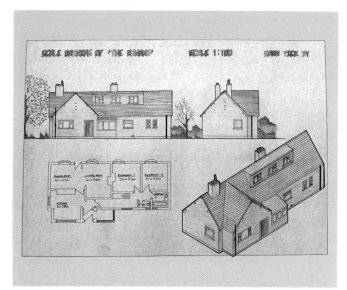

A pupil's home, drawn by Sara Vick in orthographic projection with an isometric drawing added later.

Computer Aided Design to design a printed circuit board. A utility program for AMX Super Art by Clwyd Technics.

NOTES TO THE TEACHER

EZI-DUN Construction System used in this book*

In the course of writing the electronics section of this book, it was necessary for the author to carefully test and select circuits. Over the years the author has tried and tested nearly every kit on the market and found them all wanting in some way. This situation led to the development of the EZI-DUN Construction System that overcomes nearly all of the problems normally encountered. It has the following merits:

- It is a very versatile electrics/electronics/micro-electronics/computer interface construction system that is very quick to assemble and dismantle, easy to use and to adapt as required.
- It is non-dedicated, allowing all popular construction kits to be used in conjunction with it.
- It allows electronics/mechanisms/structures to be incorporated on the board; individual components and/or systems boards can be used directly as required.
- It can be incorporated into mobile projects (eg vehicles).

- The joints require no soldering – the reliable sockets require only single strand wire.
- The boards are modular and can be electrically linked and/or bolted together, allowing very complex circuits to be assembled.
- The circuits when assembled very closely resemble standard theoretical schematic circuit diagrams.
- It allows for true 'open ended problem solving' when used with other popular construction kits and equipment.
- It can be used by ten-year-old children and above and is ideally suited for secondary school and tertiary ages.
- The standard kit is suitable for the Electronics part of the GCSE Technology syllabus.

Computer Interfaces

The Basic programs used in this book assume the User Port is being addressed. Some interfaces also use the Printer Port.

The author mainly uses the Pilot One interface and the Beasty control interface (from Commotion) for programs in Basic. The LEGO® interface and Barnet Box (from Commotion) were also used, but with their own Logo-like programs.

*The EZI-DUN system is patent pending.

SAFETY

GENERAL SAFETY RULES IN CDT

- **Ask if unsure.**
- Wear **apron, goggles, strong shoes** and other **safety clothing** as and when needed. If you have **long hair** it needs to be tied up.
- **Ties** and other **loose clothing** must be either removed or tucked in.
- Do **not fool about** in the workshop/studio.
- Do **not rush about** – walk.
- Do **not interfere with other people's work**.
- Tidy tools and materials away after use.
- Wear **goggles** when using machines or when dust is likely to get in your eyes.
- Use a **face mask** if working conditions are dusty.
- Report any **breakages** at once.
- **Stop buttons** are for **emergency** use only.
- **Sharp edged** tools such as chisels must be handled carefully, keeping both hands behind the blade at all times.
- **Clamp** your workpiece firmly when drilling or turning down on a lathe etc.
- **Paints** and **resins** can cause an awful mess. **Plan ahead** and work on a sheet of polythene or newspaper in a well ventilated place.
- Be specially careful if **acids** are used – ask your teacher about the special dangers involved.

FIRST AID

All injuries **must** be reported to the teacher who will advise on what has to be done. **Do** you know where your **First Aid box** is?

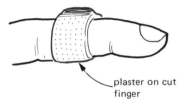

plaster on cut finger

FIRST AID

Below are some basic first aid measures you should know about.

Burns – Place in cold running water for at least 10 minutes then add a medicated cream.

Severe Bleeding – Try to raise the cut part above heart level to reduce bleeding for example lift a bleeding leg up with the patient lying down.

Fainting – Lay patient down to increase blood flow to the head (lifting the legs up will help).

Eyes – If something gets in your eye, try to wash it out with an 'eye bath' rather than rubbing your eye. If **acids**, **alkalies** or a **catalyst**, such as **organic peroxide**, gets in your eyes, **you MUST see a doctor or an eye specialist without delay.**

Electric Shock
Turn the power off, lay the person down and, if necessary, try **artificial respiration** until a doctor arrives.

SAFETY RULES

WEAR SAFETY CLOTHING
DO NOT FOOL ABOUT
BE TIDY
WORK SENSIBLY
REPORT ACCIDENTS
ASK IF UNSURE

goggles

long hair tied up

tie tucked (or removed)

loose jewellery removed

apron

strong shoes

face mask

leather gloves

WHAT SAFETY FACTORS ARE WRONG?

DON'T USE THIS WINDOW

ACID

DESIGN SHEET

PAINT

QUESTIONS/EXERCISES

① Design a **'Safety Rules'** notice for a general workshop using not more than 30 words.

② What action should be taken if you had: (a) a **burn**, (b) something in your **eye**, (c) an **electric shock**?

③ Draw a person wearing **five pieces of safety clothing**.

SAFETY WITH MACHINES

Machines can be very dangerous if care is not taken in their use. **Never use a machine until you have been instructed in its safe use.** Check with your teacher every time you want to use a machine in case it has been set up for a particular purpose (speed and tools may have been selected for a special reason etc). Some machines may only be operated by CDT-trained teachers eg the circular saw and a machine planer.

General rules

- Only **one person per machine**.
- **Safety guards** and goggles **must** be used.
- **Double-check** before starting a machine.
- **Tidy up** after use.
- **Do not leave a machine switched on and unattended** at any time.
- Use the foot switches, if they are supplied.

Speed of a machine

The speed that a machine spindle turns must be considered carefully – ask for help if needed.
The general rule is:
Large holes being drilled, or large diameters being turned in a lathe, require **slower spindle speeds**.

The **material** being drilled or turned also has to be considered; for example brass can be drilled faster than steel.

Drilling machine

- **Hold the work firmly** – Machine vice or clamp.
- Ensure drill is **central and tight**.
- Remove **chuck key** before starting.
- Use **guards** and **goggles** provided.

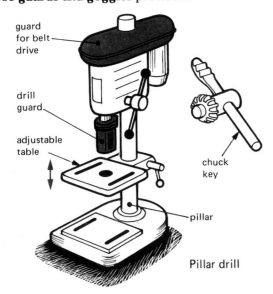

Pillar drill

Notes on drilling:
Centre punch metal before drilling. Support **thin metal** with a piece of scrap wood underneath. Withdraw the drill occasionally when drilling a deep hole to remove swarf and clear the drill flutes.

Heating (eg brazing hearth)

Plan ahead so as to avoid too much movement (eg have the flux and brazing rod ready if brazing).
Use the **extractor fans** if fumes build up.

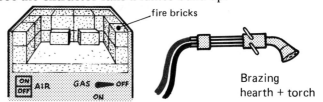

Brazing hearth + torch

Polishing machine (buffer)

- **Never** hold your work in your apron or other loose clothing.
- Use the **bottom quarter** of the polishing wheel nearest to you. Never use the top half.
- Beware of sharp corners catching on the wheel.

Lathes

- **Hold the work close to the chuck**.
- **Hold the work firmly** – If the work is long, extra support will be needed.
- Your teacher may need to **check** before turning the lathe on.
- Remove the **chuck key** before turning on.
- Ensure **cutting tools are set at centre height**.

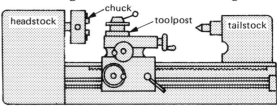

Casting

Casting must only be carried out under strict teacher supervision with all the leather safety clothing on – An explosion can result if the proper precautions are not taken. (Oil bound sand is safer than other types.)

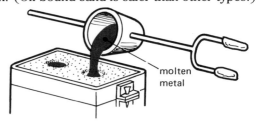

Abrasive wheel (sanding disc)

- Use the **dust extractor** and wear **goggles**.

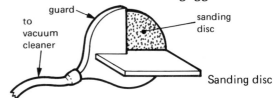

Sanding disc

QUESTIONS/EXERCISES

① What **five general safety rules** would you use if writing a 'machines safety' notice for a general purpose workshop?
② Make a **safety notice for a drilling machine** which is to be placed next to the drilling machine.
③ What special safety precautions need to be considered when using: (a) **Brazing hearth**, (b) **Lathe**, (c) **Polishing (or buff) machine**?

Electrical safety

Electricity can be very dangerous. The danger will depend on the **voltage** supply and the **current** flow available. **Mains electricity** (240 volts) is especially dangerous unless a very sensitive **earth leakage circuit breaker** is available. They are now becoming more widely available from DIY shops. Small **low voltage batteries** as used in small radios and stereos are safe to handle.

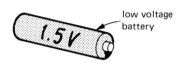

low voltage battery

Mains electricity

All equipment must have:
- The **correct size fuse** (see calculation below).
- **Good electrical insulation** – **Portable equipment** such as electric drills are now made **double insulated** and do not require an **earth** wire.
  The double insulated symbol as found on equipment.
- 110 or 120 volt **mains electricity**, being safer, is becoming standard practice for use on building sites and some workshops.
- Keep away from **wet areas**.
- Any **home made equipment** needs to be checked by a qualified electrician before use.

Fuse calculation example

What is the correct fuse for a **mains (240 V) hairdrier** rated at 720 watts?

Answer – Using the following formula

$$\text{Current (amperes)} = \frac{\text{power (W)}}{\text{volts (V)}}$$

Therefore $\textbf{current} = \dfrac{720\,\text{W}}{240\,\text{V}} = 3$ amp fuse needed

fuse

rating marked here

Electric plugs

A **plug** has **three wires**. The **brown wire** is the **live wire** and goes to the **fuse**. The **green/yellow** connects up to the **earth** terminal connection. The **blue** wire connects to the **neutral (N)** terminal.

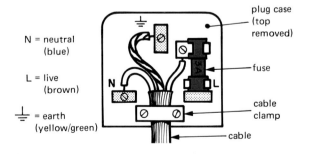

N = neutral (blue)

L = live (brown)

⊥ = earth (yellow/green)

plug case (top removed)

fuse

cable clamp

cable

Plastics

Plastics can cause particular problems. Below are factors that you should know about.

Breathing hazards

Work in a **well ventilated area** when working with:
Polyester resins (GRP work etc) – When a **resin** is mixed with a **hardener** (catalyst) it gives off **styrene fumes** which can reach harmful levels if **good ventilation** is not provided.
Hot wire cutter – Dangerous **styrene fumes** are produced when cutting **expanded polystyrene** or **styrofoam**.
Machine standing – Reduce this to a minimum. GRP work can be cut with a knife when at the soft **'Green stage'** to avoid the need for standing.
Wet and dry emery – Used wet, helps avoid dust problems.

Burning plastics give off **deadly fumes**.

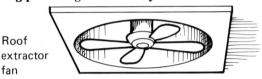

Roof extractor fan

Skin hazards

It is advisable to use a **barrier cream** and **disposable polythene gloves** when working with **resins** such as polyester, polyurethane and epoxy resins. Skin complaints such as **dermatitis** can result if care is not taken. The resin hardener **organic peroxide** is extremely dangerous (as are all organic compounds) and must only be used under strict teacher supervision.

disposable glove

BARRIER CREAM

Hot plastic – When used in injection moulding machines and glue guns etc, may burn on contact with the skin due to their high 'heat capacity'. If this happens remove the molten plastic and cool quickly if possible and treat as a burn (see page 1). **Leather gloves** can be worn.

Fire and explosion risks

Many plastics catch fire if exposed to a naked flame. **Cleaners** and **solvents** are **highly flammable** and must be kept in a **fireproof** (steel) cabinet.
Resins and **catalysts** (hardeners) must not be stored together in case they react and cause a fire due to heat build up – **store in fireproof cabinets**.

Only mix enough **resin** and hardener for about 10 minutes work. If the **plastic resin** starts to **set** too quickly and **heats up** put it in **cold water**.

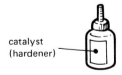

catalyst (hardener)

PLASTIC RESIN

ACETONE CLEANER

QUESTIONS/EXERCISES

① What **safety advice** could be given to a person who has been given an **old electric drill**?

② What size **fuse** would you recommend to protect a small plastic heater rated at 480 **watts** and connected to the **mains** (240 volts AC)?

③ Design a **'plastics safety notice'** using no more than 100 words (no drawings).

EXAMINATION PROJECT GUIDE

1 PROBLEM (SPECIFICATION)

1A Identify the situation or need

A separate sketch of the **situation** and **need**, the **problem** and any initial **market research** could be included here.

1B Brief

- Write the brief in one or two sentences then give:
- **A detailed specification** with the **main functions** listed such as: – to be portable, to cost less than ten pounds, to be rainproof.
- list any **limitations** such as: – to be made less than 100 mm long and made in six weeks.
- **A list of questions** that need to be researched and answered later.

2 INVESTIGATION AND RESEARCH

This stage investigates the **problem** and possible ways of solving it.

2A Investigation and research into the factors involved

The **checklist below** will help you at this stage.

Investigation checklist in no special order.	
Appearance	What could it look like?
Environment	Will it get hot/dusty/wet?
Ergonomics	What **human factors** are involved?
Time	To make and order part etc.
Safety	Will it be safe in use?
Strength	Which parts need to be strong?
Form	What parts could be used?
Materials	What materials could be used?
Finish	What surface finishes could be used?
Cost	In time and money.
Manufacture	What construction methods could be used?
Fittings	Will you need to buy parts?
Power	Possible power requirements.
Society	Effect on people and living things.
Other factors	Is the equipment needed available?

Also make use of help from teachers, magazines, libraries, companies, parents, and people who have tackled similar problems before.

Research – This may involve reading books and magazines, asking other people, sending away for information etc. **Experiments** can be carried out using scrap materials and construction kits etc.

Note – **Evidence of research must be kept as notes photocopies etc.**

2B Ideas and solutions

Ideas and **possible solutions** (at least **three**) are considered in **sketch** and **note** form. Even seemingly silly ideas should be included at this stage, they may form the basis of a great idea later.

Explain why you **like** or **dislike** the ideas usually as notes next to the sketches.

2C Development (development of selected ideas)

- Give reasons for your choice and check with your teacher that it fits the examination requirements.
- **Develop** the selected **ideas** and **solutions** by **considering** as **detailed sketches** or as **models** if more appropriate.

2D Working drawing (or working model) and planning of work

A **working drawing** (or **model**) must provide enough detail to enable somebody else to make it. It will need to show:

- The **important sizes**.
- How the parts are **assembled**.
- The **surface finish** and **appearance details**.
- A **parts list**.

Note 1 – **Working drawings** usually consists of:
- An 'assembly sketch'
- **A detailed drawing** of the whole product assembled; separate **part drawings** may also be needed.

Note 2 – **Detailed drawings** can be presented as **Orthographic drawings, exploded drawings, cross sections, isometric drawings, clear detailed sketches** etc.

Note 3 – Photographic evidence will be required by the examination board if **models** are made.

The planning stage

Plan your work, this can be carried out using an **activity chart** but there is no need to explain how to solder etc. (See next page for example.)

3 MAKING (manufacturing)

Remember when **making** that the work will be **marked** for **quality, attention to detail, good use of materials** as well as **subject** knowledge.

Do not rely completely on construction kits.

4 TESTING AND EVALUATION

This can be carried out as follows:

- Compare against the original **specification** and **list of functions** indicating successes and failures.
- Report on any difficulties encountered.
- **Tests** completed – Report on tests carried out.
- **Conclusion** – Finish with a conclusion that gives ideas for further improvements as if it were to be made again. Also include peoples's comments.

Extra An **advertisement** explaining the good features and how it is used can also be included to help the examiner know what it is all about.

General note Check against your examination board for any variations. The above are compiled after analysing all the GCSE **examination boards syllabi**. Sometimes **mass production** requirements also need to be considered.

QUESTIONS/EXERCISES

① Using the **investigation checklist** above to help, sketch the design of a pair of holiday **fun sunglasses** that could be made by a small firm.

② Make a list of all the page numbers that have **working drawings** on them in this book.

OTHER PROJECT HELP

What? When? Where? How? Questions to ask yourself.

Planning work

Most examinations now require evidence of planning in the project work. Below is an example of a method that can usefully be used; for more detail see pages 38, 40 and 43.

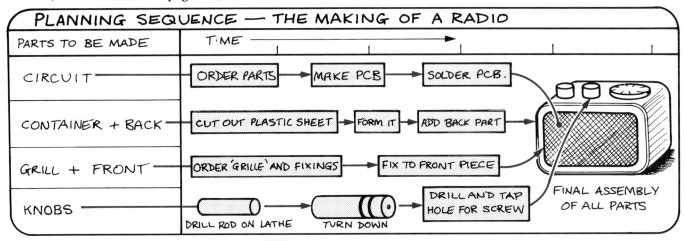

PLANNING SEQUENCE — THE MAKING OF A RADIO

PARTS TO BE MADE	TIME
CIRCUIT	ORDER PARTS → MAKE PCB → SOLDER PCB.
CONTAINER + BACK	CUT OUT PLASTIC SHEET → FORM IT → ADD BACK PART
GRILL + FRONT	ORDER 'GRILLE' AND FIXINGS → FIX TO FRONT PIECE
KNOBS	DRILL ROD ON LATHE → TURN DOWN → DRILL AND TAP HOLE FOR SCREW

FINAL ASSEMBLY OF ALL PARTS

EXAMINATION TIMES

In **order to plan your work effectively you should know the time of examinations etc.** Below are two checklists that will help you. Ask your teacher to give the dates and insert them in the boxes provided.

Example 1 – CDT Technology

Major project brief submitted for approval by the examination board about May the year before the final examination. ☐

Course/project work is marked during April ☐ (use March ☐ to do the final evaluation/testing).

Paper 1 $1\frac{1}{2}$ hours, general examination questions ☐ (in the examination hall).
Paper 2 More specific questions based mainly on the Technology modules ☐ (in the examination hall).

Example 2 – Design and realisation

Course/project work marked during April ☐ selection of work made during the final two years before the examination.

Paper 1 **Design paper** – given in December ☐
Designs folders are sent for assessment at end of February ☐
Realisation of Paper 2 must be completed by beginning of May ☐
Evaluation of design is done after this ☐

Paper 2 **Written paper** – covering all the syllabus ☐

EXAMINATION TECHNIQUES

1 Project work

(a) Find out the date it must be handed in for assessment.
(b) Make sure you allow time to **make it, test it** properly and complete any final presentation getting photographs developed etc.

2 Papers 1 and 2

Find out the examination dates and allow time for revision. (Mark them in your diary.)
(a) Before each examination make sure you know what **type of questions** that are to be asked in each paper.

(b) **Look at past papers** and find out which topics occur most often. Also see the questions at end of each section in this book.
(c) Carefully read the **examination papers instructions**.
(e) **Calculations** should be shown.
(f) If a choice of questions is given select the ones you find easiest and will gain the most marks.
(g) **Pace yourself** when in the examination room; do not spend an hour on a question only worth 5 marks.
(h) Ensure you have the **equipment needed** such as – pens, pencils (HB and H), rule, rubber, felt tips, crayons, compass, calculator, protractor, set squares, either spare leads or a pencil sharpener, a watch and perhaps a T-square.

QUESTIONS/EXERCISES

① Copy out the **examination times** using either the **technology example 1** or the **design and realisation example 2**, then insert the **dates** for your examination.

② What **examination aids/tips** would you give a student about to take a technology examination in a few weeks' time?

PROJECT WORK – EXAMPLES

The three examples given in this section have been selected because they show many of the techniques used in **Craft Design and Technology**.

The desk tidy
This example shows how a fairly common design problem is carried out. It is based mainly on the manipulation of materials to produce a functional and attractive design.

The personal disco system
This example shows how an electronics design problem can be tackled.

The wheelchair buggy
This example shows the application of computer control in problem solving. The control program printout on page 16 is a very useful program and could be a useful starting point for other pupil projects that involve the control of two DC motors and the use of up to four inputs. The buggy is controlled by a joystick, or the arrow direction keys. The path the buggy travels can be replayed.

General comments
A variety of drawing and presentation techniques are shown in these examples. Some of the techniques are: heavy outlines, colouring, adding shadow, use of circuit symbols.

For more help on presentation see the sections on **appearance and graphical communication**.

DESK TIDY

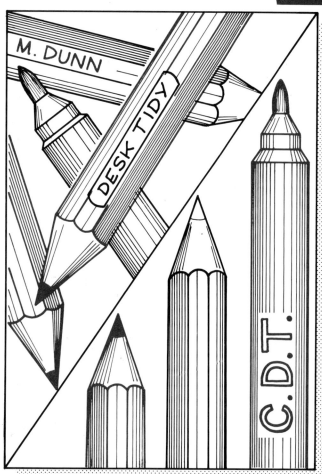

Cover for desk tidy folder

1 PROBLEM (SPECIFICATION)

1A IDENTIFY THE PROBLEM
My homework desk is difficult to keep tidy because I have so many pens and other writing and drawing equipment.

UNTIDY AREA

WORKING AREA HERE

THE PRESENT SITUATION

1B BRIEF
Design and make a desk tidy system that solves the problem illustrated above.
It must be : easy to use
portable
attractive
reasonably priced

LIMITATIONS
To be made in the school workshop before Christmas, otherwise no limitations.
QUESTIONS
Will all the coloured pens need to be stored in it?
How can the things be arranged for easy access?
What materials could be used?
What forms of materials are available? (e.g. tube)
Where can I obtain more ideas?
How could it be carried?

QUESTIONS / EXERCISES

① **Design a folder cover** for a desk tidy that includes your **name**, the title **desk tidy** and the **subject**. (See page 20 for other ideas.)

② **Identify a problem** that occurs in your house or bedroom that needs some form of tidy. Decide what needs to be kept tidy then draw the **problem** together with explanatory text.

---

2 INVESTIGATION AND RESEARCH

2A INVESTIGATION AND RESEARCH

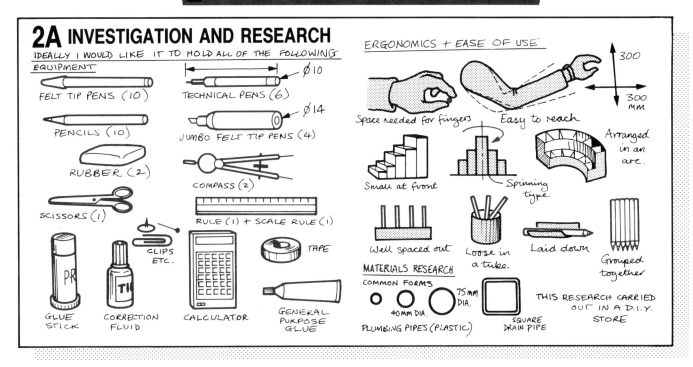

2B IDEAS AND SOLUTIONS

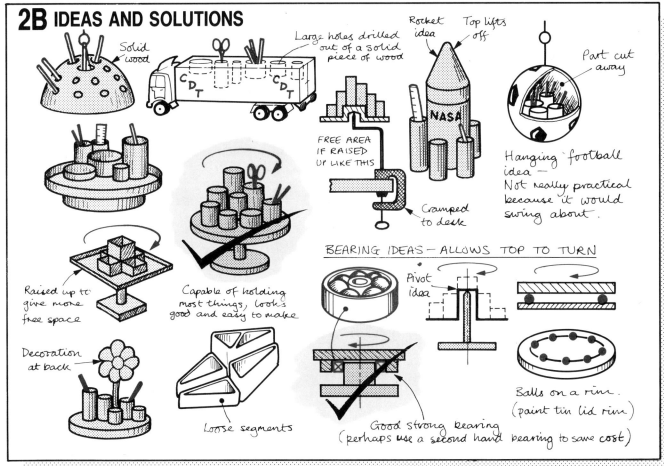

QUESTIONS / EXERCISES

① If you were to make a **desk tidy** what **equipment** would you like to store in it?

② Sketch in some detail three different ways of **arranging** six colouring pens that are often used and are easy to use.

③ Sketch in detail then colour two **ideas suitable** for a **desk tidy** that a person keen on sport, computers or animals may like as a present.

2C DEVELOPMENT

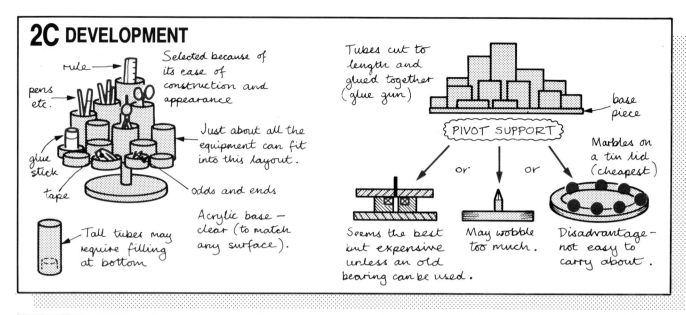

rule

pens etc.

glue stick

tape

Selected because of its ease of construction and appearance

Just about all the equipment can fit into this layout.

odds and ends

Acrylic base – clear (to match any surface).

Tall tubes may require filling at bottom

Tubes cut to length and glued together (glue gun)

base piece

PIVOT SUPPORT

or   or

Marbles on a tin lid (cheapest)

Seems the best but expensive unless an old bearing can be used.

May wobble too much.

Disadvantage – not easy to carry about.

2D WORKING DRAWING OR MODEL AND PLANNING

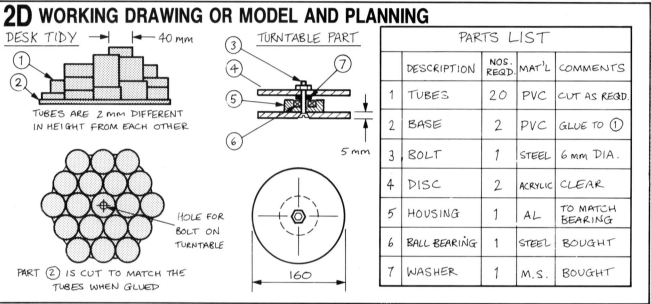

DESK TIDY — 40 mm

①
②

TUBES ARE 2 mm DIFFERENT IN HEIGHT FROM EACH OTHER

HOLE FOR BOLT ON TURNTABLE

PART ② IS CUT TO MATCH THE TUBES WHEN GLUED

TURNTABLE PART

③
④
⑤
⑥
⑦

5 mm

160

PARTS LIST				
	DESCRIPTION	NOS. REQD.	MAT'L	COMMENTS
1	TUBES	20	PVC	CUT AS REQD.
2	BASE	2	PVC	GLUE TO ①
3	BOLT	1	STEEL	6 mm DIA.
4	DISC	2	ACRYLIC	CLEAR
5	HOUSING	1	AL	TO MATCH BEARING
6	BALL BEARING	1	STEEL	BOUGHT
7	WASHER	1	M.S.	BOUGHT

A desk tidy model made from old kitchen containers etc, to test out initial ideas.

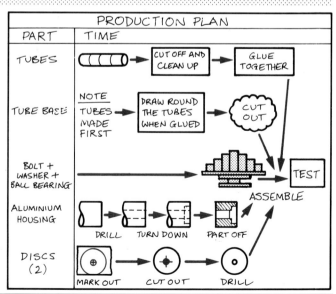

PRODUCTION PLAN

PART	TIME
TUBES	CUT OFF AND CLEAN UP → GLUE TOGETHER
TUBE BASE	NOTE TUBES MADE FIRST → DRAW ROUND THE TUBES WHEN GLUED → CUT OUT
BOLT + WASHER + BALL BEARING	→ TEST
ALUMINIUM HOUSING	DRILL → TURN DOWN → PART OFF → ASSEMBLE
DISCS (2)	MARK OUT → CUT OUT → DRILL

QUESTIONS/EXERCISES

① (a) **Draw a desk tidy** that is to be made from four separate parts. Each part must be capable of being made by itself before being assembled.

(b) Make a **parts list** like the one above for your desk tidy (also see page 29).

(c) Draw a **production plan** like the one above for your desk tidy design (also see page 32).

3 MAKING

Making the desk tidy - a tube belonging to the desk tidy being 'squared off' on a sanding disc.

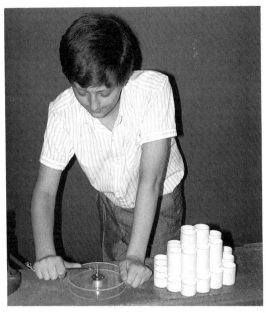

The desk tidy being assembled - the 'ball race' being joined to the base plates.

4 TESTING

Does it satisfy the design brief?

The result is very pleasing and satisfies the main functions namely :-

To be easy to use. It turns round easily and is fun to use.

To be portable. All the equipment stays in place if it is moved by sliding it along or by lifting it up in the air.

To be attractive
Various people have said it looks good and say they want one too.

Cost Luckily, I managed to get a free 'ball bearing' which would have cost about £3.00. The other materials cost £2.50.

Tests made

The force needed to turn it round is very little. It turns for a long time if pushed hard. Everything except the calculator fits into the tubes. The compass has to be closed before it can fit into a tube.

Conclusion The desk tidy works well but a few minor improvements could be made. The base could have a felt bottom and a larger tube could be added for larger things.

Friends testing the desk tidy for ease of use.

QUESTIONS/EXERCISES

① Carry out 'tests and an evaluation' on four writing materials such as – soft absorbent paper, shiny drawing paper, plastic material and newspaper. Tests to be carried out using a felt tip pen and a HB pencil on each piece of material.
Tested samples to be glued on the answer sheet. Tests could include suitability for 'colouring in', smudge resistance, time to dry, mixing of colours etc.

PERSONAL DISCO SYSTEM

1 PROBLEM (SPECIFICATION)

1A IDENTIFY THE PROBLEM

Quite a lot of my time is spent in my bedroom playing music — I would like to have some disco effect to add interest.

1B BRIEF

Design and make a disco lighting effect that responds to music.

<u>Limitations</u> Must not cost too much and should match present décor.

<u>Functions</u>
- To look good when in use and when not on.
- To be portable — to friend's house —
- Easy to operate — sensitivity, on/off etc.
- Easy to change batteries if need be.

2 INVESTIGATION AND RESEARCH

2A INVESTIGATION AND RESEARCH

<u>Display Ideas</u> — also see ideas page

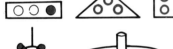

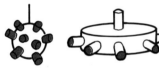

SYSTEM — POSSIBLE

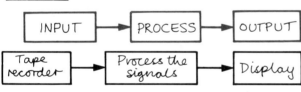

COST Must not be more than £15.

TIME To be finished before Easter.

SAFETY NO MAINS electricity is allowed so batteries may be needed. Alternately a power pack could be used. I have one at home that could be tried.

POWER REQUIRED Experiments are needed to find out the effects different bulbs have. It may be possible to use small 6 V bulbs. 0.06 W

ERGONOMIC FACTORS
Must be easy to carry about
Easy to adjust sensitivity, on/off change batteries.
Easy to clean and tidy up — no dust traps.

SOUND
Could be split up into various levels such as High, Low and Medium notes.

RESEARCH
Must find out the power output of my cassette recorder.

┌ SPACE FOR ANSWER ─────┐
It depends on volume and varies between 0 and about 1 watt.
└──────────────────────┘

Circuit seen in a magazine

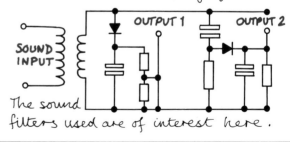

The sound filters used are of interest here.

QUESTIONS/EXERCISES

① (a) **Identify a problem** in a couple of sentences, that arises when using a telephone or a music centre, then illustrate it with a sketch.
(b) Write a possible design **brief** that could arise out of 1 (a).

② Carry out an 'investigation and research' into a modern desk lamp using a similar approach to that shown above. Also see the **investigation** stage on pages 23 to 26.

2B IDEAS AND SOLUTIONS

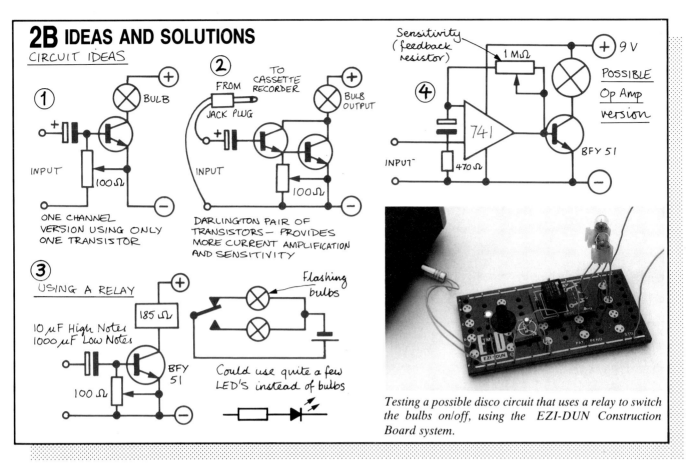

CIRCUIT IDEAS

① BULB
INPUT
100 Ω
ONE CHANNEL VERSION USING ONLY ONE TRANSISTOR

② FROM JACK PLUG
TO CASSETTE RECORDER
BULB OUTPUT
INPUT
100 Ω
DARLINGTON PAIR OF TRANSISTORS — PROVIDES MORE CURRENT AMPLIFICATION AND SENSITIVITY

③ USING A RELAY
10 μF High Notes
1000 μF Low Notes
185 Ω
BFY 51
100 Ω
Flashing bulbs
Could use quite a few LED's instead of bulbs

④ Sensitivity (feedback resistor)
1 MΩ
9 V
POSSIBLE Op Amp version
741
INPUT
470 Ω
BFY 51

Testing a possible disco circuit that uses a relay to switch the bulbs on/off, using the EZI-DUN Construction Board system.

DISPLAY IDEAS

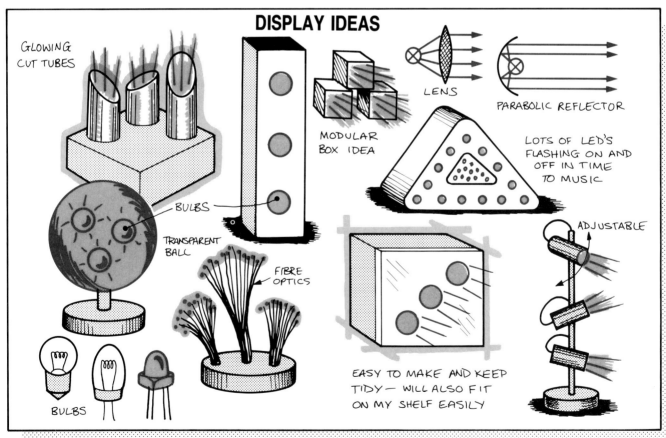

GLOWING CUT TUBES

BULBS

TRANSPARENT BALL

BULBS

MODULAR BOX IDEA

LENS

PARABOLIC REFLECTOR

LOTS OF LED'S FLASHING ON AND OFF IN TIME TO MUSIC

FIBRE OPTICS

EASY TO MAKE AND KEEP TIDY — WILL ALSO FIT ON MY SHELF EASILY

ADJUSTABLE

QUESTIONS/EXERCISES

① (a) Draw a **circuit diagram** for a flashing light circuit (for help see electronics section) then,
(b) Draw four **ideas** for a container to put the circuit in that could then be sold in a novelty shop.

② Draw one of the container ideas above (about 150 mm high), then make it look as **attractive** as possible with the use of coloured felt tip pens or inks.

2C DEVELOPMENT

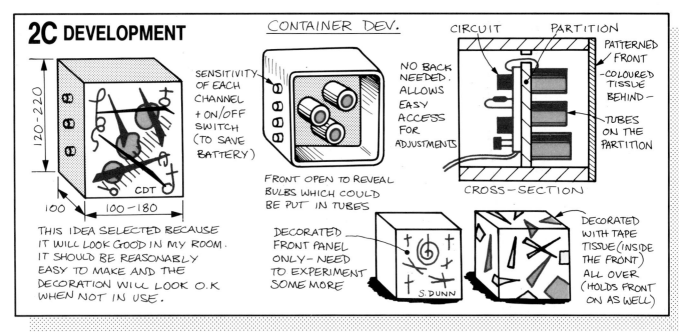

CONTAINER DEV.

120—220
100
100—180
CDT

SENSITIVITY OF EACH CHANNEL + ON/OFF SWITCH (TO SAVE BATTERY)

FRONT OPEN TO REVEAL BULBS WHICH COULD BE PUT IN TUBES

NO BACK NEEDED. ALLOWS EASY ACCESS FOR ADJUSTMENTS

CIRCUIT   PARTITION
PATTERNED FRONT
-COLOURED TISSUE BEHIND—
TUBES ON THE PARTITION
CROSS—SECTION

THIS IDEA SELECTED BECAUSE IT WILL LOOK GOOD IN MY ROOM. IT SHOULD BE REASONABLY EASY TO MAKE AND THE DECORATION WILL LOOK O.K WHEN NOT IN USE.

DECORATED FRONT PANEL ONLY— NEED TO EXPERIMENT SOME MORE

S. DUNN

DECORATED WITH TAPE TISSUE (INSIDE THE FRONT) ALL OVER (HOLDS FRONT ON AS WELL)

2D WORKING DRAWING (OR MODEL) AND PLANNING

CIRCUIT DIAGRAM
—AS A SYSTEM—

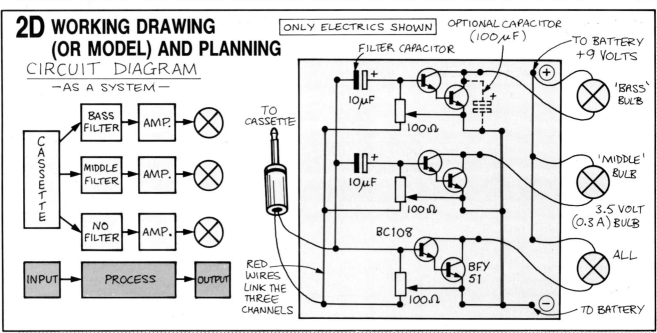

ONLY ELECTRICS SHOWN

OPTIONAL CAPACITOR (100μF)

FILTER CAPACITOR

TO BATTERY +9 VOLTS

BASS FILTER → AMP. → ⊗

MIDDLE FILTER → AMP. → ⊗

NO FILTER → AMP. → ⊗

CASSETTE

INPUT → PROCESS → OUTPUT

TO CASSETTE

10μF
100Ω
10μF
100Ω
BC108
BFY 51
100Ω

RED WIRES LINK THE THREE CHANNELS

'BASS' BULB
'MIDDLE' BULB
3.5 VOLT (0.3A) BULB
ALL

TO BATTERY

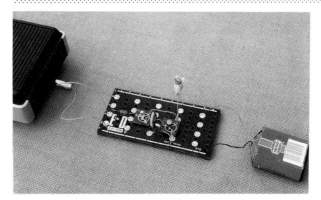

Testing a simple disco circuit idea before going on to make the three-bulb version. Made using the EZI-DUN Construction Board system.

Testing out a circuit that operates three electric bulbs independently (bass, middle and high notes). Made using the EZI-DUN Construction Board system.

QUESTIONS/EXERCISES

① Choose a **disco container idea** from the last page then **develop** it in a way similar to the example above.

② Explain with the aid of a **pictorial sketch** how the container idea you choose for number 1 above could be made into a model. Name the materials and joining methods used.

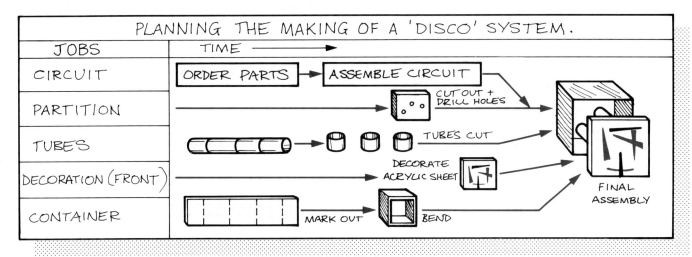

3 MAKING

The container was hard to get square because the bends need an allowance for the plastic thickness. The circuit worked first time once the variable resistors had been adjusted. The decorative panel took a long time to get right. Many experiments with coloured plastic, coloured tissue and crayons were tried to get the best effect.

The photograph shows 'RUB ON TRANSFERS' being placed on the container for the ON/OFF switch positions.

Adding the words 'Personal Disco' using rub-down transfers to the disco container.

4 TESTING

DOES IT SATISFY THE ORIGINAL BRIEF?
It looks reasonably attractive when not in use.
It can be carried about but the battery needs fixing in better.
The controls on the side are easy to use but a free space is needed for hand access on the left side.

TESTS MADE
A 2.5 volt bulb was tried and it gave a better light but soon 'blew'. A TIP 141 DARLINGTON PAIR transistor was tried with good results, but it is expensive compared to two cheap transistors.
The cassette output at max. volume was about 5 volt. When the TIP 141 transistor was used many more bulbs per channel could be used (more cost). In order to get maximum effect the cassette had to be on high volume. If too loud, books were placed on the speaker so that the voltage output could still be high for the bulbs to work.

CONCLUSION
It could be made a lot better if more money used. I am very pleased with it and use it regularly at home. Cost £12 for everything.

The finished disco system on a bedroom bookshelf next to the tape recorder which provides the sound signals.

QUESTIONS/EXERCISES

① (a) Select one of the container ideas on page 7, then make a **working drawing sketch** of it explaining how you would make it, then add a **parts list**.

(b) **Plan the making** of your chosen container idea using the example above to help you (also see page 32 for help).

WHEELCHAIR BUGGY

1 PROBLEM (SPECIFICATION)

1A IDENTIFY THE PROBLEM

Physically handicapped children who need to use a powered wheelchair need to practice controlling it without crashing into things.

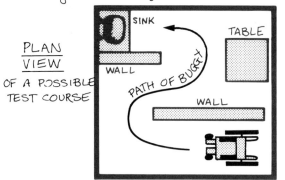

PLAN VIEW OF A POSSIBLE TEST COURSE

1B BRIEF

Design and make a model computer controlled buggy that can be operated by a handicapped child who has lost the use of his/her legs.

FUNCTIONS
1. To work and look like a full sized 'powered' wheelchair.
2. To be able to replay the program on the computer.
3. To use a control system like that used on real powered wheelchairs.
4. To indicate when the wheelchair has reached a certain place.

LIMITATIONS
To be fairly robust and cheap.

2 INVESTIGATION AND RESEARCH

2A INVESTIGATION AND RESEARCH

To look like a real wheelchair.

The normal wheelchair with electric conversion

A 'special' powered wheelchair

SIZE
A doll could be used with the model. The doll used will determine the buggy sizes. Possible dolls:- Action man, Sindy dolls. Any doll used must be able to bend.

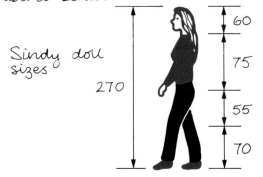

Sindy doll sizes

270

60
75
55
70

POWER SUPPLY - This could depend on the interface used. What is available?

> Space for answer
> A 4 input and 4 output interface using the 'USER PORT'.
> It has its own power supply of 5V. which can be used to drive the motors.

MOTORS To keep costs down cheap DC motors could be used. Other possibilities are stepper motors and gear motors.

THE COMPUTER PROGRAM
It needs to be easy to use.
It should be as foolproof as possible.
The screen must have something on it at all times.
It should run on a BBC computer using either LOGO or BBC BASIC language.

QUESTIONS/EXERCISES

1. Write a **design brief** similar to the one above for a particular 'teaching aid' for a blind person.
2. Design a room layout for a flat that has a living room, a kitchen, a bathroom and a bedroom for a wheelchair bound person to live in. Allow plenty of room for turning the wheelchair.

2B IDEAS AND SOLUTIONS

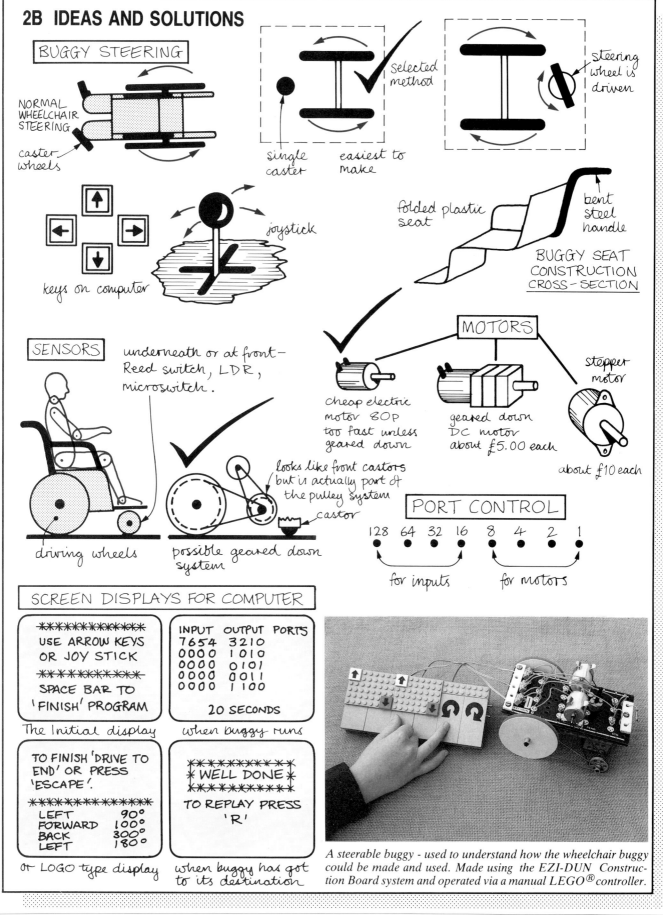

BUGGY STEERING

NORMAL WHEELCHAIR STEERING

caster wheels

selected method

single caster

easiest to make

steering wheel is driven

keys on computer

joystick

folded plastic seat

bent steel handle

BUGGY SEAT CONSTRUCTION CROSS-SECTION

SENSORS

underneath or at front – Reed switch, LDR, microswitch.

MOTORS

stepper motor

cheap electric motor 80P too fast unless geared down

geared down DC motor about £5.00 each

about £10 each

looks like front castors but is actually part of the pulley system

castor

driving wheels

possible geared down system

PORT CONTROL

128 64 32 16   8 4 2 1

for inputs   for motors

SCREEN DISPLAYS FOR COMPUTER

```
************
USE ARROW KEYS
OR JOY STICK
************
SPACE BAR TO
'FINISH' PROGRAM
```
The Initial display

```
INPUT  OUTPUT  PORTS
7654    3210
0000    1010
0000    0101
0000    0011
0000    1100

  20 SECONDS
```
when buggy runs

```
TO FINISH 'DRIVE TO
END' OR PRESS
'ESCAPE'.
**************
LEFT        90°
FORWARD    100°
BACK       300°
LEFT       180°
```
or LOGO type display

```
*************
* WELL DONE *
*************
TO REPLAY PRESS
'R'
```
when buggy has got to its destination

A steerable buggy - used to understand how the wheelchair buggy could be made and used. Made using the EZI-DUN Construction Board system and operated via a manual LEGO® controller.

QUESTIONS/EXERCISES

① Sketch neatly two **ideas** of a motorised **wheelchair buggy** that a teenager could use to travel to the local shopping centre, along a pavement in any weather.

② Improve two of the screen displays for computer shown above using standard keyboard letters and symbols which can be made into patterns as required.

2C DEVELOPMENT

Note **only part of the development shown.**
This wheelchair buggy program can be used to control any DC motor buggy.
The 'user port' of a BBC Computer is used via a control interface.
The program is quite long because it has been designed to have **screen help** notes for the user at every stage as well as being able to **replay** a given route. It uses **sensors** which when triggered stops the program and makes a **sound**. The printout below is taken directly from the computer.

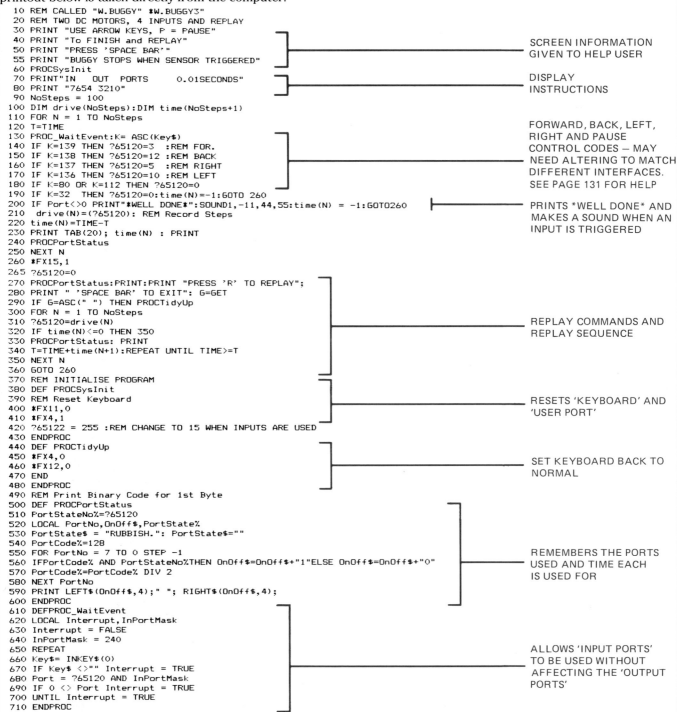

```
 10 REM CALLED "W.BUGGY" *W.BUGGY3"
 20 REM TWO DC MOTORS, 4 INPUTS AND REPLAY
 30 PRINT "USE ARROW KEYS, P = PAUSE"
 40 PRINT "To FINISH and REPLAY"
 50 PRINT "PRESS 'SPACE BAR'"
 55 PRINT "BUGGY STOPS WHEN SENSOR TRIGGERED"
 60 PROCSysInit
 70 PRINT"IN   OUT PORTS     0.01SECONDS"
 80 PRINT "7654 3210"
 90 NoSteps = 100
100 DIM drive(NoSteps):DIM time(NoSteps+1)
110 FOR N = 1 TO NoSteps
120 T=TIME
130 PROC_WaitEvent:K= ASC(Key$)
140 IF K=139 THEN ?65120=3  :REM FOR.
150 IF K=138 THEN ?65120=12 :REM BACK
160 IF K=137 THEN ?65120=5  :REM RIGHT
170 IF K=136 THEN ?65120=10 :REM LEFT
180 IF K=80 OR K=112 THEN ?65120=0
190 IF K=32  THEN ?65120=0:time(N)=-1:GOTO 260
200 IF Port<>0 PRINT"*WELL DONE*":SOUND1,-11,44,55:time(N) = -1:GOTO260
210  drive(N)=(?65120): REM Record Steps
220 time(N)=TIME-T
230 PRINT TAB(20); time(N) : PRINT
240 PROCPortStatus
250 NEXT N
260 *FX15,1
265 ?65120=0
270 PROCPortStatus:PRINT:PRINT "PRESS 'R' TO REPLAY";
280 PRINT " 'SPACE BAR' TO EXIT": G=GET
290 IF G=ASC(" ") THEN PROCTidyUp
300 FOR N = 1 TO NoSteps
310 ?65120=drive(N)
320 IF time(N)<=0 THEN 350
330 PROCPortStatus: PRINT
340 T=TIME+time(N+1):REPEAT UNTIL TIME>=T
350 NEXT N
360 GOTO 260
370 REM INITIALISE PROGRAM
380 DEF PROCSysInit
390 REM Reset Keyboard
400 *FX11,0
410 *FX4,1
420 ?65122 = 255 :REM CHANGE TO 15 WHEN INPUTS ARE USED
430 ENDPROC
440 DEF PROCTidyUp
450 *FX4,0
460 *FX12,0
470 END
480 ENDPROC
490 REM Print Binary Code for 1st Byte
500 DEF PROCPortStatus
510 PortStateNo%=?65120
520 LOCAL PortNo,OnOff$,PortState%
530 PortState$ = "RUBBISH.": PortState$=""
540 PortCode%=128
550 FOR PortNo = 7 TO 0 STEP -1
560 IFPortCode% AND PortStateNo%THEN OnOff$=OnOff$+"1"ELSE OnOff$=OnOff$+"0"
570 PortCode%=PortCode% DIV 2
580 NEXT PortNo
590 PRINT LEFT$(OnOff$,4);" "; RIGHT$(OnOff$,4);
600 ENDPROC
610 DEFPROC_WaitEvent
620 LOCAL Interrupt,InPortMask
630 Interrupt = FALSE
640 InPortMask = 240
650 REPEAT
660 Key$= INKEY$(0)
670 IF Key$ <>"" Interrupt = TRUE
680 Port = ?65120 AND InPortMask
690 IF 0 <> Port Interrupt = TRUE
700 UNTIL Interrupt = TRUE
710 ENDPROC
```

SCREEN INFORMATION GIVEN TO HELP USER

DISPLAY INSTRUCTIONS

FORWARD, BACK, LEFT, RIGHT AND PAUSE CONTROL CODES — MAY NEED ALTERING TO MATCH DIFFERENT INTERFACES. SEE PAGE 131 FOR HELP

PRINTS *WELL DONE* AND MAKES A SOUND WHEN AN INPUT IS TRIGGERED

REPLAY COMMANDS AND REPLAY SEQUENCE

RESETS 'KEYBOARD' AND 'USER PORT'

SET KEYBOARD BACK TO NORMAL

REMEMBERS THE PORTS USED AND TIME EACH IS USED FOR

ALLOWS 'INPUT PORTS' TO BE USED WITHOUT AFFECTING THE 'OUTPUT PORTS'

Note The program shown above will run with or without the interface being connected but line 420 will need altering to 420 ?65122 = 15 if input sensors are to be used; it sets the eight ports so that four are used for output, to control the two buggy motors, and four for input use.

QUESTIONS / EXERCISES

① Using a computer guide book, or similar, find out what the following abbreviations or codes mean or do.

| REM | PROC | ENDPROC |
| GOTO | ASC | PRINT |

② Copy the lines using **print** statements, then suggest three changes you would like to make to the information given within the quotation marks, to make the program more fun or more informative.

2D WORKING DRAWING (part of)

WHEELCHAIR BUGGY BY Maja Oving
Drawn to scale

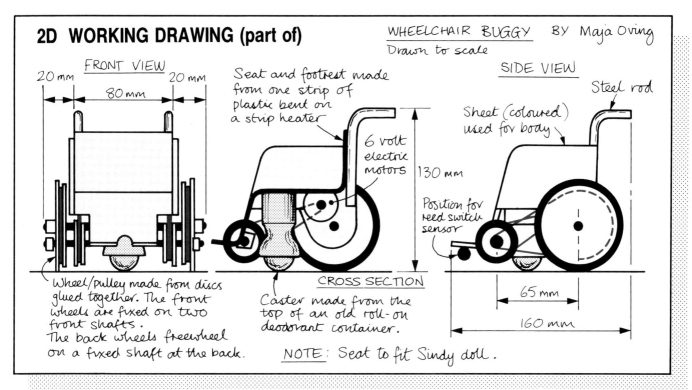

FRONT VIEW

20 mm   80 mm   20 mm

Seat and footrest made from one strip of plastic bent on a strip heater

6 volt electric motors

130 mm

SIDE VIEW

Steel rod

Sheet (coloured) used for body

Position for reed switch sensor

Wheel/pulley made from discs glued together. The front wheels are fixed on two front shafts.
The back wheels freewheel on a fixed shaft at the back.

CROSS SECTION

Caster made from the top of an old roll-on deodorant container.

NOTE: Seat to fit Sindy doll.

65 mm

160 mm

3 MAKING

Brief report on the making of the wheelchair buggy

Some of the dimensions were first checked by making a card model and sitting a Sindy doll in it. The small 'under-arm deodorant' container type, used for the caster, just fitted in. A circle cutting jig for use in the sanding disc was used to ensure perfect wheels were made. The wires terminated in a quick release plug and socket.

4 TESTING

Does it satisfy the original design brief?
① It looks fairly realistic especially when a Sindy doll is in the seat.
② The program can REPLAY the last journey made by the operator as many times as required.
③ The buggy can be controlled by either the keyboard keys ⬆⬇➡⬅ or a joystick.
④ The buggy stops as required when the reed switch sensor is triggered by a magnet.
The cost was lower than my teacher expected but would have been quite expensive if geared down motor used.

THE COMPUTER PROGRAM
It took a long time to write a suitable program. I had to get some 'expert' advice at times.
The people who have tested the buggy and the program think it is easy and fun to use.

POSSIBLE IMPROVEMENTS
Something to hold the wire up so that it does not get tangled up. The elastic bands are a little too stretchy — better ones

could be used. Geared motors could be used and a better caster found.

The finished model of the wheelchair buggy being tested in a model room which was made to match the scale of the buggy.

QUESTIONS/EXERCISES

① (a) Why do you think a simple **caster** is needed on a simple buggy like the one above? Note – the wheels revolve forwards or backwards in the example above.

(b) What is the **length, height** and **width** of the buggy?

② Draw the **pulley drive system** in outline as used in the wheelchair buggy above.

DESIGN AND PROBLEM SOLVING

Design and Problem Solving is very important in Craft, Design and Technology and as such is explained in some detail in this book. It is sometimes called 'Product Design' because products are being designed. To design successfully we need to take into account many factors such as: human factors, size, cost, appearance, safety etc.

The diagram below shows the four main stages used in the design process used in this book. These stages are sometimes subdivided. It is presented like this to show that design is not really a linear series of events but a fluid interdependent process. The rest of this book shows design as a linear process for convenience. A summary presented in a linear way is given on the next page.

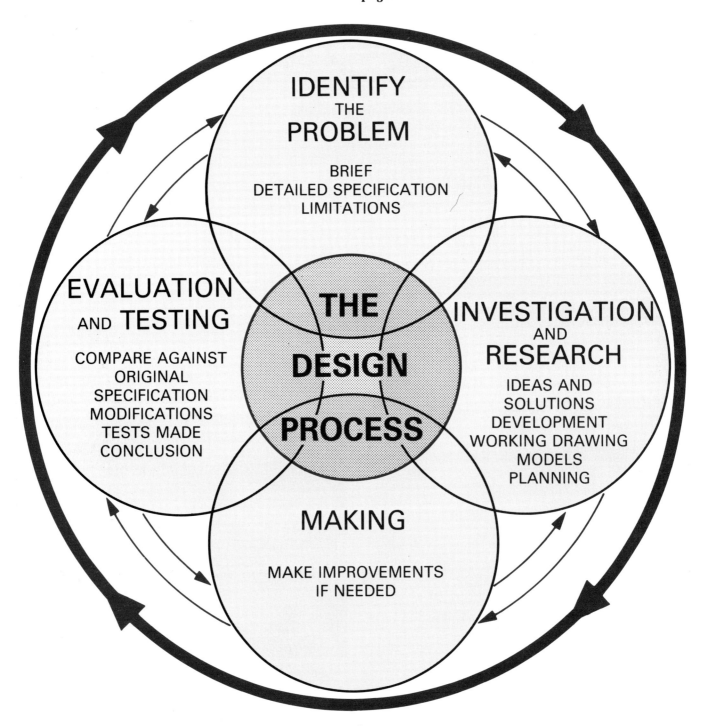

IDENTIFY THE PROBLEM
BRIEF
DETAILED SPECIFICATION
LIMITATIONS

EVALUATION AND TESTING
COMPARE AGAINST ORIGINAL SPECIFICATION
MODIFICATIONS
TESTS MADE
CONCLUSION

THE DESIGN PROCESS

INVESTIGATION AND RESEARCH
IDEAS AND SOLUTIONS
DEVELOPMENT
WORKING DRAWING
MODELS
PLANNING

MAKING
MAKE IMPROVEMENTS IF NEEDED

QUESTIONS/EXERCISES

① What are the four main parts of the **Design Process**. List them starting with **identify the problem.**

② Redraw the diagram above then colour it in using five colours, one colour for each circle. The lettering must be neat (ie use guide lines to help you).

DESIGN PROCESS – A SUMMARY

1 PROBLEM (SPECIFICATION)

(1A) Problem (specification)
Identify a **problem** or **human need**. A sketch of the situation or problem could also be included.

(1B) Brief
1 Write the **brief** in one or two sentences then give:
2 A **detailed specification** with the **main functions** listed,
3 A list of any **limitations**,
4 A **list of questions** that need to be researched and answered later.

2 INVESTIGATION AND RESEARCH

(2A) Investigation and research
Checklist (in no special order)
Appearance, environment, ergonomics, time, safety, strength, form, materials, finish, cost, manufacture, fittings, power, society, other factors.
Research May involve reading books, asking other people etc.

(2B) Ideas and solutions
Ideas and **possible solutions** (at least **three**) are considered in **sketch** and **note** form. Even seemingly silly ideas should be included.
Explain why you **like** or **dislike** the ideas given.

(2C) Development
Giving **reason for your choice, develop** the selected **ideas** and **solutions** as **detailed sketches** with notes (or as models).

(2D) Working drawing (or model) and planning
The **working drawing** (or model) will need to show:
(a) How the parts are **assembled**,   (b) The **important sizes**,
(c) **Surface finish** and **appearance details**,   (d) A **parts list**.
Note Photographs of models may be needed.
The planning state
This can be carried out using an **activity chart** or **production plan chart**.

3 MAKING (MANUFACTURING)
Remember when **making** that the work will be **marked** for **quality, attention to detail, and good use of materials.**
Note Don't rely completely on construction kits.

4 TESTING AND EVALUATION
This can be carried out as follows:
a Compare against the original **specification** and **list of functions**.
b **Report** on any difficulties encountered.
c **Tests completed** – Report on tests carried out.
d **Conclusion** – Write a conclusion that also gives ideas for further improvements.

QUESTIONS/EXERCISES

① (a) Copy the **design process** above, then place it in your design folder so that it is easy to refer to when needed.

(b) Beside 1(a) just copied, add the percentage marks each part is allocated by your examination board when carrying out project work.

POSSIBLE DESIGN FOLDER LAYOUTS

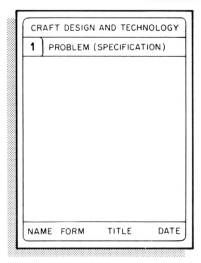

CRAFT DESIGN AND TECHNOLOGY

1 PROBLEM (SPECIFICATION)

NAME FORM   TITLE   DATE

CRAFT DESIGN AND TECHNOLOGY

2A INVESTIGATION / RESEARCH

NAME FORM   TITLE   DATE

CRAFT DESIGN AND TECHNOLOGY

2B IDEAS AND SOLUTIONS

NAME FORM   TITLE   DATE

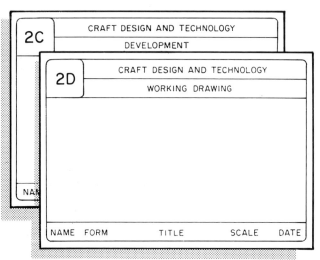

2C CRAFT DESIGN AND TECHNOLOGY
DEVELOPMENT

2D CRAFT DESIGN AND TECHNOLOGY
WORKING DRAWING

NAME FORM   TITLE   SCALE   DATE

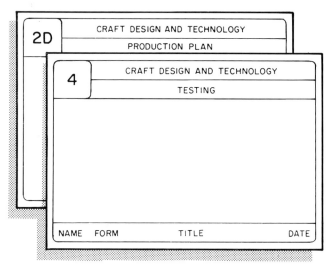

2D CRAFT DESIGN AND TECHNOLOGY
PRODUCTION PLAN

4 CRAFT DESIGN AND TECHNOLOGY
TESTING

NAME FORM   TITLE   DATE

Your design folder layouts can be in any style as long as they are attractive and acceptable to your teacher and the examination board.

To avoid having to produce borders every time, design sheets can be reproduced using a photocopier. You may need to allow space for punched holes.

The design folder cover can be made very attractive, a few examples are given below.

FOLDER COVER DESIGNS

A4 folders

Make it look attractive and presentable

A3 folder with ribbon holding papers together

QUESTIONS/EXERCISES

① Design an attractive **page layout** system that you could use for your future design work.

② **Design a folder cover** that could be used either on your current work or your next design.

DESIGN PROCESS – AN INDUSTRIAL EXAMPLE

This page briefly explains how the design/problem solving approach is used in industry.

① Identify problem/need

There are many ways of identifying problems and needs that a firm could use. In large firms this task is mainly the responsibility of: the **directors, market research** and the **sales department**.

> The staff of NEW PRODUCTS think there may be a market for a new pocket torch suitable for carrying in the pocket or a handbag. The beam should be adjustable (i.e directional when not held).

② Brief

After much discussion an initial **design brief**, usually agreed by the directors, will be published and sent to interested parties.

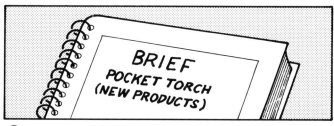

③ Investigation/research

The design brief is now **investigated** and **researched**. This will involve departments such as: **research, design, sales, costing** as well as potential **customers** etc.

④ Ideas/solutions

Ideas and **possible solutions** can be considered by the firm's own **design team** or by outside specialist **design consultants**.

⑤ Best idea(s)

The most promising ideas are developed in much more detail. Prototypes are often made at this stage of the whole product or parts of the product.

⑥ Production plans

Plans are made so that it can be produced for real. This usually involves **detailed drawings, models** and deciding when and where it will be made.

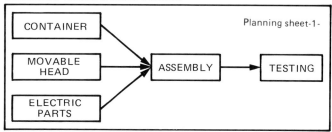

⑦ Make it/production

Usually working from **working drawings**, the manufacturer, who may have no connection with the firm who designed it, will make a prototype to the firm's specifications.

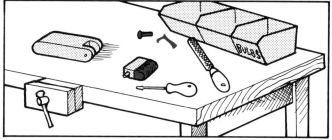

⑧ Testing/evaluation

Before a product is sold it needs to be **tested** to see if it does its job properly. Is it the right price and is it acceptable to potential customers? Alterations are usually required before **mass production** can be started. This may involve the training of new staff and negotiating new rates of pay with the Unions etc.

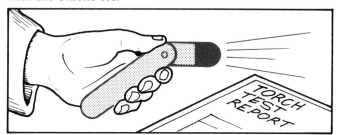

QUESTIONS/EXERCISES

① Replace each of the design stage diagrams above with diagrams that illustrate the stages in designing a new **direction compass**.

② Make a list of the personnel you think are involved with the different stages in the design of the torch above (eg directors are involved in agreeing the design brief).

DESIGN AND PROBLEM SOLVING
(IN MORE DETAIL)

This section will help you when designing a product and solving problems in school or at home. A DESIGN/PROBLEM SOLVING PROCESS is explained step by step together with CHECKLISTS and EXAMPLES. NOTE Three practical design examples are given earlier in the book (pages 6–17).

1 PROBLEM (SPECIFICATION)

The **problem** stage can be split into two or more parts as explained below.

1A Identify the problem
1B Brief

1A IDENTIFY THE PROBLEM

First **identify** a real **problem** or **human need(s)**. A sketch of the original **situation** the problem arises from can also be included at this stage.

Example of A1 PROBLEM

Having just recieved my new bicycle for a birthday present, I am keen to avoid having it stolen when I cycle to the shops and down to the river etc.

OPEN

My bike at the shop.

My bike on the river bank.

1B BRIEF

- This is the second part of **1 Problem (specification)**. It is done by writing the design **brief** in one or two sentences followed by:

- **A detailed specification** with the **main functions** listed. (Eg To be attractive, portable, to cost less than ten pounds, to be waterproof etc.)

- Listing any **limitations** that will influence the design. (Eg To cost less than £10, to fit in my pocket and to be completed in six weeks time.)

- **Questions** – jot down questions which come to mind that can be researched and answered later such as:
  Who else will use it?
  Does it need to be portable?
  Where will it be used?
  To help think of questions ask yourself the following questions:

Who? When? Where? What? How?

Example of 1B BRIEF

- **Design Brief**
  Design and make a product that will deter a thief from stealing my bicycle.

- **Detailed Specification** and **Main Functions**
  To be easy to carry about.
  To help prevent a thief from stealing my bike.
  To be strong enough.
  To immobilise my bike or clamp it to things like railings or trees.
  Must not rust.
  Be easy to use.

- **Limitations**
  To be made in the school workshop.
  To be completed by Christmas.

- **Questions and things to I need to find out.**
  How strong will it need to be?
  What is already on the market? (Must visit Halfords)
  What do my friends use?
  What is a reasonable cost?
  In what way can a bike be immobilised besides being locked up?

QUESTIONS/EXERCISES

① Write a **specification** to be sent to a firm for two large signs which will be made and attached onto the side of the town's new leisure centre. The examples above may help with **specification** and **limitations**.

② Think of a **handicapped person** you know (or your teacher knows) then write two possible **design problems/specifications** for a device that could help improve their quality of life.

2 INVESTIGATION AND RESEARCH

This stage **investigates** the design problem.
It can be tackled in many ways. There is no perfect method for solving **all** problems. The method used here is based on the new CDT syllabi and works well in practice with most project work.
Note Photographs of any models and research helps produce a good design folder.

The stages that come under the general heading of **investigation** and **research**, for examination purposes are:

2A Investigation and research into the factors involved.

2B Ideas and solutions – Ideas and solutions are considered in sketch/model and note form.

2C Development – Development of the selected ideas/solutions.

2D Working drawing (or model) and planning – This stage finalises the plans and details needed before making the product.

Research can be carried out at any of the above stages.

2A INVESTIGATION AND RESEARCH

The topics in the **checklist** below are explained more fully on the next few pages.

1 Appearance	9 Finish
2 Environment	10 Cost
3 Ergonomics	11 Manufacture
4 Time	12 Fittings + equipment
5 Safety	13 Control
6 Strength	14 Power
7 Important sizes	15 Society
8 Materials	16 Other factors

For notes on research see page 26.

1 Appearance (aesthetics)

(Also see section on Appearance, pages 44 to 48.)
The **appearance** or **aesthetics** of a product is always important and sometimes it is the most important factor. The appearance of any product depends on some or all of the following factors:

> Line, Shape and Form
> Colour
> Texture
> Decoration

A product's appearance is also effected by the background or place it is used.

2 Environment

The **environment** or **situation** the product or system is used in can play a major part in a products requirements. Below are examples of environments that you may need to consider.

Hot	or **Cold**
Wet	or **Dry**
Dusty	or **Dust Free**
Acid	or **Alkali**
Light	or **Dark**
Modern	or **Old Fashioned**
Untidy	or **Tidy**
Public	or **Private place**
Kitchen	(Food and Hygiene)

Example
It would be useless making a mild steel knife or fork for the kitchen because it would rust.

3 Ergonomics (human factors)

Ergonomics is a technical word used to describe the **human factors** involved in design work such as comfort and ease of use of things like handles, dials and seats. Humans vary a great deal, from helpless babies to olympic athletes. Humans are capable of running, sitting, and kneeling, but there are also things people cannot do such as lift very large loads, see in the dark, or fly. Humans like to be reasonably comfortable, have their own interests, to be loved and feel important (our ego). Humans change a great deal during their lifetime so it is important to know for whom you are designing. The needs of a small child are quite different from those of an old person.

Anthropmetrics – Is a related science that quantifies human physical dimensions.

Size
Size must be taken into account (eg hand or finger sizes may be important to know).

Movement
Is movement important? Can you reach the parts wanted, move the controls easily etc.?

Sight (eyes)
Are there parts that need to be seen easily? (colour and shape and clarity are important here).

Sound (ears)
Is noise likely to be a problem (eg sound can be either annoying, like a squeak, or pleasant, like music.)

Feel (skin)
The parts touched will need to be comfortable. Sharp edges will need to be removed. Textures can be rough, smooth, soft or hard to touch.
The ergonomic diagrams are on the next page.

QUESTIONS/EXERCISES

① List four important **functions** you think a family car must fulfil.
② List five **functions** an electric kettle must fulfil.

③ What **human factors (ergonomic factors)** need to be considered in the design of a bicycle? Consider the seat, the brakes and the pedals in turn.

2A INVESTIGATION AND RESEARCH (CONTINUED)

Smell (nose)
Is this likely to be a problem or an aid to your design?

Taste (tongue)
Some materials are **toxic**. Do not use them if they might be put in the mouth especially if babies are likely to use it.

Temperature
Humans like to be comfortable: about 21°C in a room. Parts may need insulating from hot or cold sources.

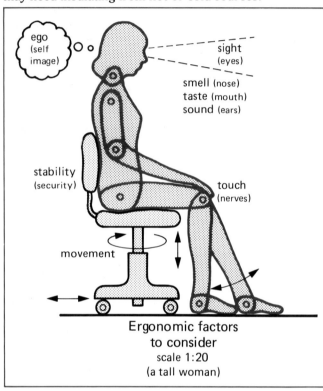

Ergonomic factors
to consider
scale 1:20
(a tall woman)

Making a human model

① Trace and label each part

② Glue tracings onto thick card

③ Cut out parts

④ Make 'pin joint' holes

⑤ Assemble parts with bent wire or drawing pins

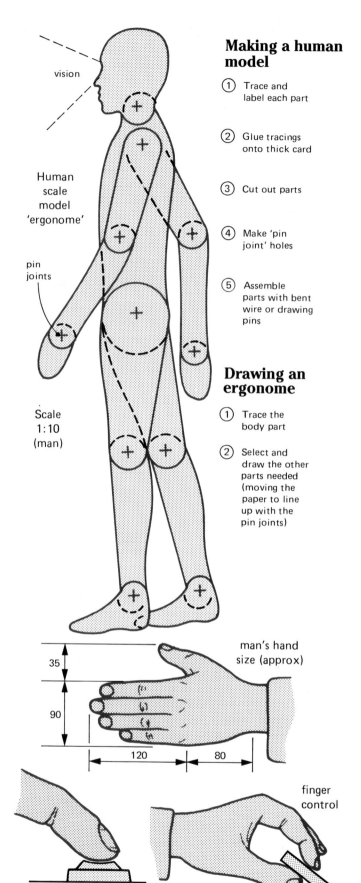

Human scale model 'ergonome'

pin joints

Scale 1:10 (man)

Drawing an ergonome

① Trace the body part

② Select and draw the other parts needed (moving the paper to line up with the pin joints)

trace and then cut out to make folded model

model after folding to required form

Folded card model (paper) scale 1:25

man's hand size (approx)

35

90

120   80

finger control

finger control

QUESTIONS / EXERCISES

① Make a simple folded card model of a person like the one above then make it look as realistic as possible using felt tip pens.

② Using the 1:10 scale **ergonome** above, trace the ergonome sitting in an easy chair. He must look comfortable, (the woman illustration above may help you).

2A INVESTIGATION AND RESEARCH (CONTINUED)

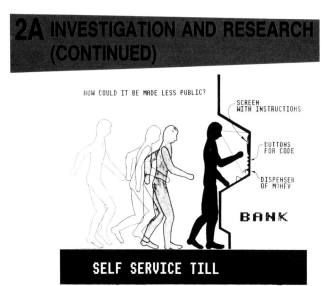

An 'Ergonome' drawing showing a self-service till being used.

4 Time

The **time** needed can be reduced by:
- Simplifying the design.
- Buying parts (allow for ordering and delivery).
- Ensuring any machines needed will be available when required – check with your teacher for lathes etc.
- Some parts could be made at home or after school.
- Planning your work into a logical work sequence. (See page 38 for help with this.)
- Use **templates** and **jigs** to avoid the need to mark out on the workpiece.

5 Safety (also see pages 1, 2 and 3)

All your projects need to be safe.
The checklist below will help.

- **Edges** – avoid or protect any sharp edges.
- **Stability** – will it fall over easily?
- **Fire** – Is there a fire risk?
- **Electric dangers** – Avoid **mains** electricity unless a qualified electrician is able to check it.
- **Guards** – moving parts may need guarding.
- **Materials** – avoid dangerous materials like lead.

6 Strength (also see pages 93 to 101)

A good designer anticipates the kind of forces a product is likely to encounter during use; for example a shopping bag should be capable of carrying a full load, being knocked about and being dropped. The forces that affect the strength of a product are classified as:

Tensile	(pulling forces)
Compression	(pushing forces)
Shear	(cutting forces)
Bending and **Twisting**	

One simple but dramatic test is called the **drop test**.
To allow for possible breakage due to wear and tear a **factor of safety** is used (see page 98 for explanation).

7 Important sizes

Important sizes need to be determined. The following may help you:
If a container is needed, what is to be put in it?
Is access important (eg for batteries replacement).
Where will it be stored? Is there a critical size?
How will it be carried or moved about?
How much room are any bought parts going to take?
How much room will the controls take?

8 Materials (also see pages 66 to 74)

At this stage it is a good idea to:
- List the properties required from a list such as:
  Hard, soft, stiff, tough, corrosion resistant, colourful, heavy, transparent, heat resistant, electrically insulating or conducting.
- List materials that could be used.
- Indicate suitable **surface finishes**.

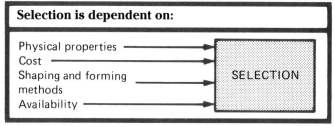

9 Finish

The surface finish of a product will affect the final appearance and protection given to the material underneath, some materials such as acrylic do not need an added finish. Some finishes are tough while others soon wear away or chip off.
Below is a check list of possible finishes you can choose from:

	OTHER:
Varnish	
Paint	
Stains	Polishing
Bluing (of steel)	Cloth
Lacquering	Fur
Plastic dip coating (on metal)	Lino/Vinyl
Anodising (aluminium only)	Carpet
Enamelling (usually on copper)	Flocking
Hammered	

10 Cost (economics)

In industry the time taken to make it, machinery costs and overheads such as transport have also to be taken into account. In schools only the cost of materials is charged. The choice between buying some parts or making them may need to be made. Buying certain parts can save time. Catalogues and local shops will provide you with prices (remember postage and VAT) but ask your teacher first, he/she may know a cheap supplier.
Note Some examination boards restrict the use of bought parts for use in projects.

QUESTIONS/EXERCISES

① Comment on the **desk tidy** design example on pages 6 to 9 with regard to the headings found on this page (numbers 4–10).

② Using your current design work. Comment on it with regard to the headings 4–10 on this page.

2A INVESTIGATION AND RESEARCH (CONTINUED)

11 Construction (manufacture) (Also see pages 75 to 90)

What method(s) of manufacture do you think are suitable for the various parts of your design? The four main methods are listed below:

- **Cutting out (material removal)**
  The parts can be cut out by sawing, drilling, filing, lathework, etc.
- **Moulding**
  The parts can be moulded by the application of a force to form it (eg vacuum forming, injection moulding, blow moulding, beaten metalwork, forging, plastic strip heater, GRP, wood lamination etc).
- **Casting**
  A liquid is poured into a prepared mould and then sets hard: metal casting, plastic embedding, 'plaster of Paris' casting etc.
- **Fabrication**
  Parts can be joined together: using screws, bolts, clip together joints, glues, solder, etc.

12 Fittings and equipment

Are there any fittings or equipment that must be specially obtained such as electronic parts or a compressor that the school does not already have.
Questions to ask yourself:
Are the parts easy to obtain?
What alternatives could I use?
When will the parts arrive if ordered?
How much will the parts cost?

13 Control (Also see page 134)

How is your design going to be controlled?
It could for example be manual, automatic, digital (ON/OFF) analogue or remote controlled.

14 Power (Also see pages 112 to 115)

Some products will need a power source.
How much power will be needed?
Will batteries be sufficient or will a mains operated power supply unit be needed?
Experiments are usually needed to find out.

15 Society (Also see pages 135 to 136)

The effects on society need to be considered with some project work such as a wind powered electric generator which would create a lot of noise and could be an eyesore.
Local and national laws have been passed which may effect what we design, a flashing neon advertising display board would not be allowed in a conservation area without special planning permission. Will your design be anti–social or simply annoy people?

16 Other factors

There may be other factors to consider.
Can you think of any?
Will it need maintenance?
Can local firms help?
If used outdoors will the materials last more than a couple of years?

RESEARCH

Research is not a separate topic, it should be carried out as and when required. Research can consist of things like: – looking at catalogues, books, measuring basic sizes, sketching details, finding out what is available in the shops that may be of interest, asking people for their points of view, collecting data, etc.

Market research

In industry **market research** departments are employed full time to find out what is marketable by keeping tabs on the competition, asking potential consumers what they like/dislike, how much they would be prepared to pay for various alternatives and asking for opinions on appearance etc. Some of this work is done by using questionaires and visiting exhibitions, libraries and so on.

In school it is important that any research done is recorded in the design folder. This can be done by obtaining photocopies of relevant information, keeping a diary with comments of places visited and sending away for information. Technological information about a particular part or system may also be required.

Practical research can also be carried out by making models to try and solve particular problems, recording the results as photographs, graphs and drawings.

Typical letter asking for information

> TO
> FAST SALES LTD
> P.O. BOX 1
> NEW TOWN
> COUNTY
>
> FROM
> JENNIFER DUNN
> 89 PRESTON ST.
> HIGH TOWN
> COUNTY
>
> DATE
>
> Dear Sir/Madam,
> Please could you send me details of your new range of products as described in New Products magazine. Code number 062.
> Thank you.
> Yours faithfully
> Jennifer Dunn

QUESTIONS/EXERCISES

① (a) Research the following torch types – pocket, camping or car and handbag torch by looking in current mail order catalogues.
  (b) Sketch one of each type, then comment on each one's suitability.

② Write an imaginary letter to a firm that sells electric motors asking for motor type AB123.

INVESTIGATION AND RESEARCH (CONTINUED)

2B IDEAS AND SOLUTIONS

This stage is best completed by drawing various **ideas** and **possible solutions** as shown in the two examples on this page, together with some explanatory notes.

If good ideas came to you before this stage you should have made a note or sketch of it at the time and include it here.

This stage should stretch your imagination using original and not so original ideas

Even seemingly silly ideas should be included, they may turn out to be very original and important.
Models can also be very useful at this stage.
The following points will help produce good work:
- Look at library books, magazines, etc.
- Ask other people for ideas and comments.
- Visit shops and exhibitions to see what useful ideas they have.
- Use a method called '**brainstorming**', where a group of people sit round and put ideas forward – nobody is allowed to criticise anybody else. Notes and sketches are made at the same time.

Indicate which ideas and solutions you **like**, it can be done with a large tick, together with notes giving reasons why they are selected.

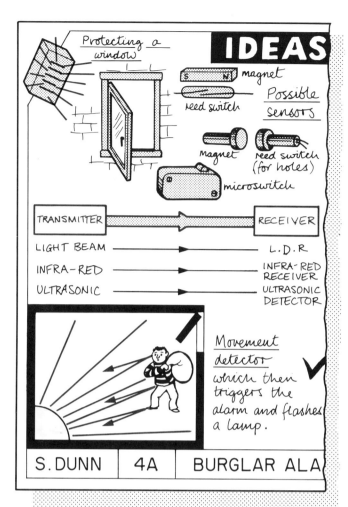

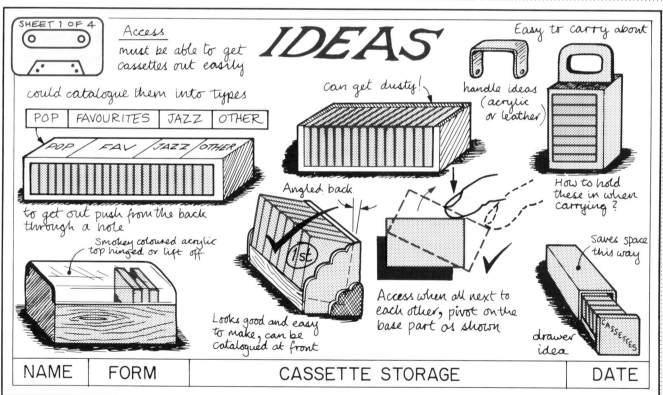

QUESTIONS/EXERCISES

① Sketch three possible *ideas* of a toy suitable for use in the bath by a 3 year old child.

② Sketch three possible **ideas** suitable for a game that makes use of either: – a magnet, marbles or an elastic band.

INVESTIGATION AND RESEARCH (CONTINUED)

2C DEVELOPMENT

This stage of the design process develops the best ideas and solutions further.

You may want to combine the best ideas and solutions already considered to form a new solution.

First give reasons for your choice and check with your teacher to see if he/she agrees. It is also wise to ask others for their opinion at this time. The wrong selection at this stage will result in a lot of wasted time.

Develop the selected ideas and solutions as detailed sketches with notes, or as models, if more appropriate. The following questions can be used as a checklist:

1 **Does it satisfy the original design brief?**
2 **Could it look better? a 'presentation drawing' could help here.**
3 **What materials could be used and why?**
4 **Indicate the important sizes.**
5 **How can each part be made?**
6 **What joints could be used?**
7 **What surface finish and texture could be used?**

Models and **mock-ups** are sometimes essential at this stage to make sure it does what you expect it to.

Good **graphical communication** techniques, including the use of colour should be used. (See pages 49–65 for help with graphical communication techniques.)

If problems develop it may be better to select another idea or to modify the idea being developed.

This page show to examples (part only) of the development.

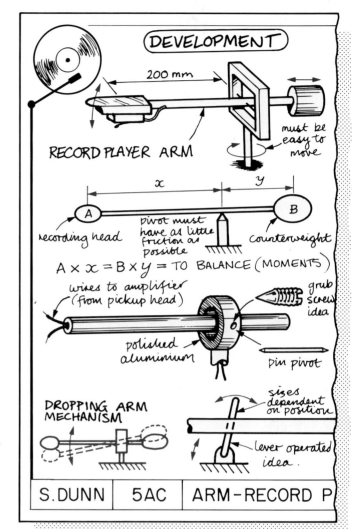

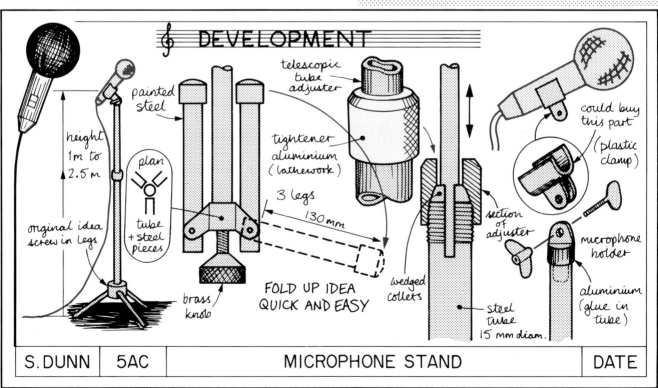

QUESTIONS/EXERCISES

① Design a **game** that makes use of at least six marbles.
  (a) Sketch various ideas that could be used.

(b) Develop the best idea in some detail in sketch form with colour.

INVESTIGATION AND RESEARCH (CONTINUED)

2D WORKING DRAWING (OR MODEL) AND PLANNING (Also see pages 57 to 62.)

The **working drawing** (and/or **model**) **must provide enough information to enable somebody else to make it if required.**

Working drawings will show:
- How the parts are **assembled** or **made**.
- The **important sizes**.
- The **surface finish** and **appearance details** (colour, texture etc).
- A **parts list** or **cutting list** may also be required.
- **What the parts do** if not obvious.

Sometimes **working models** can do all or part of the above more effectively.

Working drawings are usually drawn as:
- **Assembly drawing** (Parts are drawn assembled).
- **Parts drawing** (Parts are drawn separately).
- **Assembly** and **parts drawings combined**.

It is usual to **draw to scale** so that sizes can be checked at the same time as the drawing is being done. If possible draw **full size**.

Drawing techniques include:
Orthographic projection,
Sectioning,
Exploded views,
Isometric, oblique or **perspective drawings.**

The examples below on this and the next page show three methods of presenting working drawings.

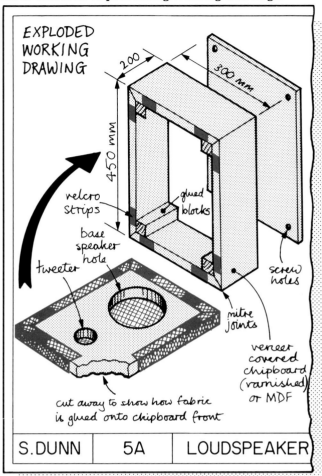

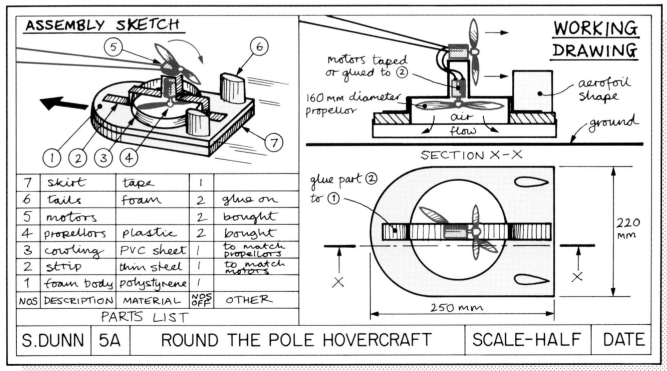

QUESTIONS/EXERCISES

① Draw a **working drawing** of something you have made recently. Two views are required, eg **front view** and a **plan view**.

② Copy either the **exploded working drawings** of the loudspeaker or the **hovercraft working drawing** (not including the assembly sketch or the parts list) shown on this page as neatly as possible.

WORKING DRAWING (OR MODEL) AND PLANNING (CONTINUED)

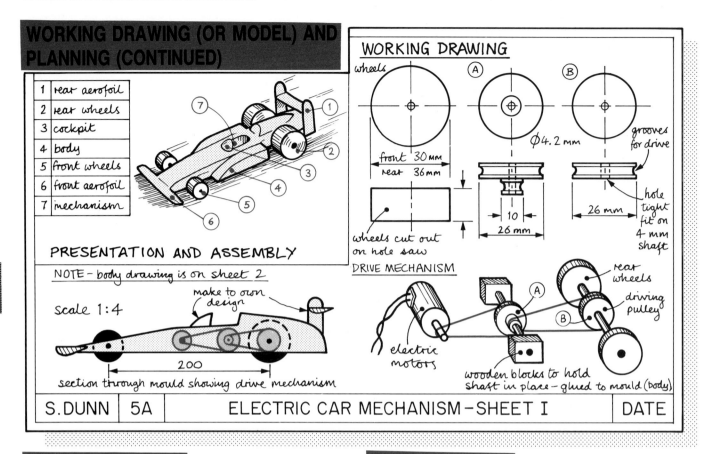

1	rear aerofoil
2	rear wheels
3	cockpit
4	body
5	front wheels
6	front aerofoil
7	mechanism

PRESENTATION AND ASSEMBLY

NOTE - body drawing is on sheet 2

scale 1:4

make to own design

200

section through mould showing drive mechanism

WORKING DRAWING

wheels

(A)

(B)

front 30 mm
rear 36 mm

Ø4.2 mm

grooves for drive

hole tight fit on 4 mm shaft

10
26 mm

26 mm

wheels cut out on hole saw

DRIVE MECHANISM

rear wheels

driving pulley

(A)

(B)

electric motors

wooden blocks to hold shaft in place - glued to mould (body)

| S. DUNN | 5A | ELECTRIC CAR MECHANISM – SHEET I | DATE |

WORKING MODELS

Working models are sometimes preferred to **working drawings** because:

- They are sometimes easier and quicker to produce than working drawings.
- They can be moved about and viewed from various angles.
- Problems such as stability, ease of use and whether it works are usually more obvious in a model.
- They can be touched.
- Errors are usually more obvious and can be corrected.

Note Parts of a design can be modelled separately to check that a particular part works (eg mechanical design problems).

The disadvantages of making models are:

- Appropriate modelling materials and construction kits may not be available.
- The materials used are more expensive than paper.
- Safe storage space is needed.
- Copies cannot be made quickly like a working drawing.
- Photographs are needed for examination purposes.

Making a model

Before making a model you will need to consider:

- The size/scale it should be.
- The kind of materials the model should be made.

Modelling materials

When selecting modelling materials it is important to try to use materials with properties similar to the materials you hope to use in the finished product. The following materials are commonly used:

paper, card, plasticine, clay, wire, strips of wood, balsawood, old packing materials such as drink containers etc, sheet plastic, foamed plastics such as expanded polystyrene, plaster of Paris, fluted polypropylene, construction kits such as LEGO® Technical Kits, Meccano, Fischertechnik etc.

Joints may be made with glue, tape, pins, clips, string and interlocking joints but of course any method can be used.

A selection of modelling materials. Can you think of any more?

QUESTIONS/EXERCISES

① Make a card model of a **high fashion wrist watch,** paying particular attention to detail and appearance.
Note To be made full size.
The watch face is best made separately and glued on.

Colours must be used.

② Using a sheet of cardboard and some glue, make a model of a radio or of a board game.

Working drawing (or model) and planning (continued)

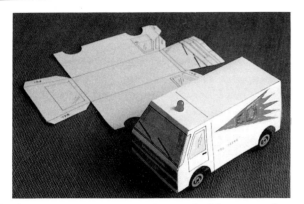

Modelling in card - the card 'development' of the van can be seen. An EZI-DUN Construction Board with circuit is placed inside, enabling a flashing light to be used on top.

Modelling a light-searching buggy using the EZI-DUN Construction Board system. Motors used: from Vento Solenoids Ltd.

A LEGO® based robot made by Jeremy for his main examination project. It selects and lifts bottles from the turntable.

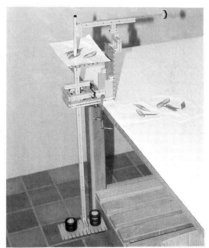

Harmonograph made from a Fischertechnik kit. It draws pictures when given a swing. A pen rests on the paper as the platform moves about.

A model of a burglar alarmed room. The door and windows are 'alarmed'. The EZI-DUN Construction Board is used underneath to mount the control circuitry on.

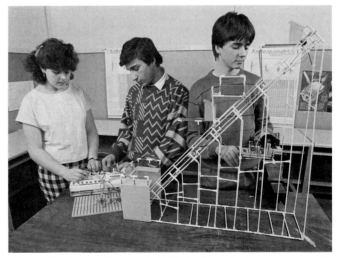

Plawco used to make a model hill-climbing device using movable 'cars'. (Picture taken by Commotion who supply Plawco.)

QUESTIONS/EXERCISES

① Using a suitable construction kit **model** your bedroom or a crane.

② What materials do you think would be suitable to model the following: – a pair of scissors, a toy elephant, a toy buggy, a house, a bridge, a chair, a bowl–shaped candle holder and twice full size jewellery.

Working drawing (or model) and planning (continued)

PLANNING

(Also see pages 38 to 40 for more help.)
Planning can save time and help ensure that the equipment and the materials needed are available when required.

The more complex a design the greater the need for forward planning.

Marks are allocated for this stage in the design process so it is worth recording the planning carried out.

Planning can be carried out:

- **For individual parts (see below).**
- **Against time for the whole product (second example below).**
- **By deciding which parts have to be made first.**
- **By making a 'critical path analysis' chart (see page 38) this is a favourite method in industry.**

It helps if the teacher is consulted early on in this process to point out any possible problems such as materials or parts not being available from school stock.

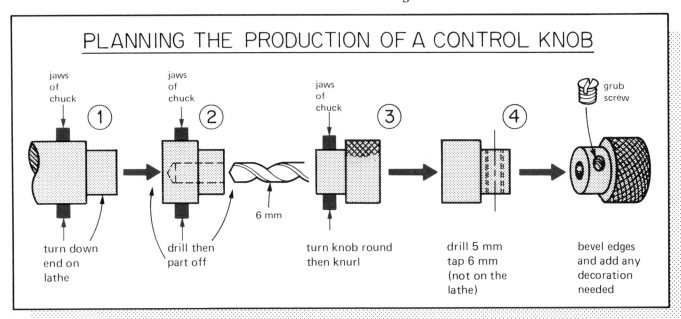

PLANNING THE PRODUCTION OF A CONTROL KNOB

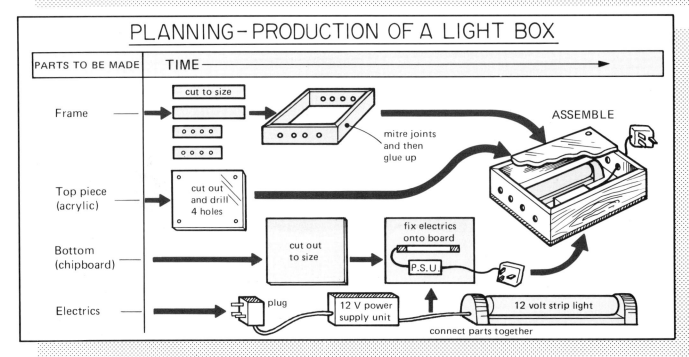

PLANNING – PRODUCTION OF A LIGHT BOX

QUESTIONS/EXERCISES

① **Plan**, using drawings, **step by step** how a home-made **Christmas card** is made. It must include at least five stages in the making of it.

② Plan the **production** of your **current design** using the examples above to help you.

3 MAKING (MANUFACTURING)

The **making** stage, sometimes called **manufacture** or **realisation**, is when the design is made, using '**working drawings**' or '**working models**' to refer to when required.

Before starting, **ask your teacher to approve your design**, and **plan** how you intend to make the individual parts, if not already done. It is important to realise that some jobs are best done in a certain sequence for example, it is easier to polish the edges of a piece of plastic before it is bent.

Do not be afraid to consider improvements to your design as it is being made, but first ask your teacher to approve the changes needed and make a note for use at the **Evaluation** stage.

Note **1** Where possible use methods that can make your job easier, for example, **templates** can make **marking out** easier.

2 Ensure work is carried out **safely** and you wear the correct protective clothing.

A versatile C R Clarke vacuum former being used to make a container for electronic circuits.

Questions to ask yourself

In what order should the parts be made?
Will parts need to be bought or ordered?
Do you need help or to learn new skills?
Where can the pieces be stored between lessons?
What special equipment will be needed?
Will a **jig** or **template** make the job easier?
See pages 75 to 89 for help with ways of **shaping and forming**.

See the last page for **planning help**.

Examples of equipment that may be needed are shown on this page and the next page.

Checking the diameter of a turned piece of solid nylon on a lathe with a micrometer.

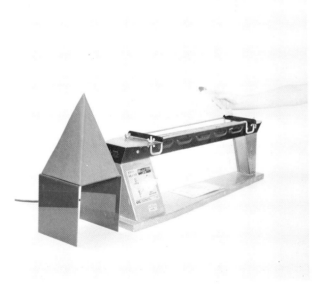

A strip heater being used to bend an acrylic 'fun hook'. The pyramid form and its stand were also made using the strip heater. The heater shown is made by C R Clarke and Co Ltd.

QUESTIONS / EXERCISES

① Using the **questions to ask yourself** on this page, answer the questions for your present design job.

② Make a list of the machines you have used in the workshop, then draw two of them using a drawing method that shows it off to best advantage.

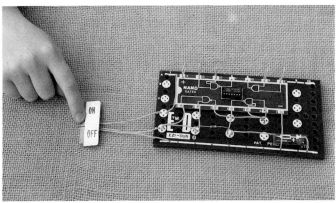

A sensitive switching circuit using one chip mounted on an EZI-DUN Construction Board. (Circuit diagram on page 127.)

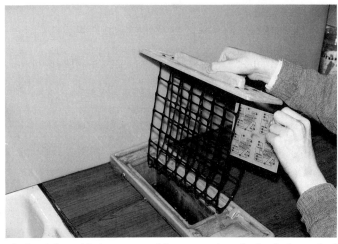

A circuit board being removed from an etch tank after being etched in ferric chloride liquid.

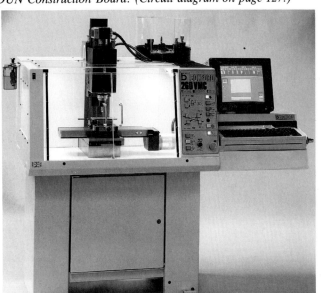

CNC milling machine. The whole operation can be carried out easily via the computer. (Boxford Ltd)

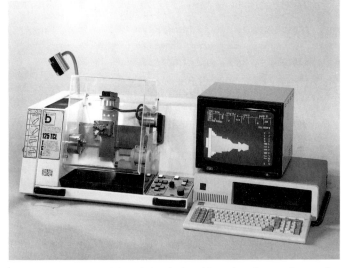

The Boxford 125/TCL training lathe. Note that the product to be made is dislayed on the screen.

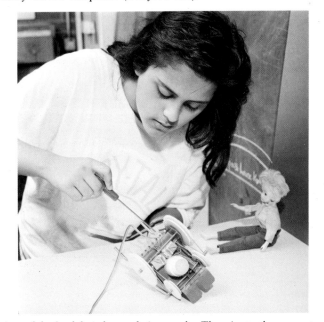

A model wheelchair buggy being made. The wire to the computer interface are being screwed into place.

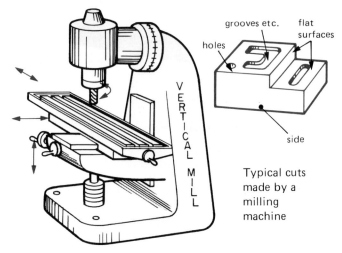

Vertical milling machine
movement indicated by red lines

QUESTIONS / EXERCISES

① Make as neat a drawing as you can of the CNC **lathe** shown above.

② Make as neat a drawing as you can of the **vertical miller** shown above.

4 TESTING AND EVALUATION

It is important that designs are **tested** and **evaluated** (sometimes called **appraisal**). In industry people spend a great deal of time **testing** and **evaluating** products before they appear on the market. Once products do appear for sale they are sometimes tested by consumer organisations and the results published in magazines such as '**Which**'.

In schools **testing** and **evaluating** is usually completed on A4 sized plain or lined paper. It is not expected that your design will be perfect, in fact it would be very strange if it were, considering it was your first attempt.

An honest, critical **test** and **evaluation** is required.

The **tests and evaluation** can be carried out as follows:

1 Compare against the original specification

You will need to refer back to the original list of functions made at the **brief** and **investigation** state. This will include things like: – appearance, function and economics. Make sure the important functions are included.

2 Report on any difficulties and modifications

During the **making** stage various changes will have been made – comment on these and say why they occurred.

3 Report on any tests carried out

Examples of tests that can be carried out include:
Ease of use, power required, efficiency, speed, distance, peoples reactions, strength.

4 Conclusion with suggestions for possible improvements

A short conclusion summarising the above together with suggestions for possible improvements, as if it were to be made again.

Allow **time** to do the **tests and evaluation**, it takes longer than most people think – at least a month on a complex job.
Note

- It helps if notes are kept as the design is being carried out, they could be in the form of a diary.

- A **presentation drawing** in the form of an advert or a '**how it works**' drawing is a useful extra for display purposes such as parents evenings; It can also be included in your design folder.

- You may only be able to test it in its proper setting.

Typical questions to ask yourself

How easy is it to use? (ergonomic factors)
Does it look **attractive**?
Is it **strong** enough in use?
Is it **safe** in use?
Is the **construction** satisfactory?
Is it easy to **maintain** in good condition?
Did it **cost** more than expected?
What **tests** still need to be carried out?
What **improvements** can still be made?
Were the best **materials** used in its construction?
Is the **surface finish** used satisfactory in use?
Can it be controlled as expected?
Is it likely to last as long as expected?
Remember to ask the eventual users for their opinions too.

The final folder check

Are all the **pages** in the proper places?
Are there any **photographs** to be added?
Are all the **pages titled** correctly?
Is there a **contents page?**
Are there any **loose pieces** that need glueing in?
Does the **front cover** need doing again?
Would some pages look better if **colour** were added?

Method of assessment

Assessment may be required to ascertain the degree of success a design has achieved.
Below are several ways of doing it:
1 **Description** – excellent, good, fair etc
2 **Percentages** – 20%, 50%, 90% etc
3 **Letters** – A, B, C, D, E
4 **Stars** – *****, ****, ***, **, *
5 **Out of 10** – 2/10, 5/10, 7/10, 9/10

PRESENTING TEST RESULTS GRAPHICALLY

Various methods are shown below and on the next page.

Assessment table

	SUBJECT	PERSON A COMMENTS	PERSON B COMMENTS
1	COMFORT	GOOD	FAIR
2	APPEARANCE	VERY GOOD	GOOD
3	STABILITY	FAIR	POOR
4	OTHER COMMENTS	JOINTS LOOK STRONG	BACK SUPPORT IS POOR

Assessment – Of a chair by two people.

QUESTIONS / EXERCISES

① Test a **felt tip** and a **ball point** pen on various surfaces and in different conditions; results to be recorded in a visual way, eg as a graph.

② As far as possible, answer the **Typical questions to ask yourself** above on this page about your last completed design work.

Histogram or bar graph

Below is a histogram showing **People's opinions of a sculpture** (marked as a percentage).

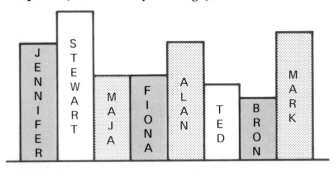

Pie chart

It looks like a round pie with parts cut into slices. It is useful for showing **percentages**.

The pie chart below shows the results of tests made on the **Energy consumed in a house** expressed as a percentage.

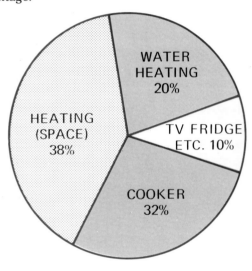

Drawing with test results and comments added

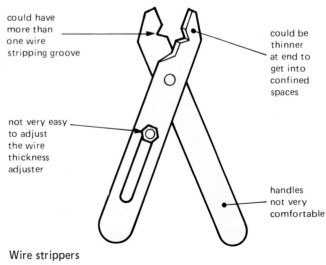

Wire strippers

Line graphs

These graphs show the relationship between **variable quantities** (eg speed, height, temperature, strength) against an axis with increments in time or distance etc.

The line graph below shows the results of **two batteries being tested**. During the test both batteries were connected to an electric motor.

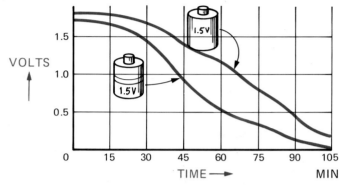

A model vehicle being tested to see how a steep a slope it can climb. Could you make a vehicle climb as steep a slope as this?

An amphibious buggy being tried out by the pupil using a hand controller.

QUESTIONS / EXERCISES

① Ask six people to mark your current design, then present the results as a **histogram** like the histogram shown above.

② Test two toy cars down the same slope at 10 degrees, then 30, 40, and 50 degrees, recording the distances travelled as a **line graph** (X–axis for **angle**, Y–axis for **distance**).

MASS PRODUCTION

Mass production means producing a lot of the same product such as thousands of dolls or hundreds of kettles which are all the same. In industry, expensive specialist machinery and equipment is used to save **time** to make good use of a person's working hours.

Ways of reducing time

Below are some simple ways of reducing time and making the work being done easier, that could be used in schools or in industry. Most methods require time to make the aid initially, but once made, they can be used over and over again. Eventually the production aids will wear out or get damaged.

A template

A template is a shape that can be drawn round.

Below is a template used to mark out the **development** (or net) shape of a container.

finished container

A drilling jig

When drilling holes a **drilling jig** can ensure holes are drilled accurately through the guide holes. If this method is used make sure the locating pins are held against smooth accurate surfaces.

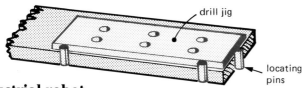

drill jig

locating pins

Industrial robot

Large industrial robots are becoming common in industry. Some schools may have one too. They are used to move parts about, to paintspray etc.

Robots helping to test a car for any gaps. Using helium gas, the robot sensors detect leaks around windows etc. (Haymarket Motoring Photo Library)

The economics of mass production

In the world of work the cost of labour can be very high. By careful planning and organisation production can be speeded up considerably so that each worker produces more in a given time. This will reduce labour costs per article, overhead costs for buildings, rents, rates, transport, heating and lighting.

The main disadvantage of mass production is that individuality is much more difficult to achieve. It would be difficult to mass produce artificial legs because they all need to be made differently.

Below are graphs showing the cost of a radio **made by hand** and by **mass production**. The read line shows how much it costs to produce 10 radios by each method and how much it costs if 300 are made. If only five radios are to be made it would be cheaper to have them **hand made** but if more than 100 are to be made **mass production** is cheaper. **Mass production** is cheaper after the **break even point** is reached.

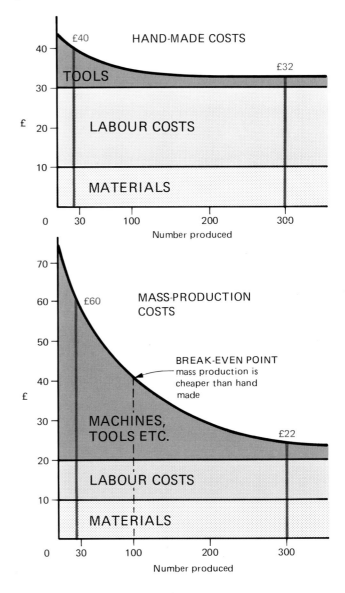

QUESTIONS / EXERCISES

① Copy the two graphs on this page showing **hand made costs** and **mass production costs**, then explain using the graphs to help you, in a few sentences why most commercial products are **mass produced**.

② Make a template to make a container similar to the one above. Make sure the sides are all 30 mm high and corners are rounded.

OTHER DESIGN AIDS

1 PLANNING USING FLOW CHARTS

2 Simplifying complex problems
(On next two pages.)

1 Planning using flow charts

This page shows various planning and flow process charts that can be used to help explain how systems or processes work.

The first flow chart shows a family chart which you probably know as a **family tree**.

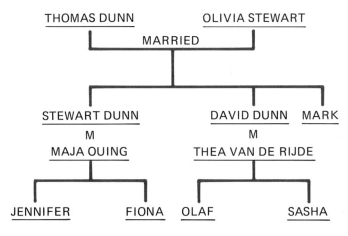

The **school rotation chart** below shows how the rotation for three groups is arranged and the change over dates.

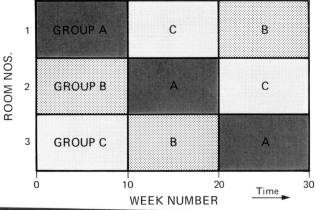

Critical path analysis (CPA)

When a project is complex a method known as **critical path analysis** can be used to find the time to make something, called the **critical path**. By studying the critical path decisions can be made to see if the time can be reduced by altering the way the product is made.

The example below shows the critical path (thick line) of a product made up of three parts. It takes four weeks from start to finish.

The length of arrow does not indicate the length of time it takes. Time is indicated separately on the connecting lines.

Critical path analysis (CPA)

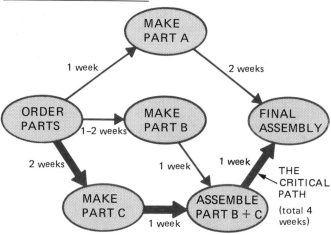

Planning using flow charts

Flow charts explain a process in logical steps. All sorts of processes can be made into a flow chart from **making a phone call** to the **assembly of an aircraft**.

The flow chart below is the kind used in computer programming. Different symbol shapes are used to indicate certain things such as **start, stop, process** and **decisions**.

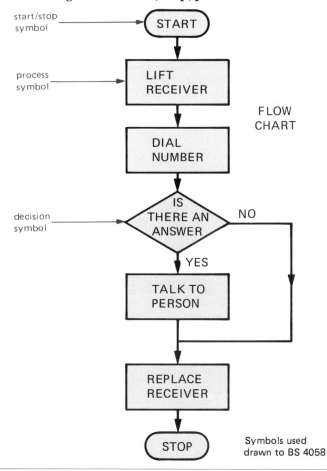

QUESTIONS/EXERCISES

① Design a **flow chart** that could be used to help a child cross the road. Use the example above to help with the use of the correct symbols.

② Use the **critical path analysis** method of planning for your current design work or a design that your teacher chooses.

2 SIMPLIFYING COMPLEX PROBLEMS

Using a systems approach

This section will help you simplify and understand complex problems or **systems** such as the workings of a record player, a robot or an aircraft. It is done by breaking the **problem** or **system** into understandable blocks of information.

Two systems you have probably heard about include the 'solar system' and the 'London Underground system'.

What is a system?

In the context of this book it can be taken to mean **a complex whole made from a set of connecting parts or things**.

Modelling a system

Before a system is modelled it is important to decide how broad to make the model. For example if trying to model a **broad system** concerning '**transport**' things such as lorries, aircraft, ships, would be included. It could be made broader still by including the effects of pollution caused by transport etc. A **narrow system** or **sub-system** is a limited version of a **broad system**. A transport **sub-system** example could include **brake** or **light systems**.

The diagram below shows how a **broad system** with its **sub-system** can be drawn out.

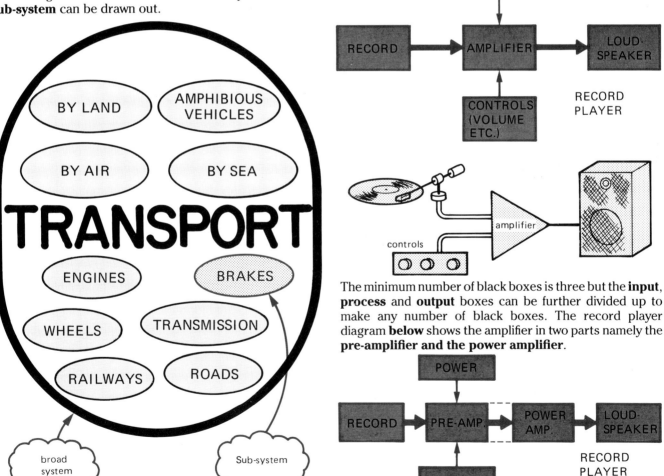

Using the 'black box' (or block diagram) approach to model systems

This is a very useful way of studying systems, especially electronic and computer systems. Control systems can be simplified into three main '**black boxes**' which are labelled **input**, **process** and **output** as shown below.

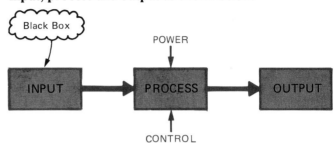

For example a record player can be analysed using the **black box** approach as shown below, the **input** comes from the needle resting on the record, the amplifier **processes** the signal, the amount of amplification is determined by the user pre-setting the **controls** such as tone or volume. The **output** state, the **loudspeaker**, converts the amplified voltage into sound.

The minimum number of black boxes is three but the **input**, **process** and **output** boxes can be further divided up to make any number of black boxes. The record player diagram **below** shows the amplifier in two parts namely the **pre-amplifier** and the **power amplifier**.

QUESTIONS/EXERCISES

① Model a **broad system** like the **transport** one above with the topic of **energy** with **sub-system** headings like windmills.

② Using the **black box** or **block diagram** of the record player above as an example, draw a **block diagram** of a **disc player**. (Two amplifiers and two loudspeakers needed.)

Black box (or block diagram) approach (continued)

Three more example systems are drawn below using the black box or block diagram approach.

1 A simple telephone system
2 A rain alarm
3 A burglar alarm

Can you identify the **input**, **process** and **output** stages.

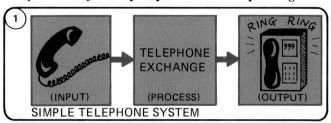

SIMPLE TELEPHONE SYSTEM

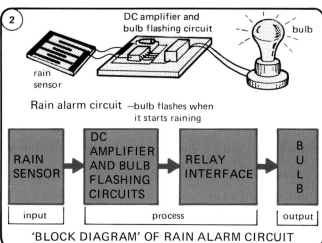

'BLOCK DIAGRAM' OF RAIN ALARM CIRCUIT

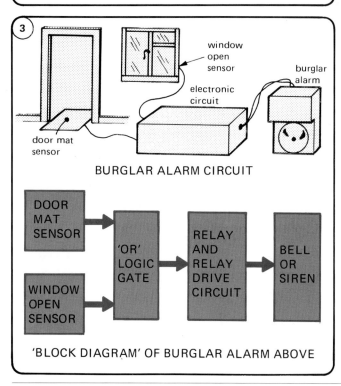

'BLOCK DIAGRAM' OF BURGLAR ALARM ABOVE

Feedback in systems

In order to have **automation** feedback is normally needed. Imagine being blindfolded and then being told to walk along the edge of a cliff. It would be difficult because our eyes (and our other senses) normally provide constant feedback enabling corrective action to be made as needed. An electric heater without any form of feedback is said to be an **open ended** control system. A heater once turned **on** stays **on** even if the room is too hot. If a heat sensor is added to provide **feedback** about the room's temperature it can be made to turn **off** automatically when the **set** temperature is reached and **on** again when the room cools down again. In control work it is sometimes important to control accurately the number of turns a normal DC electric motor makes. **Open loop** motor control would not be suitable but if **feedback** control is fed from the output shaft to the supply voltage a reasonably accurate control can be obtained as illustrated below:

'Open loop' electric motor control
(very difficult to control accurately)

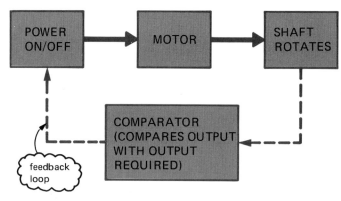

Electric motor control with 'feedback'

An automatic height-measuring device made using LEGO® Technical kit 1090. The height is calculated by counting the black and white strips passing the optical sensor. The readout is given on the computer screen.

QUESTIONS/EXERCISES

① Model an **electronic thermometer** using a **block diagram** similar to the ones shown above.

② Draw a model of a **room fan heater** with **feedback** to control the temperature using the **black box** approach as shown on this page.

DESIGN AND PROBLEM SOLVING QUESTIONS

Folder design

(1) Design a suitable **border layout** for your design sheets which could be used for future design work. It can reflect your own personality or the kind of work you will be designing.

(2) Design a **folder cover** for your project work which reflects your own personality or the work you are currently designing.

(3) Copy out the **Design Process Summary** on page 19 and then place it in your design folder so that it can be referred to quickly.

(4) Write three design briefs that could arise from the needs of:

(A) A member of your family.
(B) A handicapped person.
(C) A member of staff.

(5) (a) Make a **folder card human model** (see page 24) and then fashion it to make a modern man or woman using coloured pens, card etc.
(b) Make a second **folded card human model** that is twice as big as the first one.

(6) Design a **storage unit** to hold something of your own choice (eg records, tapes, books etc.)

(a) Write your own **design brief**.
(b) **Investigate** and **research** the problem.
(c) Sketch at least three **ideas** and **possible solutions**.
(d) **Develop** the best solution indicating how it could be made.

(7) Design a **modular sculpture** that is based on four or more parts that have the same basic form. No restrictions on materials but must fit in a 0.25 m cube.

(8) Design a **bedside light** that makes use of a 40 watt **mains** or a **car headlight bulb**. It must be safe in use.

(a) **Investigate** the important design features with special emphasis on safety.
(b) Sketch **three possible solutions** in the situation(s) they will be used.

(9) **A desk tidy** is required for a director of a toy factory. It must look impressive and have '**director**' written on it. **Investigate** the problem then sketch three **possible ideas/solutions**.

(10) The school shop wants a **money container** that keeps coin types separate so that it is easy and quick to count the money taken in each day.

(a) **investigate** this problem in some detail.
(b) Sketch three **possible solutions**.
(c) Develop the **best idea** showing construction details.

Notes Bank notes can be ignored.

It must be portable and capable of being made in the school workshop.

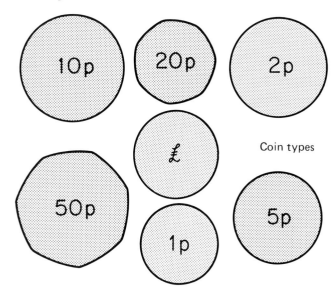

Coin types

(11) A food manufacturer wants a cheap self service 'nut bar' dispenser that they can give free to shopkeepers; to help sell the new nut bar called '**munch**'. The dispenser should fold flat when not in use, so that it does not take up much room when being transported to the shops. It must hold 100 bars when full. Details of the new '**Munch**' bar are given below:

Ø 25 × 100 mm long

Nut bar drawing

(a) Sketch **three possible** ideas with an advertising slogan added etc then;
(b) Make a **card model** of the best idea.
(Test using rolled up tubes of card made to the size of a 'Munch' bar.)

(12) Design a **waste paper container** that could be **mass produced** suitable for use outside sweet shops.

(a) **Investigate** and **research** the problem.
(b) Sketch at least three **ideas** and **possible solutions**.
(c) **Develop** the **best solution** indicating how it could be made and what materials are suitable.

DESIGN PROCESS QUESTIONS

(13) Design a **trophy** for a competition run by a television program called '**Future Technology**'. The trophy must be modern and appealing to the viewer. It is to be made from plastics and steel, which will be chromium plated.

(a) Sketch **four possible ideas**.
(b) **Develop the best idea** with details of construction and materials added.
  (It should be well presented and coloured in.)

(14) The school **assembly hall doors need to be held open** when pupils leave or enter the hall.
Design a device that will keep the door open, which is easy and quick to operate. The user should not have to bend down to use it.

Notes

The doors open 90 degrees; so a hook cannot be used to hook it onto a nearby wall.
The doors should not close by mistake as students walk past them.

(15) What design features do you think important in the design of a family car used for camping holidays. Draw a suitable car loaded up ready to go on holiday with the features you think important.

Mainly technological questions

(16) The basic layout of a **washing machine** is given below. Using the information below make a **flow diagram** of the **system** so that dirty clothes can be put in the washing machine, are washed and then spin dried ready to be removed and put on the washing line.

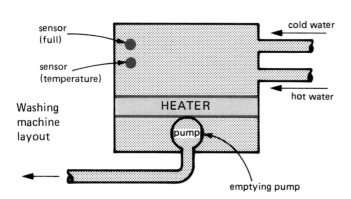

Washing machine layout

Water enters via hot and cold water solenoid valves, the water heater heats the water to the correct temperature as required, the drum provides either a washing motion or a spinning motion at 800 rpm for spin drying. A pump is used to pump the waste water out.

(17) Design a **container for an electric or electronic circuit** of your own choice.

(a) Draw and name the circuit to be used.
(b) **Investigate** the design factors.
(c) Sketch **three possible solutions** for the container.

(18) Below are three containers which could be used to enclose an electronic circuit

(a) Which one would you choose to make in a school workshop? Give reasons why you selected it and rejected the others.
(b) Make a possible CPA (Critical Path Analysis) chart for the production of one of the containers below (times need not be shown).

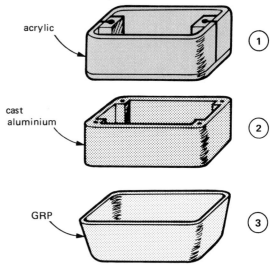

acrylic ①

cast aluminium ②

GRP ③

(19) Design a device that converts the small hand held PCB (Printed Circuit Board) drill shown below into an accurate drill that can be made to move under control 40 mm up and down (the motion being rather like the workshop pillar drill). The design must have a flat area where PCBs can be placed and drilled.

Note
The device must not be very expensive. Kit parts can be used in a limited way if required.

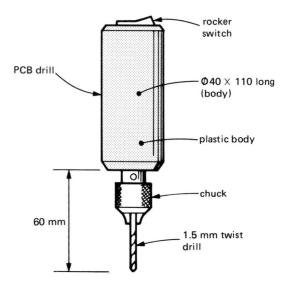

PCB drill

rocker switch

Ø40 × 110 long (body)

plastic body

chuck

60 mm

1.5 mm twist drill

DESIGN PROCESS QUESTIONS

CRAFT PROJECT IDEAS   Over 150 ideas here

Mainly craft

Action Man type toy
Artificial hand
Backgammon game
Bedroom furniture
Bird box/table
Bookcase
Bracelet
Briefcase
Bubble machine for disco
Candle holder
Car or bike anti-theft device
Cardbox
Cards (for an occasion–Greetings)
Chair
Chair ergonomics
Cheese boards
Chess set
Clamp
Climbing frame
Clip – Decorated
Clock
Compass (drawing or directional)
Condiment set
Container – Nuts, ash, fruit
Container – Pens, casettes, cards
Cosmetic display
Cutting board – Bread, cheese etc.
Cutting board – Bread
Cutting board – Cheese
Daughts
Desk tidy
Dice or spinning top
Dishes
Drawing instruments
Drilling aid
Drums
Educational aids
Elastic band bounce game
Enamelling
Executive toys
Exerciser
Figures – Animal/human
Fishing stools/box
Flying 'pull' bird
Fun hook
Game in a container
Games – Draughts, O's and X's etc.
Garden equipment
Greenhouse extras
Guitars
Gyroscope
Hardness tester
Holiday pack/tent
Inclinometer
Jewellery case or tree
Jewellery – Pendants, rings, braclets
Jigsaw
Joint tester
Jumping jack – Pull toy
Keyfob
Kinetic art
Kitchen – Cutlery
Kitchen – Foil dispensers
Kitchen – Herb rack

Kitchen – Racks
Kitchen – Steps
Laminated wood – Salad spoons
Lamp
Magazine rack
making use of recycled cans etc.
Marble games
Marble roller coaster
Materials testers
Milk indicator
Mirror stand
Mobile
Model house
Models of futuristic houses etc.
Modern lighting
Money box
Nameplate
Nine mens Morris game
Notepad holder
Notice board
Pad saw holder
Pattern maker on paper
Pecking woodpecker toy
Pen holder
People counter/recorder
Percussion instruments
Photograph display or holder
Picnic bench
Pivoted toy
Plant containers
Plant pot holder
Play bricks
Play equipment
Polystyrene (expanded) model town
Pop-up cards
Pottery
Puzzles – Jigsaw, interlocking
Rack – cassettes, books etc.
Radiator shelf
Resin casting
Room name
Room plaque
Salad servers
Sculpture – Abstract – Human etc.
Security system
Sewing container
Shoe tidy
Signs
Sledge
Something for the disabled
Sports aids
Stand for something, eg Mike
Stationery – Calender
Stationery – Date diary
Stationery – Desk
Stationery – Notepad
Stationery – Tape dispenser
Stool
Sundial
Survey of people's habits
Table
Table mats
T-square for homework
Theme based on nature
Tiles

Toast rack
Tool box
Tools – hammer, hacksaw, screwdriver
Toys – Tipping lorry, cars, puppets
Trolley
Try square
Using a given part design a?
Vehicles
Wastepaper container
Wire shapes soldered eg a man shape
Wire strippers
Workbench
Xylophone

Graphical communications

2D drawings from 3D
3D drawings from 2D
Architectural drawings
Axonmetric drawings
CAD on computer
Car badge
Communication
Computer animation
Customized illustrations
Design illustration
Development
Enlarging and reducing
Ergonome model
Ergonomic line drawings
Flow chart
Flow of pupils or work
Geometric patterns
Graphs and charts
House number
Ideograms
Ikon design
Lettering for effect
Loci
Logograms
Models in card
Optical illusions
Packaging developments
Packaging for effect
Pantograph work
Patio layout
Perspective drawings
Record cover
Safety poster
School plan
Sectional drawings
Simplified process
Sundial
Symbols
Symbols and conventions
Tessellations
Tile design
Using a grid to aid work
Using a light box
Vectors
Workshop layout

For mainly Technological Projects see pages 137 and 138.

For mainly Technological Projects see pages 137 and 138.

QUESTIONS/EXERCISES

① Which **ten project ideas** would you like to make yourself? Use the lists above to help you.

② Which **two project ideas** would like to make if you only had one day to make them. Sketch your favourite idea.

③ Which **graphical communication drawing** from above would you like to draw next for homework? (Sketch neatly.)

APPEARANCE (AESTHETICS)

This section is about the appearance, or aesthetic appearance, of shapes and forms that need to be considered when designing. The appearance of a product may be the most important consideration to a purchaser of a product. This is particularly true of fashionable products such as clothes, jewellery and other decorative items. Products that are not considered fashionable also have to be reasonably attractive or else they will not be as popular to the user or purchaser.

This section is divided up as follows:

1 Lines, shapes and forms

2 Texture

3 Patterns (if any)

4 Colour

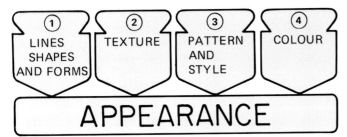

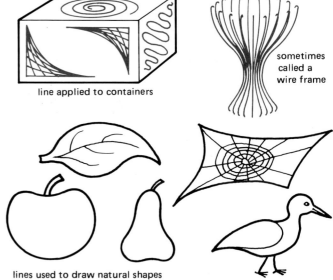

sometimes called a wire frame

lines used to draw natural shapes

1 LINES, SHAPES AND FORMS

Each of these terms are described below.

Lines

Lines are basic to all drawings and many products. Below are examples of lines used to produce various effects.

Which of the above seem to imply movement?

Shapes and forms

Shapes are **two** dimensional, the two dimensions being **length** and **width**. **Forms** are **three** dimensional, the third dimension being **depth**.

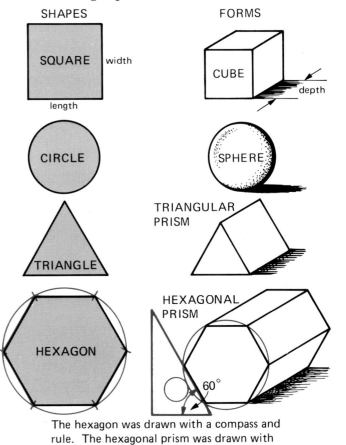

SHAPES — FORMS

SQUARE width / length

CUBE depth

CIRCLE

SPHERE

TRIANGLE

TRIANGULAR PRISM

HEXAGON

HEXAGONAL PRISM

60°

The hexagon was drawn with a compass and rule. The hexagonal prism was drawn with a compass and a set square.

QUESTIONS / EXERCISES

① List at least four factors that influence the **appearance** of a product. What is the essential difference between a **shape** and a **form**?

② Draw a **random pattern** made up of **lines** that implies **movement** (appearing to move).

③ Draw a fairly large cube then **decorate** using a **line** pattern to make it attractive.

Geometric and natural shapes

Shapes (and **forms**) can be described as either **geometric** or **natural** in appearance.

Geometric shapes and forms

They are precise and can be drawn with instruments. Examples below:

The last two shapes are impossible to make.

Natural (or organic) shapes

Natural shapes include things such as animals and plants. They are often drawn without the use of drawing equipment like a compass or a rule.

Random shapes

To produce some random shapes scribbles are drawn on pieces of paper, the interesting shapes are coloured in as required.

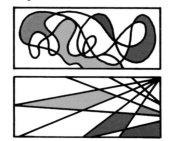

Cutting or segmenting

Drawings or photographs can be cut up and rearranged, or drawings can be drawn to make them look as they were if cut up.

Mirror images

The shape is 'mirrored' about an **axis**.

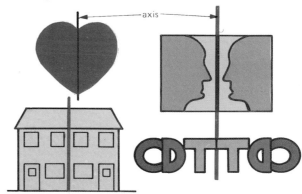

Positive and negative shapes

These are similar to **mirror images** but the colour is reversed on the negative side.

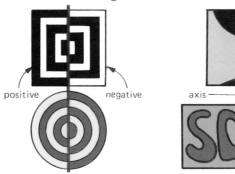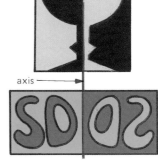

QUESTIONS/EXERCISES

① Draw a simplified outline of a person or an animal, then draw it using the following styles: **geometric, natural** and **segmented**.

② Draw **two alphabetical letters**, such as your initials, then draw its **mirror image** next to it.

Harmonious (or similar) shapes

Parts that make up the complete shape are all similar and can be said to be in **harmony** (harmonious colours also used).

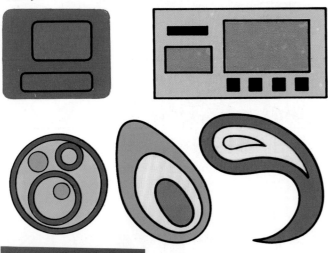

Simplified shapes

The shapes below are simplified. Can you tell what the shapes below are supposed to represent? (The long line represents a horse.)

Evolved shapes

The initial shapes below on the left were the starting point, they were then developed **step by step** moving to the right.

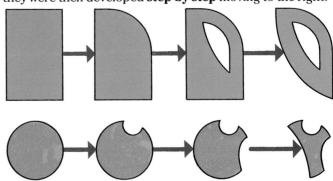

Contrasting shapes

The drawings below are made up from constrasting shapes (contrasting colours also used).

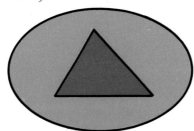

2 TEXTURE

All materials have a certain texture. Glass usually has a hard smooth texture whereas a fur glove feels soft and smooth.

It is important that the correct texture is selected or created for some situations. It would be sensible to make a seating surface out of soft smooth material rather than a hard, rough material. In design work artificial textures are sometimes applied; artificial 'old world' wooden beams can be bought which are actually made from plastic which is moulded to look like the real thing. Artificial textures are often applied to materials to produce the required textural appearance.

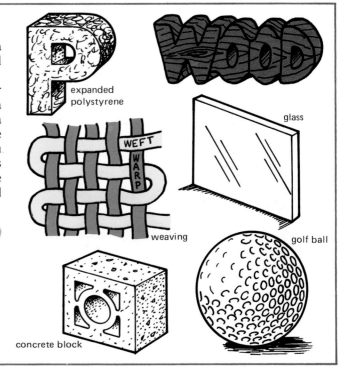

QUESTIONS / EXERCISES

① (a) Draw a group of shapes that could be said to be in **harmony**.

(b) Draw a group of shapes that **contrast** with each other.

② Draw a **simplfied shape** of a caravan or a person jumping.

③ Draw a product that could be classified as being (a) **hard,** (b) **soft**, (c) **rough** and (d) **smooth**.

3 PATTERN AND STYLE

Pattern

Patterns are made up from simple or complex shapes, they can be arranged in a **regular** or **irregular fashion**. They are often applied to products to produce the **effect** required. Examples include tiles and packaging materials.

'Units' to make a pattern

Basic **units** (such as a tile) can be arranged into a **pattern**.

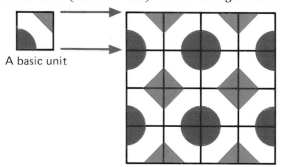

A basic unit

Patterns made using a grid

Ready made **grids** such as **graph paper** can be used.

Triangular grid

Square grid

Tessellations

These are certain types of patterns that are suitable for interlocking tiles like the example below.

Tessellation based on fish shapes

Using letters to make a pattern

Stencils and templates

They are used to '**mark out**' shapes quickly. There are also lettering stencils which can be useful in CDT work.

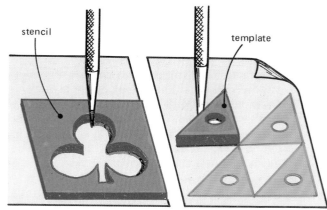

stencil

template

Style and fashion

Style and **fashion** are constantly changing. New **ideas**, **friends**, **materials**, **technology**, **lifestyle**, **politics** and **the country you live in**, play their part in what is acceptable. Below are examples of **styles and fashions** from different times.

Styles from different periods are shown below.

Classical pillars

Old English lettering and numbers

Art nouveau 1890's

1980's punk

QUESTIONS / EXERCISES

① Design and draw a **geometric tiled pattern** (using at least 16 tiles) made up from one basic tile design having only two simple shapes on it.

② Draw a **pattern based on your initials** that could be used on your design folder.

③ (a) Select and draw a **fashionable modern product**.
(b) Select and draw a very **old fashioned** household product.

4 COLOUR

When designing it is very important to consider the **colour a product** will have and **colour of the environment** it will be used in. Certain colours have associations, for example **red** is used for **STOP** and **green** for **GO** on traffic lights.

A colour is described in **three main** ways:

- **Hue** – type of colour eg red, green, blue.
- **Chroma** – Indicates its brightness.
- **Tone** – refers to the amount of **black** or **white** used. A **light colour** is usually referred to as a **pale** colour. A **dark colour** is referred to as a **darker colour** or **tone**.

Painting colours

To produce the full range of painted colours only **three primary colours** are needed, plus **black** and **white**, to obtain **tonal effects**. The **three primary colours**, for paint, are: **red, yellow**, and **blue**. The **colour circle** below is a convenient way of showing how other colours can be made. To produce the **secondary** (meaning second) **colours** such as **green** mix the **primary colours** on either side; in the example, **yellow** and **blue**, are mixed together. The **tertiary** (meaning third) **colours** are made by mixing the colours either side of the **tertiary colour** required.

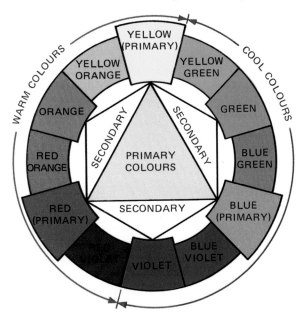

Warm and cool colours

The colours that we associate as being **warm** and **cold** are marked around the colour circle above. Red and yellow is associated in our minds with heat because of the sunheat which we see everyday. Blue is considered a cool colour because we know the night is cool and people turn blue when cold.

Contrasting colours

The biggest contrast is obtained by selecting the **opposite colours** on the **colour circle**. These colours are said to **complement** each other.

Colours in harmony

Colours **next to each other** on the **colour circle** are said to be in **harmony**.

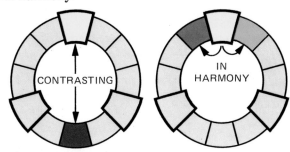

Colours involving light

The **primary colours** for the mixing of **colours using light** are: **red, green** and **blue**; usually written as RGB on the back of computer monitors and video camera cable connectors. If **red, green** and **blue** are mixed together **white** is the result. Try altering a colour TV to see what effects can be produced by varying the amount of **red, green** and **blue**.

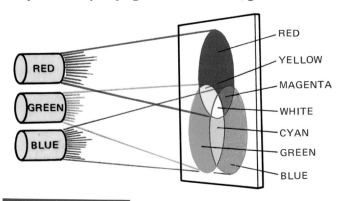

Rainbow colours

White light is **split** up into **rainbow colours** by the tiny raindrops in the sunlight. The rainbow colours can also be produced using a **prism** of glass as shown below:

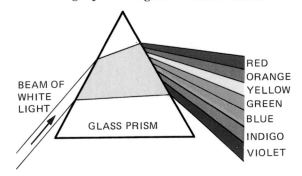

QUESTIONS/EXERCISES

① Draw and paint a **colour circle** similar to the one above using only the **three primary colours** for paint.
② Draw three blank "colour circle" diagrams then colour one with **warm colours**, the second with **cool colours** and the other with **harmonious colours** (three segments).
③ Make at least three **card spinning tops** (matchsticks in centre) then paint each half a different colour. Then spin to see mixed colours.

GRAPHICAL COMMUNICATION

This page summaries the **graphical communication** methods that are explained on the next few pages. The methods are:

1 Technical sketching methods

2 Pictorial drawings (or three dimensional)
Oblique and
Isometric
Perspective drawings

3 Axonometric projection

Notes
- **For orthographic projection (flat drawings), see pages 60–62.**
- For **models** see page 31.

A **building** form is used in each example on this page so that comparisons can be made between the different methods.

(a) Look at the drawings below and see if you can spot the difference between the drawing techniques, such as angle used.
(b) Which method do you think looks the most realistic and which the least realistic?
(c) Which drawing method would you prefer?

① Technical sketching (without instruments)

② Pictorial drawings (3D) (drawn with instruments)

ⓐ Oblique drawing

ⓑ Isometric projection

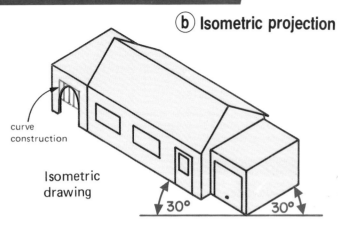

Isometric drawing

30° 30°

ⓒ Perspective drawing

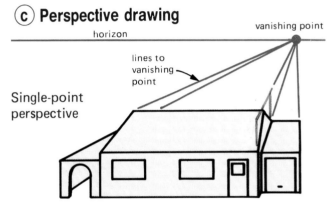

horizon — vanishing point

lines to vanishing point

Single-point perspective

vanishing point — horizon — vanishing point

Two-point perspective (estimated method)

③ Axonometric (useful for house layouts)

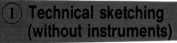

The 'plan' is drawn, then the walls are projected up

45° 45°

QUESTIONS/EXERCISES

① List the main drawing methods used to illustrate products **three dimensionally**.
③ Which drawing method do you think is the easiest to use when using drawing instruments and why?
③ **Sketch pictorially** (in 3D) your own house or a local house of interest to you.

1 TECHNICAL SKETCHING

Sketches are used to communicate thoughts and ideas quickly on paper. HB pencils can be used, they give a fairly dark line yet are still reasonably easy to rub out if a mistake is made.

Below are some techniques to help you sketch.

- **The centre line method**
- **Circles (and ellipses)**
- **The box method**
- **Using a grid**

The centre line method

This is useful for shapes like the **goblet** and **torch** drawn below where each side is the same and has curves.

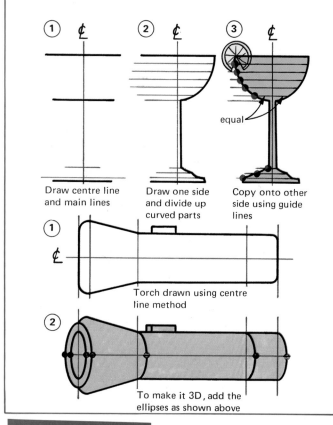

① Draw centre line and main lines

② Draw one side and divide up curved parts

③ Copy onto other side using guide lines

equal

① Torch drawn using centre line method

② To make it 3D, add the ellipses as shown above

Circles (or ellipses)

Draw a box outline as shown below to act as a guide. The short green dots are useful for more accurate circles.

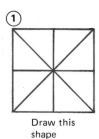

① Draw this shape

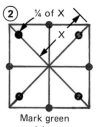

② ¼ of X X Mark green positions on diagonal lines

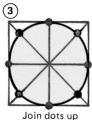

③ Join dots up

The box method of sketching

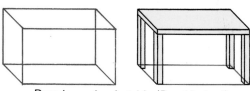

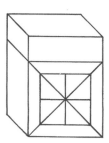

Drawing a simple table (Box Method)

Drawing house scales (Box Method)

Using a grid

Grids or graph paper can be used as shown below to help aid drawings.

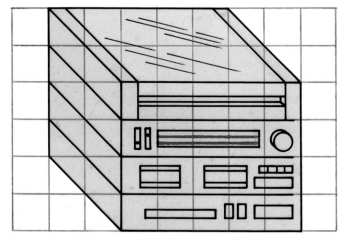

Music stack system — graph paper used

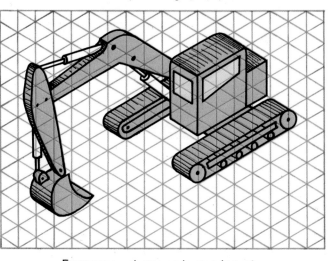

Excavator — drawn on isometric paper

QUESTIONS / EXERCISES

① Using the **centre line method** of sketching draw a vase at least 180 mm high.

② Using the **box method** of sketching draw a washing machine or a piece of furniture.

③ Draw a **music centre** or a **wooden toy**; using either squared **graph paper** or **isometric paper** as a drawing guide.

2 PICTORIAL DRAWINGS

Pictorial drawings are drawing methods that view an object three dimensionally. The methods most commonly used for pictorial drawings are:
Oblique, isometric and **perspective** drawings.

Oblique drawing

This method is the easiest to use because it starts with a single **flat front view**. The main **advantage** is that it can be drawn by direct measurement. The **disadvantage** is that the drawings are not as realistic as perspective drawings. *Note* – If circles are to be drawn, arrange them on the front view so that they can be drawn using compasses.

The stages in drawing oblique forms

(a) Draw the front view of the object (full size).
(b) Draw 45 degree lines back as shown.
(c) Mark the depth on the 45 degree lines. **Cabinet oblique** halves this distance to obtain a more realistic effect and is used below.
(d) Complete and line in as shown below.

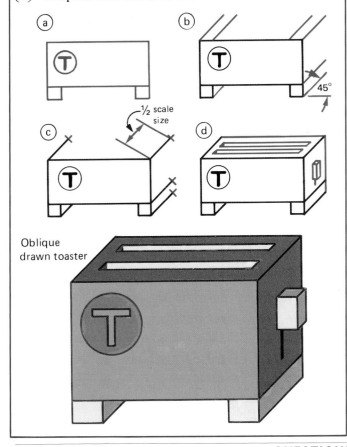

Oblique drawn toaster

Isometric drawing

This method looks more natural than oblique drawing with one corner of the object in front, yet still allowing direct measurements to be made. Curved shapes are more difficult to draw. A compass cannot be used for circles; they have to be constructed or drawn in with an isometric circle template.

Stages in drawing isometric forms

(a) Draw a vertical line and mark off the height of the object.
(b) Draw the two 30 degree lines using a 30 degree **set square**, and measure the lengths off as shown.
(c) Draw the other vertical and 30 degree lines as required.
(d) Complete the drawing and line in.

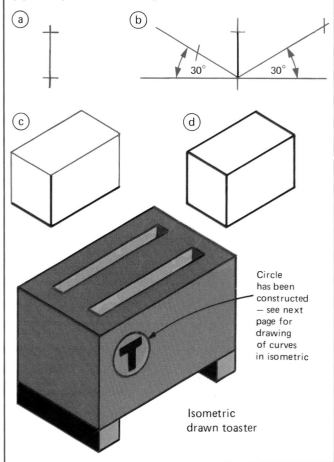

Circle has been constructed – see next page for drawing of curves in isometric

Isometric drawn toaster

QUESTIONS/EXERCISES

① Using the letters 'CDT' above as a guide, draw the letter 'E' in **oblique** and **isometric projection**, at least 100 mm high.
② Draw a toaster of your own design in **oblique projec-** **tion** with the toast as well if you like!
③ Draw a television in **isometric projection**. Extra – Draw a picture on the TV screen.

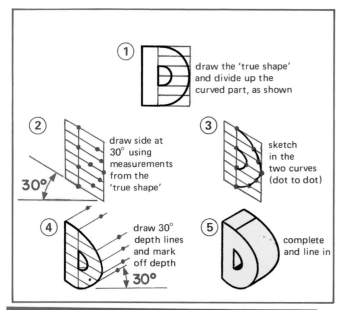

① draw the 'true shape' and divide up the curved part, as shown

② draw side at 30° using measurements from the 'true shape'

③ sketch in the two curves (dot to dot)

④ draw 30° depth lines and mark off depth

⑤ complete and line in

Stages in drawing in 'one point perspective'

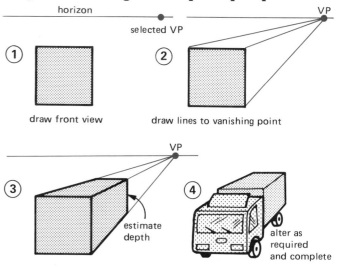

horizon

selected VP

① draw front view

② draw lines to vanishing point

③ estimate depth

④ alter as required and complete

Single point perspective (estimated method)

This is a simple but effective way of drawing **three dimensionally**. The depth is **estimated** but could be obtained by **construction** (see page 64 for a house example). The example below shows the effect of varying the objects' position in relationship to the **vanishing point VP**.

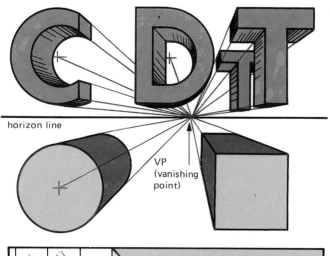

horizon line

VP (vanishing point)

S.D. INC.

Buildings in single point perspective

Two point perspective

This method uses **two vanishing points (VPs)**. The object drawn is usually **viewed from a corner** as shown. The next page shows a room drawn in two point perspective. It started out like the **internal drawing** (B) below.

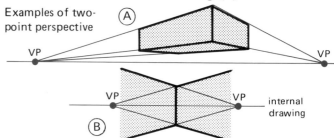

Examples of two-point perspective

Ⓐ VP   VP

Ⓑ VP   VP   internal drawing

Stages in drawing two-point perspective

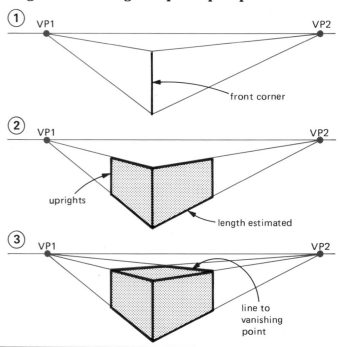

① VP1   VP2
front corner

② VP1   VP2
uprights
length estimated

③ VP1   VP2
line to vanishing point

QUESTIONS / EXERCISES

① Using the isometric letter 'D' above as a guide, draw a large letter 'P' in **isometric projection**, 150 mm high and 10 mm thick.

② Draw your own initials in **estimated single point**

perspective using the CDT example above to help you.

③ Draw a building or a city scene of your own choice in **estimated single point perspective**.

Drawing a fun camera – stages

① VP₁ ———— horizon ———— VP₂

Select a corner position then draw to the two vanishing points

② VP₁ ———— VP₂

Estimate length and thickness and draw lines to VP

③ VP₁ ———— horizon ———— VP₂

Find centre line by using diagonal lines as shown

④ Draw circle construction then add final details

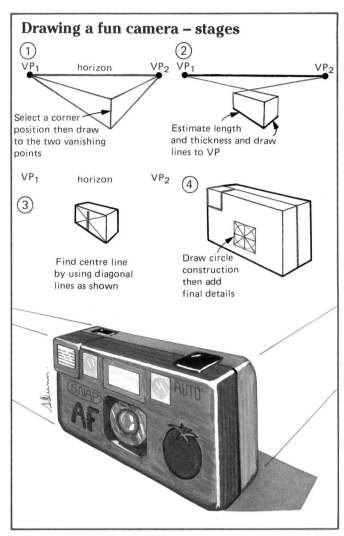

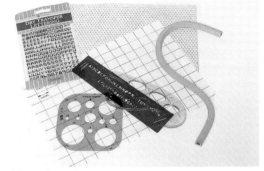

Drawing aids such as french curve, stencil, flexible curve, etc.

CDT drawn in Two point perspective

① make a grid around the letters

② a red lines to VP₁

② b green lines

divide by 14

③ transfer letters to this grid

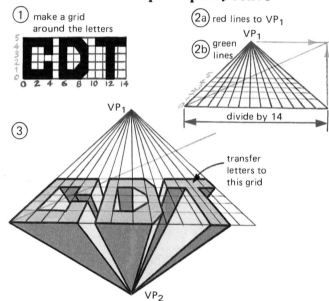

STAGES

① VP₁ ———— horizon ———— VP₂

② VP₁ ———— VP₂

③ VP₁ ———— VP₂

A **kitchen** drawn in **two point perspective**. Could you draw a similar room using **two point perspective**.

To do this a large piece of paper is needed to allow the vanishing points (VP) to be a fair distance away.

QUESTIONS / EXERCISES

① Draw a **fun camera** in **two point perspective** similar to the one drawn about on A3 paper. The camera itself to be about 80 × 60 × 30 mm.

② Draw the corner of your own bedroom in **two point perspective** using the kitchen drawing states above to help you. Pale colours can be added.

GRAPHICAL PRESENTATION

Good **presentation** is very important in design work, it helps sell an **idea** or a **product** and inform potential customers or manufacturers. This section illustrates methods that can be used reasonably easily after a little practice. **Presentation drawings** are of two main types:

(1) **Presentation** or **Artists drawings** – accuracy not being critical.
(2) **Instructional drawings** which need to be accurate and convey precise information.

Equipment needed

There is a very large selection to choose from. The photograph shows a range of equipment commonly used in presentation drawing work. Can you spot the following:

Drawing board, crayons, technical pencil, felt tip pens and compass?

Pencils

Pencil leads, now made from graphite, are supplied in a range of hardnesses. HB is the most common general purpose type. The B (Black) range of pencils are used for **freehand drawings**, such as B, 2B and 3B pencils. The H (Hard) range are used for **technical drawings**, such as H, 2H, 3H, and 4H pencils.

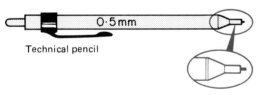

Technical pencil

Technical pens

These pens have a special point that is parallel at the tip, as shown below, this enables accurate work when used against a ruler. 0.5 mm is the most common size point.

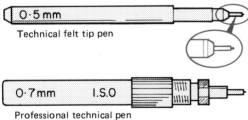

Technical felt tip pen

Professional technical pen

Colouring methods

The most convenient method is usually **felt tip pens** or **crayons** but **inks** and **paints** can also be used. Felt tips and inks are either **water based** or **spirit based** (the permanent types).

Good quality drawing equipment that can be used in graphic presentation: the A3 drawing board, set of layout markers (Marsgraphic 3000), water-soluble crayons, quick adjusting compass, technical pens and pencils are all made by Staedtler.

Presentation methods

darkened outline

crayon

light source

heavy felt tip outline

shadows — can be determined from the light source as shown

SUN

Toning
1 lightest colour
2 darker colour
3 darkest colour

cut out and mounted on black card

ground shaded in

QUESTIONS / EXERCISES

(1) What **pencil hardness** do you think is suitable for:
   (a) sketching and (b) technical drawing.
(2) Draw a greatly enlarged technical pen point then

explain why it is made like that.
(3) Copy the set of **presentation drawings** above using the same techniques.

Shiny surfaces

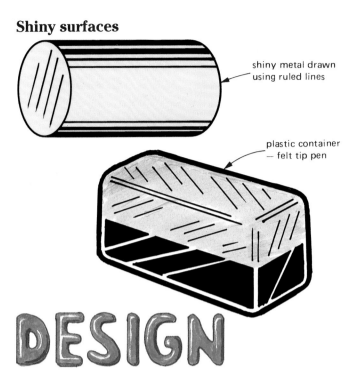

shiny metal drawn using ruled lines

plastic container — felt tip pen

Drawing on coloured card

NOTES

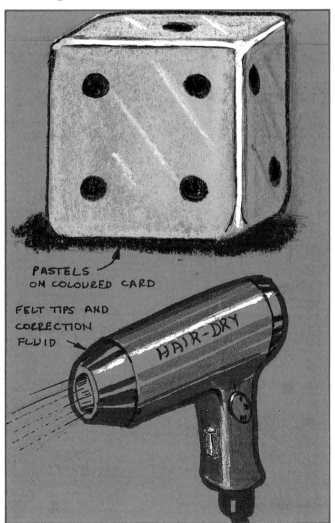

PASTELS ON COLOURED CARD

FELT TIPS AND CORRECTION FLUID

HAIR-DRY

Felt tip pen only

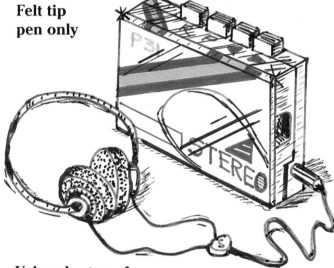

P3

STEREO

Using dry transfers (title + shading)

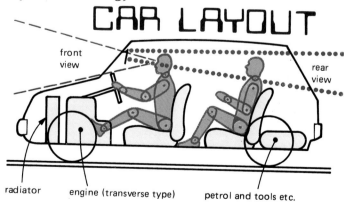

CAR LAYOUT

front view

rear view

radiator   engine (transverse type)   petrol and tools etc.

QUESTIONS / EXERCISES

① Select a simple object that is **shiny**; then draw it so that it looks realistic. Use examples above to help you.

② **Cut out a picture** from a magazine and use it as part of a design that could be made in the workshop.

③ Draw a **personal stereo system** similar to the one shown on this page using only felt tip pens.

Fashion drawings

drawn using
felt tips and
crayons

words that
illustrate
what they mean

Enlarging and distorting a grid shape

The two shapes below have been copied from the drawing on the left. The first drawing below is increased in size and the second drawing used a distorted grid onto which the person was copied.

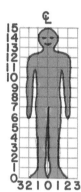

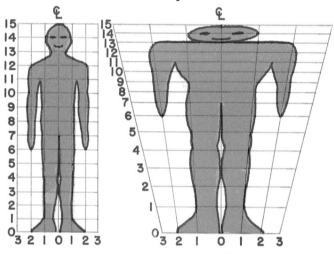

The drawing of simple **characters** on a **computer** is done by drawing an 8 by 8 grid on paper then filling in the parts required as shown below. The **binary column** values are then totalled up before using them in a BASIC program. Below is a simple program for the **BBC computer** which you could try.

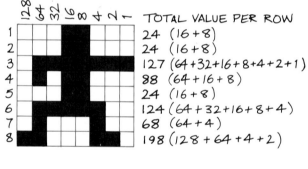

COLUMN VALUES

	TOTAL VALUE PER ROW
1	24 (16+8)
2	24 (16+8)
3	127 (64+32+16+8+4+2+1)
4	88 (64+16+8)
5	24 (16+8)
6	124 (64+32+16+8+4)
7	68 (64+4)
8	198 (128+64+4+2)

```
 1 REM CALLED "MAN" WHICH FILLS SCREEN WITH FIGURES
10 MODE 5
20 VDU23, 225,24,24,127,88,24,124,68,198
30 PRINT CHR$(225);"MAN ";
40 GOTO 20
```

Lettering styles

The **lettering style** selected should match the image you want to convey. Below is a selection from a large lettering catalogue.

Antiques   **TRENDY**

DATA   **STENCIL**

A wire frame drawing being rotated. Modern computer aided drawing programs make this reasonably easy.

QUESTIONS/EXERCISES

① After looking at fashion catalogues or similar sketch and colour a **fashion drawing** of your own using the techniques seen.

② Using the **grid method of enlarging a drawing** shown above, enlarge the person drawing (top drawing) by five times using a suitable grid.

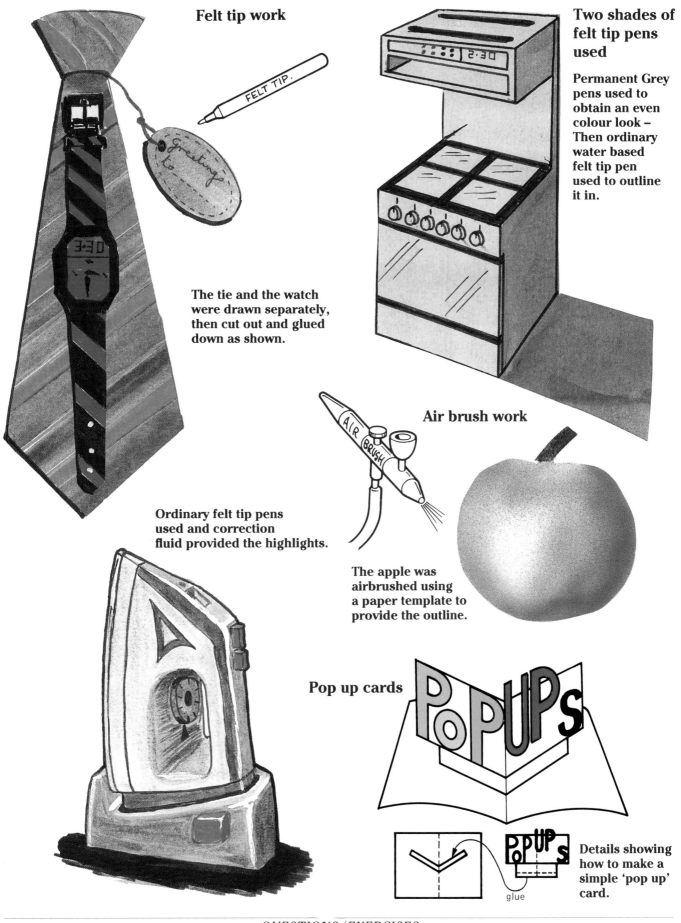

Felt tip work

FELT TIP.

greeting to

3:30

The tie and the watch were drawn separately, then cut out and glued down as shown.

Two shades of felt tip pens used

Permanent Grey pens used to obtain an even colour look – Then ordinary water based felt tip pen used to outline it in.

1:8 2:30

Air brush work

AIR BRUSH

The apple was airbrushed using a paper template to provide the outline.

Ordinary felt tip pens used and correction fluid provided the highlights.

Pop up cards

PoPUPs

PoPUPs

glue

Details showing how to make a simple 'pop up' card.

QUESTIONS/EXERCISES

① Make a full size card model of a **modern watch**. Then display it on a suitable background/display that 'shows it off'.

② Using **two felt tip pens** (eg a light grey and a dark grey), draw and colour your current design work or a radio.

A sequence showing step by step how to make a Printed Circuit Board (PCB)

The pupil who did this used a word processor for the text – The border theme and lettering style is based on the printed circuit theme. The original was drawn twice the size shown.

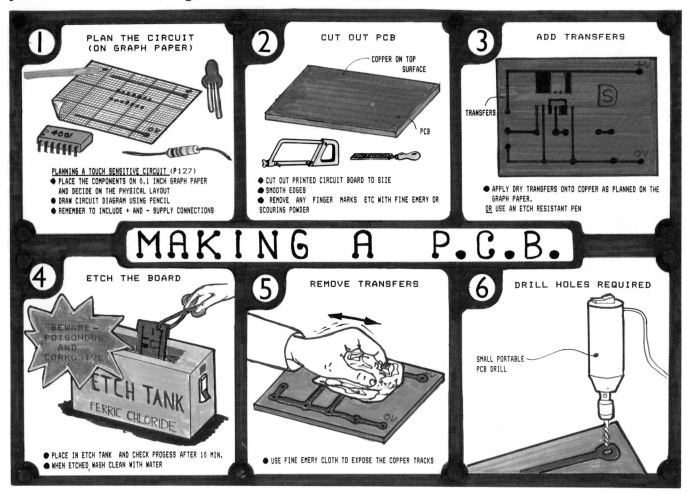

1 PLAN THE CIRCUIT (ON GRAPH PAPER)

PLANNING A TOUCH SENSITIVE CIRCUIT (P 127)
● PLACE THE COMPONENTS ON 0.1 INCH GRAPH PAPER AND DECIDE ON THE PHYSICAL LAYOUT
● DRAW CIRCUIT DIAGRAM USING PENCIL
● REMEMBER TO INCLUDE + AND – SUPPLY CONNECTIONS

2 CUT OUT PCB
COPPER ON TOP SURFACE
PCB
● CUT OUT PRINTED CIRCUIT BOARD TO SIZE
● SMOOTH EDGES
● REMOVE ANY FINGER MARKS ETC WITH FINE EMERY OR SCOURING POWDER

3 ADD TRANSFERS
TRANSFERS
● APPLY DRY TRANSFERS ONTO COPPER AS PLANNED ON THE GRAPH PAPER.
OR USE AN ETCH RESISTANT PEN

MAKING A P.C.B.

4 ETCH THE BOARD
BEWARE – POISONOUS AND CORROSIVE
ETCH TANK FERRIC CHLORIDE
● PLACE IN ETCH TANK AND CHECK PROGESS AFTER 10 MIN.
● WHEN ETCHED, WASH CLEAN WITH WATER

5 REMOVE TRANSFERS
● USE FINE EMERY CLOTH TO EXPOSE THE COPPER TRACKS

6 DRILL HOLES REQUIRED
SMALL PORTABLE PCB DRILL

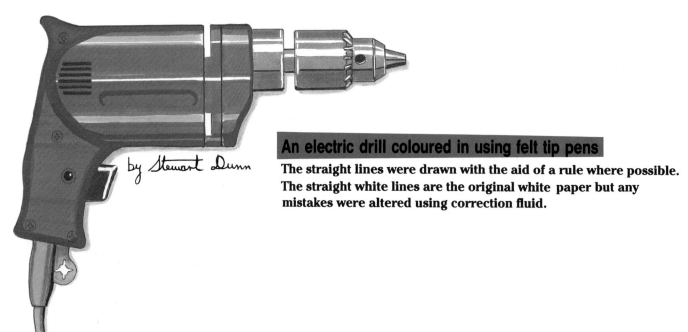

by Stewart Dunn

An electric drill coloured in using felt tip pens

The straight lines were drawn with the aid of a rule where possible. The straight white lines are the original white paper but any mistakes were altered using correction fluid.

QUESTIONS/EXERCISES

① Plan and **draw the sequence of events** for one of the following: (a) **Making a PCB** (Printed Circuit Board) in your school (use example above to help) or, (b) **Making a cup of coffee** or, (c) Describe another **CDT process**.

② Trace the outline of the **electric drill** above then colour it as shown using only felt tip pens, then 'cut out' and mount on coloured card.

A presentation drawing

Drawn by the author in pencil and then coloured in using felt tip pens. The initial colouring did not look very impressive but when the reflections and shadows were added it brought the drawing to life. The reflections were added using a white paint pen and correction fluid.

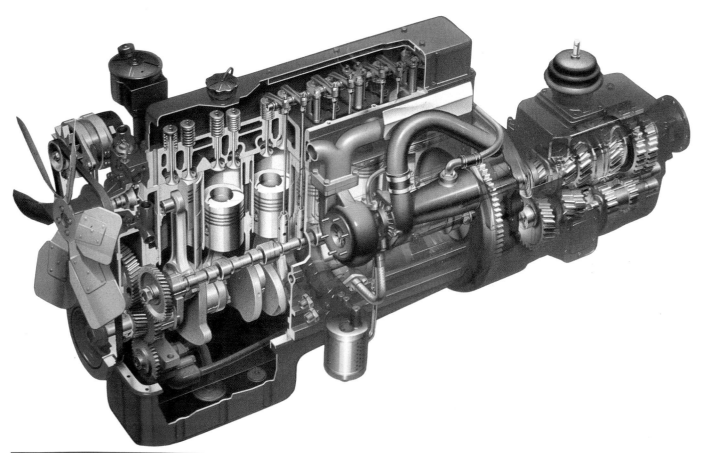

Cross sectional drawing

Of a Leyland DAF engine – Note the way different colours are used to represent different parts and how different parts are sectioned to show as much detail as possible. Can you identify the pistons, crankshaft and valves?

QUESTIONS/EXERCISES

① Trace the outline of the car above (or a car advert) then **colour** with **felt tip pens** in a similar style to that shown. Highlights and shadows can be added after the main colouring is done.

② Draw a **simplified version of the engine** above so that the following parts can be seen clearly and labelled: piston, connecting rod, valve etc.

ORTHOGRAPHIC (OR FLAT DRAWINGS)

ORTHOGRAPHIC PROJECTION

Orthographic projection (sometimes called **flat** or **multi-view drawings**) is a method of accurately drawing an object from several directions. Each view is drawn as though **flat**. **Drawing instruments** are usually used to produce these drawings. The **common views** drawn being **front view** (or **front elevation**), **plan** (or **top elevation** and **end** (or **side elevation**). Other views can also be drawn if required.

Working drawings are usually drawn in **orthographic projection** because they conveniently provide the information needed when making products.

The **two types of orthographic drawing** are called **first angle** and **third angle projection** (used in America). When planning the layout of an **orthographic** drawing allow space around the drawing for dimensions and other details.

First angle projection

The **energy saving house** example drawn in **first angle projection** has solar panels and a conservatory on the sunny south side. The three dimensional drawing below shows how the different views can be visualised. The views can be thought of as projected views (like a shadow) onto the folded paper; when opened up it produces the **first angle projection layout** as shown below.

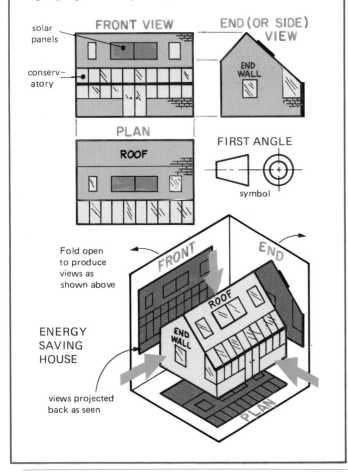

Third angle projection

The same **energy house** is drawn in **third angle projection**. Can you see the difference?

This method can be visualised by imagining that the object is being viewed through a transparent container. The **views** are seen at the **front** (like looking in a mirror), instead of behind the object.

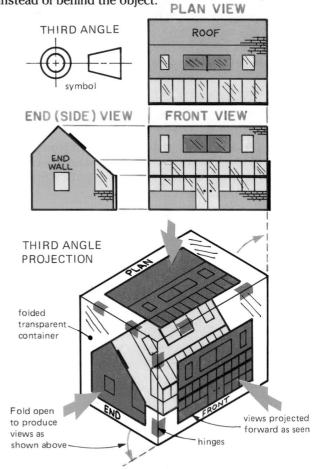

Drawing the electric vehicle

The first steps used in drawing the electric vehicle on the next page – **First angle projection** used.

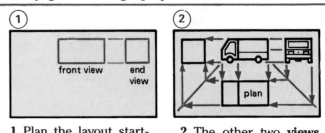

1 Plan the layout starting with the **front view** (because it has the most information on it), then **end view**.

2 The other two **views** can be constructed from the first two. The red lines show how this is done using a 45 degree line.

QUESTIONS/EXERCISES

① (a) Neatly sketch in **first angle orthographic projection** the **front, end** (or side) and **plan** views of a house of your own design. Use **squared paper** to guide you. (b) Redraw in **third angle projection**.

② Neatly sketch in **first** or **third angle orthographic projection** the **front, end** (or side) and **plan** views of a product you have made recently.

Orthographic projection continued

Electric vehicle – First angle projection

Four views are to enable the **front** and **back** of the vehicle to be seen. To avoid repeating measurements **sizes** can be transferred from one drawing to another, as shown by the red lines, the 45 degree line enables measurements to be turned through 90 degrees.

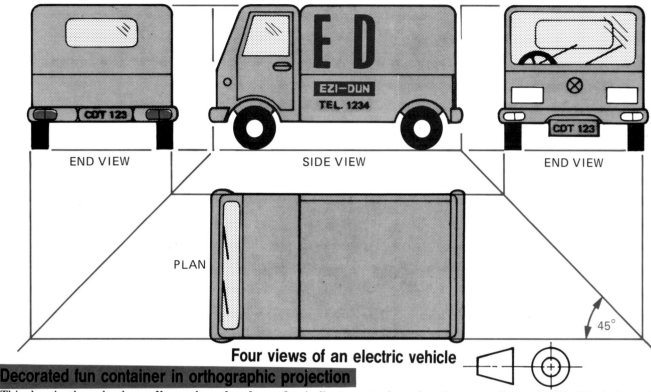

END VIEW   SIDE VIEW   END VIEW

PLAN

45°

Four views of an electric vehicle

Decorated fun container in orthographic projection

This drawing has also been **dimensioned**, **coloured** to indicate parts, has a **border**, **parts list** and a **title block**. Part of it is **cross-sectioned** (mark X–X). **Hidden detail** being shown as dashed lines.

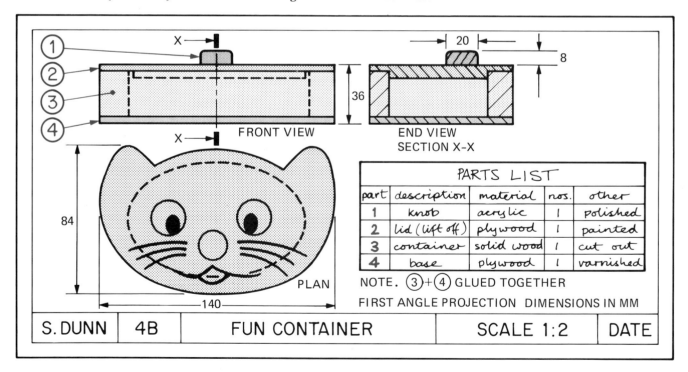

part	description	material	nos.	other
1	knob	acrylic	1	polished
2	lid (lift off)	plywood	1	painted
3	container	solid wood	1	cut out
4	base	plywood	1	varnished

NOTE. ③+④ GLUED TOGETHER
FIRST ANGLE PROJECTION DIMENSIONS IN MM

S. DUNN | 4B | FUN CONTAINER | SCALE 1:2 | DATE

QUESTIONS/EXERCISES

① Draw in **first** (or **third**) **angle projection** the **electric vehicle** above.
Use the steps described at the bottom of the last page to ensure the drawing is laid out properly.

② (a) Either draw a **container** and add a **parts list**, like the one shown above, **or** (b) Use a drawing previously drawn then add a **parts list** and add eight main **dimensions**.

Orthographic projection continued

Sectioning

Sectioning Allows us to show what an object would look like if cut. This page illustrates various ways of doing this. The **cross hatch** lines are at 45 degrees. Nuts, bolts and holes are not sectioned.

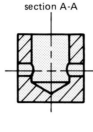

part to be sectioned

section A-A

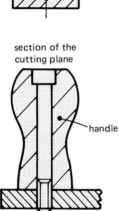

cutting plane

handle

section of the cutting plane

handle

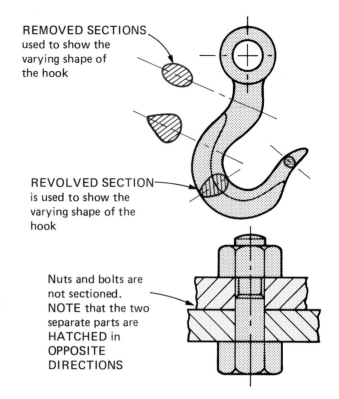

REMOVED SECTIONS used to show the varying shape of the hook

REVOLVED SECTION is used to show the varying shape of the hook

Nuts and bolts are not sectioned. NOTE that the two separate parts are HATCHED in OPPOSITE DIRECTIONS

Sectioned working drawing

The drawing below shows a simple **fuse/continuity tester** drawing that uses two methods of sectioning. Can you see the **part section** and **section X–X**? The container is made from two vacuum-formed parts that are held together with two plastic 'click' rivets. Fuses are tested by simply placing them across the two contacts. The LED lights up if it is OK.

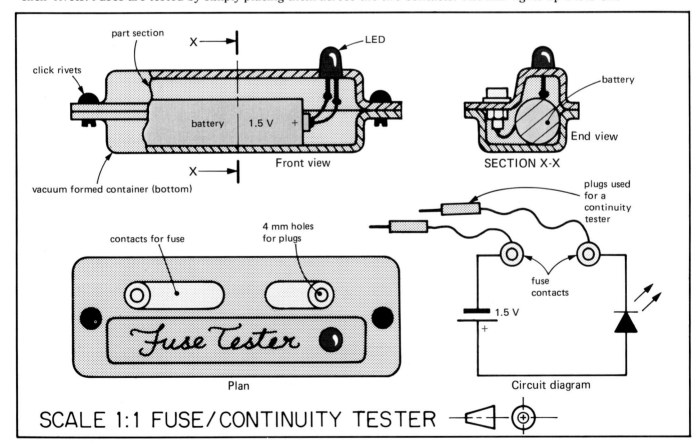

part section

X

LED

click rivets

battery   1.5 V   +

Front view

X

vacuum formed container (bottom)

battery

End view

SECTION X-X

plugs used for a continuity tester

contacts for fuse

4 mm holes for plugs

Fuse Tester

Plan

fuse contacts

1.5 V
+

Circuit diagram

SCALE 1:1 FUSE/CONTINUITY TESTER

QUESTIONS/EXERCISES

① Draw the **cross-sectional** view of the **handle** above. Cross hatch in opposite directions and leave the threaded part unhatched.

② Draw the **front** and **end view** of a simple container then indicate on the front view **section X–X**. The end view is to be drawn **sectioned** (similar to example above).

DRAWING STANDARDS

Drawing standards have been agreed nationally and internationally to ensure that the people involved in **designing and making** can communicate their ideas clearly to other people, in another country or just in the next room. In Britain the **British Standards Institute (BSI)** produces booklets covering most standards needed. These standards are the same as the **International Standards Institute (ISO) Recommendations** where possible.

British Standards you may need to use:

BS 308: Engineering Practice (some on this page),
BS 3939: Graphical Symbols for Electrical Power, Telecommunications And Electronic Diagrams – see page 128 for some of these.
BS 1192: Building Drawing Practice,
BS 4058: Flow Chart Symbols – see page 38.

This page shows some of the drawing standards used in producing **working drawings**.

Types of line used:

OUTLINES

FOR DIMENSIONS, PROJECTION AND HATCHING LINES

FOR HIDDEN DETAILS – DASHED LINES

FOR CENTRE LINES

SECTION LINES

TO REPRESENT A BREAK

Printing clearly

Neat clear printing is needed like that below

ABCDEFGHIJKLM
NOPQRSTUVWXYZ
1234567890

Example of good and bad printing

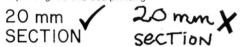

Dimensioning

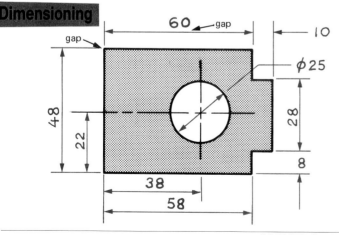

Dimensioning radii, circles and holes

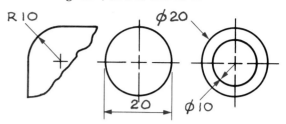

Dimensioning pictorial views

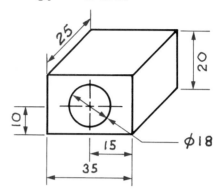

Thread conventions

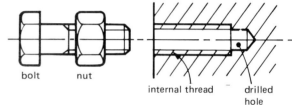

bolt   nut

internal thread   drilled hole

Cross-section of a pulley

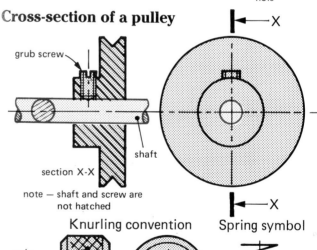

grub screw

shaft

section X-X

note – shaft and screw are not hatched

Knurling convention   Spring symbol

only part needs to be knurled

Architectural symbols – materials

brick   glass   concrete

QUESTIONS/EXERCISES

① Copy the **line types** and descriptions above then, using guide lines, neatly write the **alphabet**.
② Draw the letters 'L' and 'O' 100 mm high and thick; dimension the letters according to **British Standards**.

③ Draw a **cross-section of a wheel and shaft** to **British Standards**. The pulley shown could be converted into a wheel by adding a rubber tyre.

Small house – Downstairs plan

Drawn using architectural symbols.

ONE Metre grid
Scale 1:50

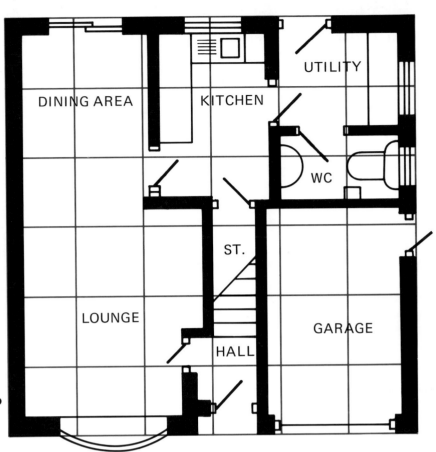

How many windows has it got?

How many doors has it got?

Where are the stairs, toilet, and garage up and over doors?

True Perspective drawing (2 point)

In order to draw **true perspective drawings** a **plan** and **side view** is needed **to obtain sizes**.
For a full explanation of this method see a book that specialises in this.

1 Draw '**picture plane**' line and **plan view** of the house.

2 Draw the **front view** on the **ground line**. (to one side.)

3 Select the viewer's **standing point** 'SP' then construct the **two points**' P–P by drawing parallel to the **plan** from SP.

4 Drop points P down onto the **horizon** line (the position is selected by user). This gives the two **vanishing points** (VP).

5 Using the information from **plan view** (where it intersects line P–P) and the **front view** as shown, construct the **true perspective view**.

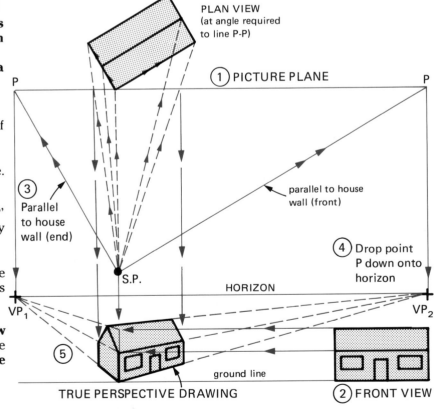

PLAN VIEW (at angle required to line P-P)

① PICTURE PLANE

③ Parallel to house wall (end)

parallel to house wall (front)

S.P.

④ Drop point P down onto horizon

HORIZON

VP₁ VP₂

⑤

ground line

TRUE PERSPECTIVE DRAWING

② FRONT VIEW

QUESTIONS / EXERCISES

① Using a sheet of graph paper draw the layout of a small '**flat**' using **architectural symbols**. (Scale of 1 square = 1 metre.). Add furniture etc if time.

② (a) Copy the drawing of the house above in **true** (two point) **perspective** on a large sheet of paper using the method described above.
(b) Draw a shed using the same method.

General questions

(1) What factors influence the **appearance** of a **shape** or **form**?

(2) **List** what you think is a **basic set of drawing equipment**, at least eight items.

(3) (a) Name two articles that are both **rough** and **hard**.
(b) Draw a pattern consisting of harmonious shapes.

(4) What are the three **primary colours**, as used when **painting**, and the **three primary colours for light**?

(5) Sketch a matchbox using the following methods of projection: **oblique**, **isometric** and **perspective** (one point estimated perspective).

(6) Explain with an example what the **box** or **crate** method of sketching is.

(7) Neatly sketch a van in **first angle orthographic projection** then repeat, but this time in **third angle projection**; **front, end** and **plan views** only.

(8) Draw and complete a **parts list** for your present design.

(9) Design in outline (ten minutes) two **possible ideas** suitable for your **design folder**; then develop the **best idea(s)** on your **design folder**. Colour to be used and drawing equipment.

(10) **Unfold a paper container** (eg a toothpaste package) then make a copy of it on a piece of white card, by tracing round it. **Redesign the package** for a different product then fold and glue it up.

(11) Using felt tips (the lighter colours) draw a good quality **presentation drawing** of your current project or a household product such as a radio.

British standards

(1) **Dimension** shape (a) below according to **British Standards**. Use a rule to find sizes. The drawing is drawn **half full size**.
(2) As question **1** above but for drawing (B) below.

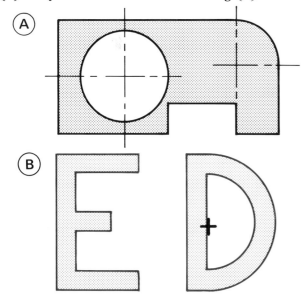

Working drawings

(Orthographic projection)

(1) The portable kitchen **timer** shown below has a digital display and flush control switches; except for the clock/timer switch and the start/stop switch both of which protrude out by 3 mm. Draw in either **First** or **third angle othographic projection** a **front, end** and **plan view** of the timer. Use a **scale of 2:1**. Obtain measurements from the **front view** using a rule (thickness is 15 mm).

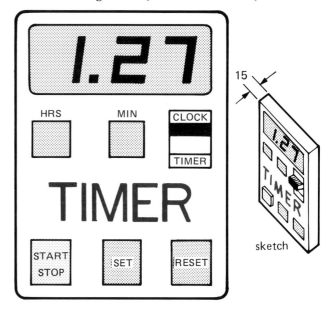

sketch

(2) A pupil produced the following drawing when asked to draw a **simple aluminium control knob** and its **small setscrew** in **orthographic projection**. Several mistakes were made as you can see. Redraw the control knob according to the correct conventions used in technical drawings. (Hints – The layout, centre lines, sectioning etc need to be redrawn correctly). Use a **scale of 2:1**. Take measurements from the views given to obtain sizes.

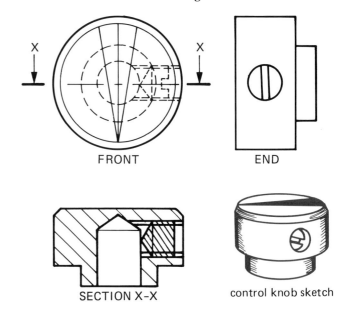

APPEARANCE/GRAPHICAL COMMUNICATION QUESTIONS

MATERIALS

During the last 200 years there has been an enormous increase in the range of materials available to us. It is therefore important that we are able to select and use the most appropriate material for a particular use.

Selecting the best material

In order to select the best material for a particular situation, we need to consider the following:

1 **Physical properties** needed
2 **Cost and time** (economics)
3 **Shaping and forming** methods
4 **Availability** (and **forms available**).

Below is a checklist for **selecting the best material**.

- **Effect of temperature** – Should the material be a **heat insulator**? Does the material need to resist **softening** or **burning**?
- **Electrical conductivity** – Should the material allow or prevent electricity to flow through?
- **Colour** – Is colour important or should light travel through? (**Opaque** or **transparent** material).

2 What cost?

Schools are mainly concerned with the cost of **materials** and parts used, but sometimes you will need to consider the **extra costs** involved such as: – paint, varnish, transfers, transport or postage if parts ordered, new tools needed, fittings and storage. *Note* When comparing cost remember that weight is important if bought by weight, for example aluminium is more expensive than steel by weight but aluminium is much lighter so the difference may not be so great by volume.

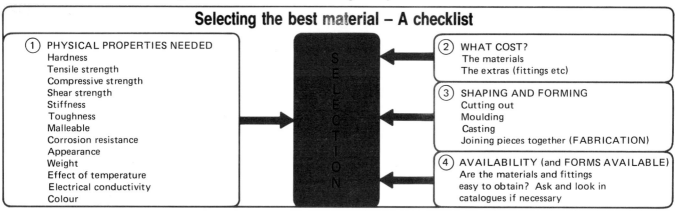

Selecting the best material – A checklist

① PHYSICAL PROPERTIES NEEDED
Hardness
Tensile strength
Compressive strength
Shear strength
Stiffness
Toughness
Malleable
Corrosion resistance
Appearance
Weight
Effect of temperature
Electrical conductivity
Colour

SELECTION

② WHAT COST?
The materials
The extras (fittings etc)

③ SHAPING AND FORMING
Cutting out
Moulding
Casting
Joining pieces together (FABRICATION)

④ AVAILABILITY (and FORMS AVAILABLE)
Are the materials and fittings
easy to obtain? Ask and look in
catalogues if necessary

Questions to ask yourself about materials

1 Physical properties needed

- **Hardness** – How hard should the material be to resist wear? *Note* Some hard materials, such as glass, are also **brittle**.
- **Tensile strength** – will the material need to resist strong pulling forces? (eg a tow rope).
- **Compressive strength** – will the material need to resist large pushing forces that tend to buckle it?
- **Shear strength** – is the material likely to be parted or sheared apart?
- **Stiffness** – do you require a **rigid** form? *Note* The form a material has effects its stiffness for example a tube is much stiffer than a flat sheet.
- **Toughness** – will it have to withstand being knocked about? If it has, do not choose a **brittle** material. Brittleness is the opposite of toughness.
- **Malleability** – does the material need to be bent or hammered without breaking?
- **Corrosion resistance** – how important is it that the material resists the weather, corrosion, rotting?
- **Appearance** – is the material's natural appearance important and what **surface finish** do you want if any?
- **Weight** – is the weight of the material important eg fishing weights need to be heavy.

3 Shaping and forming

Note See also **shaping and forming** pages 75 to 91.
Materials can be formed by:

- **Cutting out** – will the material need to be formed by removing pieces using: – a drill, a lathe, a saw, a file, etc.?

- **Moulding** – can the material be moulded into the required form using techniques such as: – vacuum forming, plastic injection moulding, wood laminating or 'laying up' on a mould with Glass Reinforced Plastics (GRP)?

- **Casting** – can the form be cast using techniques such as: – aluminium casting, and plastic casting (embedding)?

- **Joining pieces together (fabrication)** – would it be easier to assemble it from different pieces using: – joints, screws, glues, rivets, etc?

4 Availability (and forms available)

Can the materials be obtained from the school's stockroom or will they have to be bought? Sometimes special shapes and forms are required and will need to be ordered or bought from local shops, plan ahead for this. Teachers often keep special materials hidden away; so ask first before buying.

QUESTIONS/EXERCISES

① List two things that could be described as (a) hard, (b) soft, (c) heavy, (d) colourful, (e) tough (f) hard to obtain from a shop.

② What physical material **properties** do you think a **tray** for use in the home should have? – Use the checklist above to help you decide.

MATERIALS TESTING

This one page illustrates some ways of testing materials which you can try. Your school may have professional testing equipment.

Before starting any tests you will need to obtain suitable test pieces. If testing various materials choose sizes so that direct comparisons can be made.

Hardness

Two common ways of testing the **hardness** of a material are:

1 By comparing the impression made in the testpiece by a small diamond point pushing into the material for a fixed time. (Vickers hardness test).
2 Drop a weight onto a ball-bearing as shown. The harder the material the smaller the dent made.

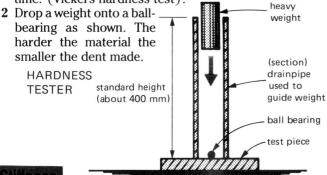

HARDNESS TESTER

Stiffness

The amount of **stiffness** is indicated by the degree of **deflection** made when a **load** is added. One way to compare materials is to add weights until the material is deflected a certain amount (say 20 mm). The larger the load required to deflect it, the stiffer the test piece is.

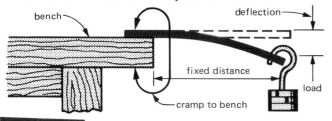

Toughness

This is the **resistance to impact**. A simple comparison can be made by holding test pieces in a vice and hitting them with a hammer (wear goggles). If **brittle**, the test piece will snap.

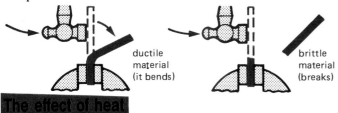

The effect of heat

Melt a drop of wax on one end of a test piece (about 100 mm × 20 mm diameter), then heat the other end. If the wax melts the material is a **conductor of heat** otherwise it is an **insulator**. (Safety – hold test pieces in tongs.)

Tensile strength

This is the ability to withstand tensile (pulling) forces. The **tensile strength** of common materials can be found in specialist text books, or test pieces can be tested. A good tensile testing machine will produce (automatically) a **tensile test graph**. The graph is important because it not only indicates the **ultimate tensile strength** (marked *) and **fracture point** (marked X) but the **elastic range** and the **plastic range** as well. Below are three graphs made on such a machine. The straight part of the graph obeys **Hooke's Law** which states that – '**Elastic materials stretch in proportion to the applied load'**. If a material is stressed beyond the **elastic limit** it will move into the **plastic stage** where the material will permanently deform (stretch). It will be noticed that **high carbon steel** can withstand a large force but cannot be stretched as easily as **mild steel** or **polythene**. The two formulae below will be useful if tests are made:

$$\text{Tensile strength (stress)} = \frac{\text{Force (newtons)}}{\text{Cross sectional area (mm)}}$$
(newtons per square mm)

$$\text{Strain } \% = \frac{\text{Increase in length} \times 100\%}{\text{Original length}}$$

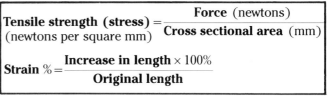

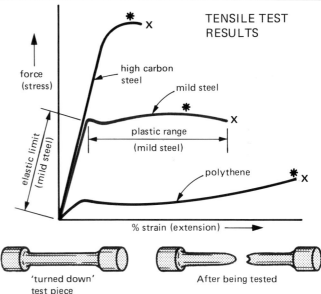

Corrosion resistance

To speed up the effect of corrosion on test pieces place one set of your test pieces half in and half out of an **acid**, such as vinegar, and the other set similarly in a moist **alkaline** environment, such as salty water. Then record results every week or so.

Electrical conductivity

To see if a material conducts electricity for a simple circuit, using a battery, bulb, test piece and connecting wires. The bulb will light up if the test piece **conducts electricity**.

QUESTIONS/EXERCISES

① How would you test two different materials for **hardness**, **stiffness** and **toughness** so that **comparative results** can be obtained? Explain with diagrams.

② (a) What is **tensile strength, Hooke's law** and the **plastic stage**?

(b) Copy the **tensile test results** graph above, then comment in some detail on the differences between the three materials.

METALS AND THEIR PROPERTIES

A brief description of the common metals used are given here. Metals can be **cast**, **machined** (cut), **moulded hot** or **cold** (eg forging and beaten metalwork) and can be **hot joined**, such as welding and brazing.

Metals are mined from the earth as **ores**. The two most common being **steel** which is made from '**iron ore**' and **aluminium** from an **ore** called '**bauxite**' the diagram below shows the stages in **making steel**.

Making Steel	
iron ore + **limestone** ↓	—melting in a **blast furnace** to produce molten iron (1500°C)
excess **carbon** and impurities removed ↓	—by the **Basic Oxygen Process**, oxygen is blown through the molten iron
steel is **rolled** or **cast**	

Alloying – Metals mixed and melted together are known as alloys, an example being stainless steel which is a mixture of chromium, nickel and steel.

Ferrous and non-ferrous metals

Metals naturally divide up into two main groups, those with iron which are called **ferrous** and those without iron which are called **non-ferrous**.

1 FERROUS METALS (metals with iron)

Cast iron and the various **steels** are **ferrous metals**. The reason for steels popularity is its great **tensile strength** and relative **cheapness**. The main problem with **ferrous metals** is that they are prone to **rust** and therefore some form of **surface protection** is needed eg paint.

RUST starting to appear in areas where the paint has been attacked by water salt and road grit

Cast iron

Cast iron contains 2–4% carbon. It is rather **brittle**, reasonably cheap and can be **cast** into intricate shapes, such as car cylinder blocks for engines. Not really suitable for school use.

Steels

Steels are classified by the small amount of **carbon** they contain. They are three main types:

Mild steel

This is the most commonly used steel. It contains 0.1%–0.3% **carbon**. It is a general purpose steel which is easy to form by cutting and bending, can be brazed, welded and soldered easily. **Low carbon steels cannot be hardened by heat treatment.**

mild steel wood screw

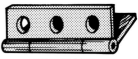

mild steel hinge

Medium carbon steel

Medium carbon steel contains 0.3%–0.7% **carbon**. It is stronger and harder than mild steel and used for hammer heads and wire ropes etc.

High carbon steel

High carbon steel contains 0.7%–1.4% **carbon**. They are naturally hard steels but can be made even harder (and more brittle) by **heat treatment** (see below). This makes them especially useful as cutting tools such as lathe cutting tools, for taps and dies threading etc. *Note* Steels with 1%–1.4% carbon are sometimes called **tool steels**.

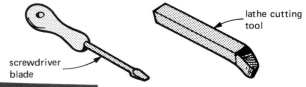

screwdriver blade

lathe cutting tool

Stainless steel

This is a special steel which is made by **alloying steel** with corrosion resisting materials such as **chromium** and **nickel**. It is a tough, hard material to cut and bend. Used for knives, kettles etc.

Annealing steel

Annealing softens steel which has been hardened by working it (eg hammering). To **anneal** steel heat to bright red heat then leave it to **soak** up the heat, then let it **cool very slowly**.

Hardening and tempering

High carbon steel is **hardened** by heating to a **bright red heat**, then **quenching** it in water. For practical use the steel is now too hard and brittle so a little of the hardness is removed by **tempering**. The amount of hardness removed by **tempering** will depend on what the metals will eventually be used for.

Tempering consists of **reheating** the steel to a certain temperature and then **quenching it again. The temperature at which steel should be quenched can be determined by the tempering colours** on the metal (see **tempering chart** at top of next page). Before heating clean the metal with emery cloth, so that the tempering colours can be seen. Allow the tempering colours to 'flow' to the end by heating next to it as shown below.

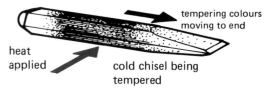

tempering colours moving to end

heat applied

cold chisel being tempered

QUESTIONS/EXERCISES

① (a) What is the difference between **ferrous** and **non-ferrous metals**? (b) How is steel made? (In outline only).

② (a) What steel would you use to make a **screwdriver** blade? (b) Explain how a new screwdriver blade is **hardened** and **tempered**.

STEEL TEMPERING CHART (oxide colours are used to indicate temperature)		
		SUITABLE FOR
	Light yellow 230°C	scribers, lathe tools
	Dark yellow 240°C	drills, taps and dies
	Purple brown 260°C	cold chisel, plane blade
	Purple 270°C	screwdriver, wood chisel
	Blue 300°C	springs, spanners

2 NON FERROUS METALS

Aluminium

Aluminium is light, has a fairly low melting temperature (650–670°C). It is a good conductor of heat and electricity, can be polished easily (eg on a polishing machine), but it is difficult to join using hot joining methods because **oxides** form on its surface. Used in aircraft construction, to make aluminium foil, road signs, window frames etc. A hard surface layer of oxides can be added by **anodizing**, for added protection.

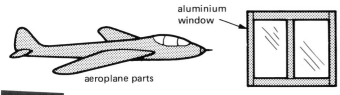

aluminium window

aeroplane parts

Copper

Copper is a very good conductor of electricity and heat. It can be worked into complex forms. It is a heavy metal, easy to solder and braze, but it is rather expensive. It is used for electric wires, waterpipes etc.

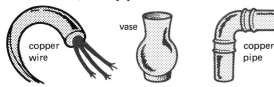

copper wire

vase

copper pipe

Brass

Brass is a yellow/brown **alloy**. One popular form is made from 60% copper and 40% zinc. It is fairly hard brittle metal, it machines and soft solders quite well. Used for screws and electrical parts.

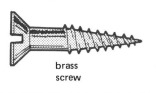

brass screw

plug with brass pins

Lead

Lead is a very heavy metal with a low melting temperature. It should not be used in school workshops because it is poisonous, causing brain damage if it gets into the blood stream.

Soft solder is an **alloy** of **lead** and **tin**. **Electrical soft solder** has flux in the centre and is made from 60% **lead** and 40% **tin**.

MULTICORE SOFT SOLDER 60% TIN 40% LEAD

Zinc

Zinc is not normally used by itself but often found as a coating on steel to prevent it rusting; this process is called **galvanising**.

Chromium

Chromium is expensive. Used to produce **chromed**, shiny, easy to clean surfaces such as bath taps, cutlery and car parts, and is a valuable alloying metal.

chromed knife

chromed kettle

Tungsten

A very high melting point metal (3400°C) that makes it suitable for electric light filaments. **Tungsten carbide** is the material brazed onto drills and saw blade tips so that they can cut hard materials. It is a compound of **carbon** and **Tungsten**.

Precious metals

Besides being used in jewellery **gold** and **silver** are very good **electrical conductors** and are used in the electronics industry. Pure gold is very soft and is therefore often alloyed with copper or silver to make it harder.

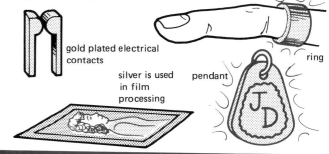

gold plated electrical contacts

silver is used in film processing

pendant

ring

3 ANNEALING NON FERROUS METALS

Annealing makes metals softer and easier to shape. Different metals require different techniques to anneal them:

Aluminium – Cover it with **common soap**, then heat it until the soap turns **black** (a temperature indicator) and then leave it to **cool**.

Copper – Heat it to **cherry red heat**, then **quench** it in water.

Brass (and gilding metal) – Heat to a **dull red**, then leave it to **cool**.

QUESTIONS/EXERCISES

① What **properties** and **uses** do **aluminium**, **copper** and **brass** have?

② (a) What is an **alloy**? (b) What metals is **soft solder** made from?

③ (a) Why do we need to anneal metals? (b) How is copper, aluminium and brass annealed?

PLASTICS AND THEIR PROPERTIES

The plastics (or polymer) story only really began about 110 years ago but now it would be hard to imagine modern life without plastics; for example carpets, clothes, tiles, bottles, bowls, raincoats, tights, toys, toothbrushes, baths etc, are usually made from plastics.

molecules

Plastics consist of **long chains of molecules** called **polymers**. The raw materials being oil, gas, coal, trees (eg rubber), and plants (eg cellulose).

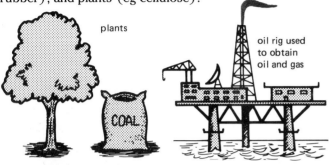
plants

oil rig used to obtain oil and gas

COAL

Advantages of plastics

(a) They are **easy to form** by moulding, casting and cutting.
(b) **No surface protection** is needed.
(c) They have **good chemical** and **weather resistance.**
(d) They can be supplied in various forms such as: sheets, liquids, resins, granules, foams etc.
(e) A wide range of **colours** and **textures** are available.

Disadvantages of plastics

(a) Some plastics (the thermoplastic types) have a rather narrow temperature range in which they can be used eg acrylic is brittle below 0°C and softens at 160°C.
(b) They **stretch** and **flex** much more than metals.
(c) Some plastics are a **fire risk**.
(d) Some plastics become **brittle** with age.

Types of plastic

There are **three** main categories of plastic (or polymer)
(1) Thermoplastics, (2) Thermosets and **(3) Elastomers (rubber)**.

1 THERMOPLASTICS

molecules free to move

They are made from long **molecules** which are free to slide about when **heat** and **force** are applied; this makes them especially suitable for moulding. In industry **injection moulding** is a very important process.

In schools plastics are moulded easily after heating in an **oven**, vacuum former, or a **strip heater**. (See pages 80/81.) **Thermoplastics** form the largest grouping of plastics.

Examples of thermoplastics

(a) Acrylic (perspex)

A rigid plastic commonly used in schools, supplied in sheet form in **various colours**, **opaque** or **transparent**, can be cut and polished using ordinary workshop tools. If heated it can be moulded at about 160°C. Used for shop signs, baths, as a glass substitute for plastic lenses etc.

keyfob

EZI-DUN
signs

shirts

magnifying glass

(b) PVC (Poly-vinyl-chloride)

It is a reasonably cheap plastic which can be a **rigid sheet** or, a **soft flexible** leathery like material if a plasticiser has been added during manufacture. It is reasonably easy to mould and cut with scissors or shears. Used to make drainpipes, hosepipes, records, raincoats and inflatable boats.

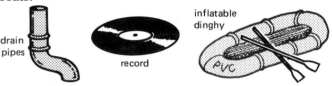
drain pipes

record

inflatable dinghy

(c) Nylon

This is a very **tough plastic**, often used for nylon zips, gearwheels, hinges, rope, door catches etc. Nylon **welds** easily but does **not glue easily**. Solid rods 'turn down' well on the lathe.

nylon socks

nylon gearwheel

(d) Polystyrene

Polystyrene can be divided into **two** main categories.
a Expanded polystyrene which is used for insulation, tiles, and for modelling. The dense foam is particularly good for model making.
b Solid polystyrene (eg sheet) **vacuum forms** easily; softening at 90°C. It is used for products such as plastic modelling kits and food containers. **Polystyrene glue** produces very strong joints on **Solid polystyrene** but dissolves polystyrene foam.

QUESTIONS/EXERCISES

① (a) List four **raw materials** that are used in the making of plastics.
(b) What **advantages** and **disadvantages** do plastics have compared with wood?

② (a) What are the three main **categories of plastics**?
(b) What **properties** and **uses** do **acrylic**, **PVC**, **Nylon** and **solid polystyrene** have?

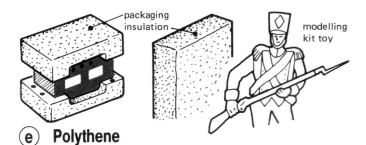

(e) Polythene

Polythene is sold either as (a) **Low density polythene** or (b) **High density polythene**. It is very **tough and flexible** but is **hard to glue**. It is used for polythene bags, bowls, milk crates and bleach bottles.

(f) Polypropylene

Polypropylene is a very tough, lighter than water plastic, which welds and 'glue guns' easily. Used for hinges (because it can be flexed thousands of times without breaking) ropes, large food containers. **Fluted polypropylene** sheet is now being used as a useful modelling material which can be quickly cut and 'glue gunned' into place.

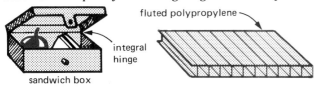

(g) PTFE (poly-tetra-fluoro-ethylene)

Used to coat non-stick frying pans and plain bearings because of its **low friction properties**. It is rather expensive.

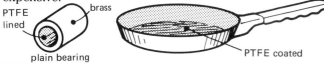

2 THERMOSETTING PLASTICS

Once made, these plastics **cannot be softened by heating**, because the molecules are **cross linked** together (see diagram below). This makes them ideally suited for electric light fittings where they must not soften when heated by the bulb.

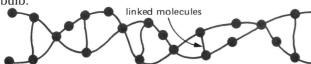

Examples of thermosetting plastics

(a) Polyester resin

Supplied as a **resin** (treacle like) with a **hardener** which is added and mixed just before use; colours can be added if required. Used for clear castings, eg embedding objects,

and for Glass Reinforced Plastics (GRP) for making canoes and GRP car bodies.

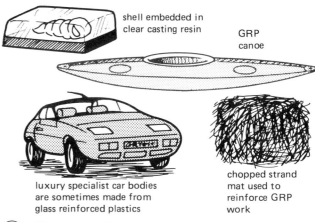

(b) Epoxy resin

This is similar to polyester resin, but it is more dimensionally stable and more expensive. It is used for glues and car repair kits.

(c) Urea-formaldehyde

Usually sold in sheet form or already glued to a surface such as a kitchen worktop (eg **Formica**), the patterns being produced during the laminating stage with patterned paper. It resists cuts and heat very well.

3 ELASTOMERS

This is the **rubber** group. Some people do not consider rubbers to be plastics but they are included because they are in the polymer family. **Elastomers** are very **flexible** and **elastic**. Used for tyres, elastic bands, oil seals etc.

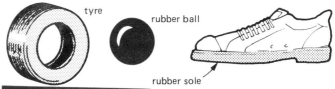

Additives to plastics

The properties of plastics can be altered by adding:

A Fillers – These alter the physical properties such as heat resistance or make the plastic cheaper; for example chalk powder can be added to polyester resin when casting chess pieces.

B Plasticisers – Can be added to make some rigid plastics more **flexible**. Flexible PVC has an oily plasticiser added.

QUESTIONS / EXERCISES

① What **properties** do **polythene**, **polypropylene** and **PTFE** have? Explain with examples.

② (a) Explain briefly what a **thermoset** (or **thermosetting**) **plastic** is.

(b) What **properties** and **uses** do polyester and epoxy resin have?

③ What are **elastomers** and what are they used for?

WOOD AND ITS PROPERTIES

Wood comes from **felled** trees which are then transported and **converted** in the **sawmills** into thick **plank** sizes. The wood is then **seasoned** outside, stacked as shown below or they are dried quicker in a special **seasoning kiln**, this reduces the **moisture content** of the wood to about 10–18% (depending on its eventual use – indoor or outdoor). The seasoned wood is then **cut up** into useful sizes and used.

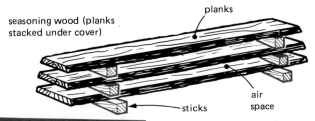

seasoning wood (planks stacked under cover)
planks
air space
sticks

Advantages of wood

1 It is **easy to work** (using common cutting tools).
2 It **glues easily**.
3 It is **warm to the touch**.
4 It has an **attractive appearance**.
5 It is **easy to obtain**.
6 It is **reasonably cheap**.
7 Wood is **electric and heat insulating**.

Disadvantages

1 **Protection** – Against insect and fungi attack is usually needed.
2 It can **warp** and **shrink** as it dries.
3 Wood easily **splits** along the grain.
4 It **cannot be cast** like metal.
5 Its **size is limited** by the tree size (**processed boards** overcome this problem eg plywood).

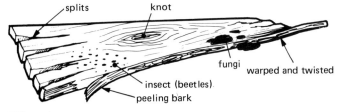

splits
knot
fungi
warped and twisted
insect (beetles)
peeling bark

Warping

Wood **shrinks** as it dries and **expands** as it **absorbs** water. This is why some wooden doors and windows 'jam' in the winter when the conditions are damp. Wood shrinks more **across the grain** than **along the grain**. Shrinkage is greater along the annular rings than across them. If a trunk is cut across it will dry as shown below.

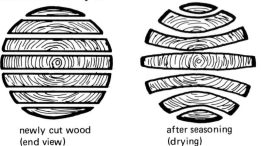

newly cut wood (end view)
after seasoning (drying)

How a tree grows

Trees need **water** and **mineral salts**, taken in by the **roots** as **sap** which rises up the tree where the action of **sunlight** on the **chlorophyll** (the green matter in the leaves) combines with **carbon dioxide** from the **air** to produce **new growth**.

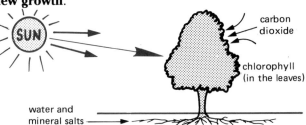

SUN
carbon dioxide
chlorophyll (in the leaves)
water and mineral salts

Every **spring** and **summer** trees make new **cells**. The **annual growth rings** can be seen when a tree is felled. Most of the trunk is **sapwood** which is living and growing but as time goes on the centre stops growing and hardens to form the **heartwood**. Most growth activity takes place in the **cambium layer** which is just beneath the protective **bark** layer.

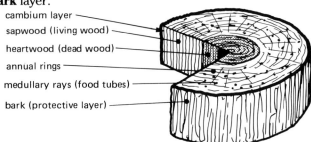

cambium layer
sapwood (living wood)
heartwood (dead wood)
annual rings
medullary rays (food tubes)
bark (protective layer)

SOFTWOODS AND HARDWOODS

Wood is either classified as 1. A **softwood** or 2. A **hardwood**.

1 SOFTWOODS (usually cheaper than hardwoods)

Softwoods come from **conifer** (cone bearing) trees. They are generally softer than hardwoods, hence their name, but not always. It is often called **Pine** in the shops. The building trade uses softwoods for most of its constructional work because of its cheapness and availability.

Softwood has a **cellular structure** made up of two cell types (tracheid and parenchyma cells) both of which look like tubes which are sealed at the ends. They carry the trees food to the leaves as well as providing the trees structural strength.

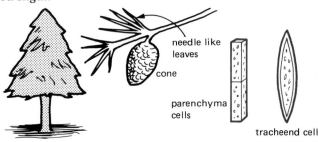

needle like leaves
cone
parenchyma cells
tracheend cell

QUESTIONS / EXERCISES

① (a) What **moisture content** does **seasoned wood** for eventual indoor use have? (b) How does the way a piece of wood is **cut for seasoning** affect the way it **warps**? Explain with an example.

② What are the **advantages** and **disadvantages** of wood compared to plastics?

③ What is the difference between a **softwood** and a **hardwood**? (Refer to leaf and cell types.)

SOME SOFTWOODS

1 Redwoods (eg scots pine) (reddish brown or yellowish). A common wood mainly used for joinery work. There are other pine types. A very hard one is **pitch pine**.

2 Cedar (reddish-brown) A very useful outdoor wood because of its natural protective oils. Used for sheds, window frames etc. It is a fairly soft wood.

3 Spruce (white to yellowish brown). It is used for constructional work, oars and gliders etc. It is strong for its weight.

4 Yew (orange to dark brown). It is fairly expensive, used for veneers and wood turning.

window frame (cedar)

bench (cedar)

picnic table

cedar or pine (with preservative)

bowl (yew)

2 HARDWOODS (more expensive than softwoods)

Hardwoods come from **deciduous** trees. These are the trees that have **broad leaves** which are shed in the winter. There are a great range of hardwoods, from the quite soft hardwoods eg balsa wood, to the very hard hardwoods such as ebony. **Hardwoods** are more complex than softwoods and have five cell types; two are illustrated.

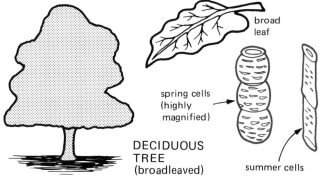

broad leaf

spring cells (highly magnified)

DECIDUOUS TREE (broadleaved)

summer cells

SOME HARDWOODS

1 Oak (light brown). A very hard wood, often used for furniture and decorative veneers and general high quality work. (Steel screws rust in oak – brass screws must be used instead).

2 Beech (light brown or pinky brown). A tough close-grained wood making it suitable for tool handles, furniture and work benches.

3 Ash (whitish). A hard tough and elastic wood used for sports equipment, handles and internal joinery.

4 Mahogany (reddish brown). Commonly used as a veneer on veneer covered chipboard. A very decorative wood used for high class furniture. (Many varieties of mahogany are available.)

5 Teak (light brown). It is used for high class furniture, tables, boats etc. It is strongly resistant to decay.

6 Balsa (white). Although it is very soft, it is in fact still in the hardwood category because it is a deciduous wood, used for model making.

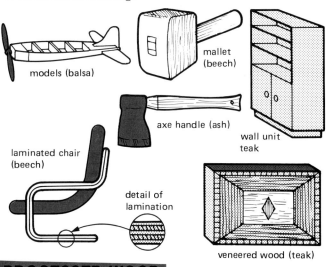

models (balsa)

mallet (beech)

axe handle (ash)

wall unit teak

laminated chair (beech)

detail of lamination

veneered wood (teak)

PROCESSED WOOD

Processed wooden boards can be supplied in **large sheets** which **do not shrink** or **warp**, often having the **final surface finish** added in the factory eg varnish, paint, decorative laminate etc.

Waterproof glues can be used to produce boards suitable for use outside (eg marine plywood).

1 Hardboard Made from pulped wood and glue which is then compressed and dried. It can be supplied already painted on one side (cheap).

2 Chipboard Made from wood chippings glued together. It is often laminated with thin veneers of wood or plastic. Different densities are available for different purposes (cheap).

3 Blockboard Made from glued strips of wood covered with veneer (fairly expensive).

4 Plywood Layers of wood veneer are glued together in alternate layers at 90 **degrees** to each other; to avoid warping. **Marine ply** is a plywood that can be used outdoors (quite expensive).

5 MDF (Medium Density Fibreboard) A fairly new material that is like a very smooth chipboard.

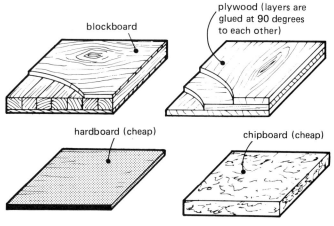

blockboard

plywood (layers are glued at 90 degrees to each other)

hardboard (cheap)

chipboard (cheap)

QUESTIONS / EXERCISES

① What **properties** and **uses** do the following hardwoods have: **Mahogany, Oak, Beech, Teak** and **Balsawood?**

② What **properties** and **uses** do the following softwoods have: **Scots Pine, Spruce** and **Cedar?**

③ What are **processed boards?** Explain with three examples.

OTHER MATERIALS

Composite materials

Materials that are combined to produce particular properties are called **composites**. **Polyester resin** when **set** is hard and brittle but **glass fibres** can be added to produce **glass reinforced plastics** (GRP) to make a very much stronger composite material (stronger than steel by weight). **Printed circuit boards** (PCB's) are also a composite of a plastic resin and woven cloth, similarly **plaster of paris** can be greatly strengthened by using it with cloth.

PCB board
(resin + cloth composite)

Ceramics

Traditionally the word ceramics refers to pottery; such as cups and plates. They are inert, good insulators, hard and usually brittle. A good surface finish can be added using a **glaze**. Some modern ceramic materials can withstand sudden changes in temperature without cracking (used for firebricks and kiln linings).

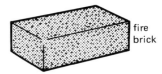

fire brick

Semiconductors

Semiconductors are made from materials whose electrical conductivity is between that of a good **conductor** and a good **insulator**. "Doped" silicon and **germanium** are two examples; they are used in the electronics industry to make **transistors** and complex logic **chips**. (See electronics page 120 for more information.)

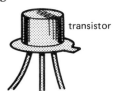

transistor

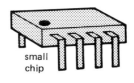

small chip

Metals questions

(1) What is the difference between **ferrous** and **non-ferrous metals**?

(2) Give typical uses for the following metals: **mild steel, high carbon steel, copper, brass** and **aluminium**.

(3) (a) What is the purpose of **annealing** and (b) How is it carried out on **copper** and **aluminium**.

(4) Explain **step by step** how a new 'screwdriver blade' or a 'cold chisel' made from **high carbon steel** is hardened and tempered.

Wood questions

(1) What do the following terms refer to in woodwork: **warping, kiln dried, cambium layer, heartwood**?

(2) What are the limitations of 'real' solid wood compared to **processed wood** such as plywood?

(3) Give typical uses for the following woods: **oak, beech, mahogany, teak, scots pine, cedar, spruce, hardboard, chipboard** and **plywood**.

Plastics questions

(1) (a) What is the essential difference between a **thermosetting** and a **thermoplastic** plastic? (b) Give two examples of each type.

(2) Give typical uses for the following plastics: **acrylic, PVC, nylon, expanded polystyrene, polypropylene, epoxy resin** and **rubber**.

(3) Explain the following terms used in plastic work: **resin, plasticisers, GRP, elastomers, chopped strand matting**.

General questions

(1) Explain how simple **tests** can be carried out to test for: (a) **hardness** (b) **Electrical conductivity** (c) **stiffness** and (d) **Corrosion resistance**.

(2) Boats can be constructed from **wood, metal** or **plastic**. Choose one suitable material from each of the above categories and then justify its use in the making of a 20 metre cross channel boat (consider: **production methods, economics, and the functional requirements of a boat**).

(3) **Tensile testing** – (a) Explain what happens to the **test piece** once it reaches the 'Plastic' part of the tensile testing graph? (b) What are the **stress** and **strain** formulae used in tensile testing? (c) What would the **tensile strength** (maximum force) of a piece of 2 mm diameter mild steel be? Given that the **ultimate tensile strength** of mild steel is 500 N/sq. mm.

(4) What **materials** would you recommend for the production of the following: 1000 **cheap chess pieces**, 2000 **saucepan lid handles**, 20 **candles**, 20 **kitchen work surfaces**, an **outdoor bench** and a **plastic magnifying glass**.

(5) Name two **composite materials** and give two typical uses for each.

(6) Explain why you think the materials indicated below were selected for their particular use?

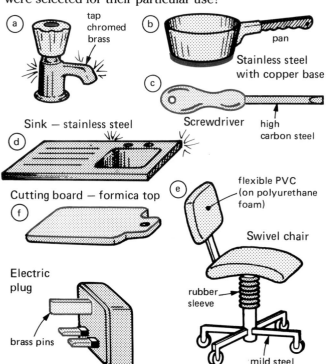

(a) tap chromed brass

Sink – stainless steel

(b) pan
Stainless steel with copper base

(c) Screwdriver high carbon steel

(d) Cutting board – formica top

(e) flexible PVC (on polyurethane foam)
Swivel chair
rubber sleeve
mild steel

(f) Electric plug
brass pins

MATERIALS QUESTIONS

SHAPING AND FORMING MATERIALS

This section summarises the main methods of **shaping and forming** under the following headings:
Marking out, measuring tools, shaping and forming by cutting, moulding materials, shaping by casting, joining methods (and containers), obtaining a good surface finish and questions.

MARKING OUT

The most common marking out tools are a **pencil**, **scriber** (mainly used on metals), **felt tip pens** and **permanent felt tip pens** for smooth plastic surfaces.

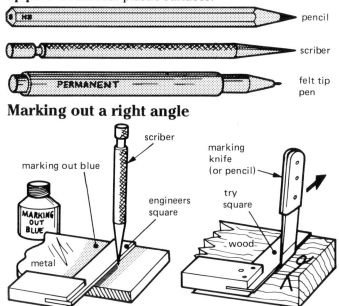

pencil

scriber

felt tip pen

Marking out a right angle

scriber

marking out blue

engineers square

marking knife (or pencil)

try square

wood

metal

MARKING OUT BLUE

Marking out angles (Other than 90 degrees)

protractor

wood

bevel gauge

adjusting screw

metal

Drawing circles

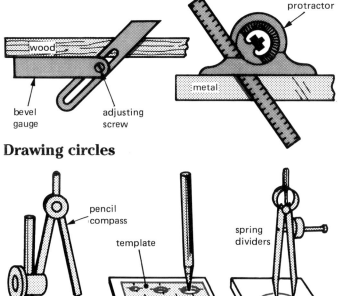

pencil compass

template

spring dividers

Other marking out tools

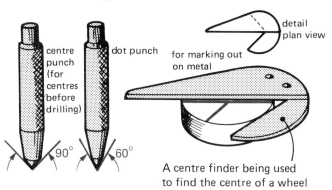

centre punch (for centres before drilling)   90°

dot punch   60°

for marking out on metal

detail plan view

A centre finder being used to find the centre of a wheel

Stages in marking out

(1) Marking out from a straight edge – metal.

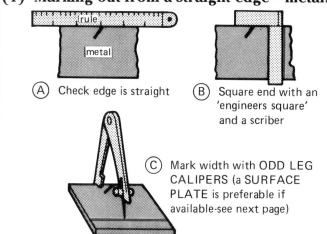

rule

metal

(A) Check edge is straight

(B) Square end with an 'engineers square' and a scriber

(C) Mark width with ODD LEG CALIPERS (a SURFACE PLATE is preferable if available-see next page)

(2) Marking out from a straight edge – wood.

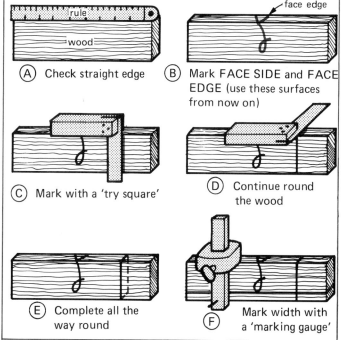

rule

wood

face edge

(A) Check straight edge

(B) Mark FACE SIDE and FACE EDGE (use these surfaces from now on)

(C) Mark with a 'try square'

(D) Continue round the wood

(E) Complete all the way round

(F) Mark width with a 'marking gauge'

QUESTIONS/EXERCISES

① On what materials would you use a **scriber, permanent felt tip pen**, a **marking knife, spring dividers** and **a dot punch**, when marking out?

② Explain the stages in **marking out a piece of wood** 150 mm long × 30 mm wide × 10 mm thick as shown above.

(3) Marking out using a template

Often used when shapes are repeated as shown.

Note — avoid wasting material

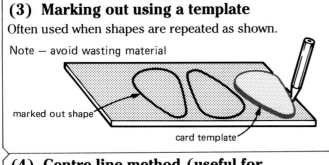

marked out shape

card template

(4) Centre line method (useful for symmetrical shapes)

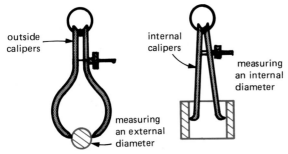

centre line

waste to be removed

(A) Start with a 'centre line'

(B) Complete shape

Notes on marking out on plastics

Pencils do not mark out very well on highly polished plastics. Scribers can be used if very accurate work is required. For general marking out 'felt tip pens' or 'chinagraph crayons' can be used.

(5) Using a surface plate to mark out

Often used to mark out parallel lines find the centres of rods as shown.

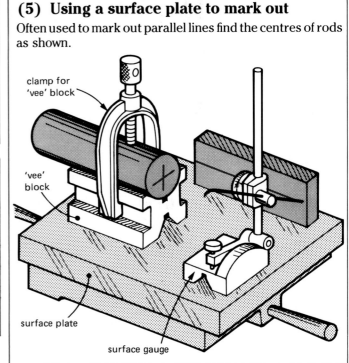

clamp for 'vee' block

'vee' block

surface plate

surface gauge

MEASURING TOOLS

A few of the common measuring tools are shown below. Metal rules are good for much of our work but sometimes a more accurate method is needed.

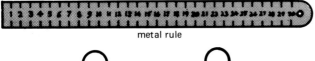

metal rule

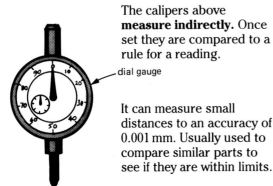

outside calipers

internal calipers

measuring an internal diameter

measuring an external diameter

The calipers above **measure indirectly.** Once set they are compared to a rule for a reading.

dial gauge

It can measure small distances to an accuracy of 0.001 mm. Usually used to compare similar parts to see if they are within limits.

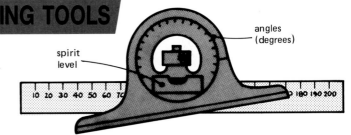

angles (degrees)

spirit level

part of a combination set — protractor (this is used to measure angles)

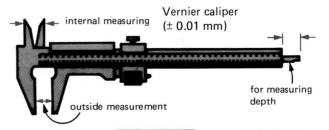

internal measuring

Vernier caliper (± 0.01 mm)

for measuring depth

outside measurement

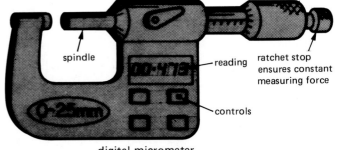

spindle

reading

ratchet stop ensures constant measuring force

controls

digital micrometer (above) (± 0.001 mm)

QUESTIONS/EXERCISES

① When would it be an advantage to use a **template** rather than mark out a shape directly on the material?

② What **measuring tools** could you select to measure the diameter of a metal rod, an angle and the inside of a metal tube?

SHAPING AND FORMING BY CUTTING

Cutting, or removal by **wasting**, is probably the most common method of shaping and forming. The main advantage is that forms can be cut out very accurately. The main disadvantage is that waste is produced eg shavings and metal filings etc. It is important to realise that the cutting tool being used must always be harder than the material being cut, for example **never** use a traditional wood saw for cutting metal. Plastics can be cut by either wood or metal cutting tools.

Saws that cut straight

These are the deep bladed saws.

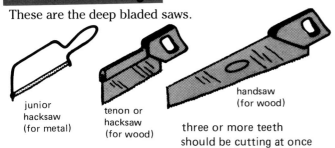

junior hacksaw (for metal)

tenon or hacksaw (for wood)

handsaw (for wood)

three or more teeth should be cutting at once

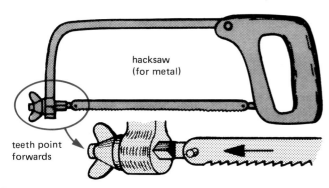

hacksaw (for metal)

teeth point forwards

Saws for cutting curves

(Narrow or round blades used)

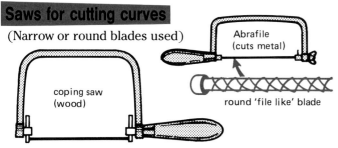

coping saw (wood)

Abrafile (cuts metal)

round 'file like' blade

Stages in cutting a large hole

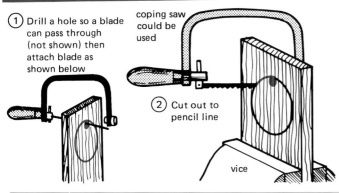

① Drill a hole so a blade can pass through (not shown) then attach blade as shown below

coping saw could be used

② Cut out to pencil line

vice

Snips or shears

Are used like scissors to cut metal or soft plastic.

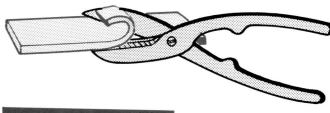

Notes on files and filing

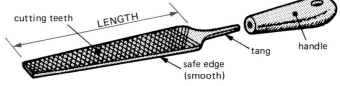

cutting teeth LENGTH tang handle

safe edge (smooth)

made from 'hardened and tempered' tool steel

File types (cross sections)

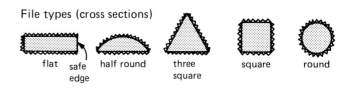

flat safe edge half round three square square round

Needle files — small files for jewellery work etc.

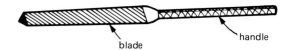

blade handle

Two methods of filing

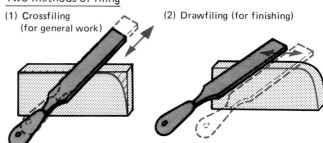

(1) Crossfiling (for general work)

(2) Drawfiling (for finishing)

Rasps and 'surform' tools

rasps are used like a file on wood

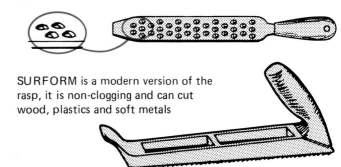

SURFORM is a modern version of the rasp, it is non-clogging and can cut wood, plastics and soft metals

---

QUESTIONS/EXERCISES

① What **saws** would you use to cut out a rectangular hole 50 mm × 100 mm in (a) wood, (b) steel and (c) acrylic? All materials 3 mm thick.

② (a) Draw and label a flat metalwork file. (b) Indicate which file types you would use on each part of this shape.

Cutting out with drill bits

Twist drill – Designed for metal but can be used for plastic and wood.

(drill bit made from high speed steel)

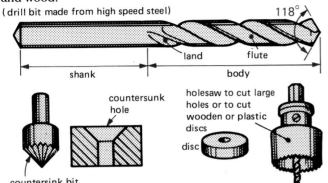

118°

land
flute

shank

body

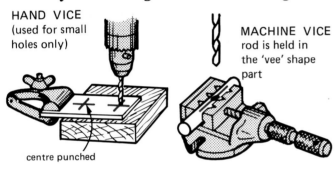

countersunk hole

holesaw to cut large holes or to cut wooden or plastic discs

disc

countersink bit

Two ways of holding work when drilling

HAND VICE (used for small holes only)

MACHINE VICE rod is held in the 'vee' shape part

centre punched

Wood boring tools

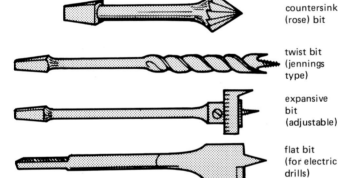

countersink (rose) bit

twist bit (jennings type)

expansive bit (adjustable)

flat bit (for electric drills)

Chain drilling

This is one way of removing pieces, holes are drilled close together and then cut (eg with an Abrafile)

WASTE

Drilling matching holes

Before the second pair of holes are drilled a pin or bolt is placed in the first pair of holes to ensure no movement takes place.

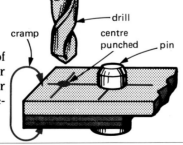

cramp

drill

centre punched

pin

Chisels and gouges for wood

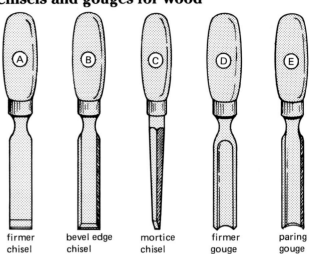

A · B · C · D · E

firmer chisel

bevel edge chisel

mortice chisel

firmer gouge

paring gouge

Chisels and gouges produced this form. Do you know which tools were used?

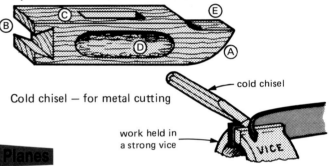

B · C · E · D · A

cold chisel

Cold chisel — for metal cutting

work held in a strong vice

VICE

Planes

Planes are primarily designed to remove wood by cutting but some plastics can also be planed as well. Precautions need to be taken to prevent the wood splitting when planing the **end grain**. There are various plane types. The two most common are the **jack plane** and the **smoothing plane**. The main difference is their length, the smoothing plane being the shorter.

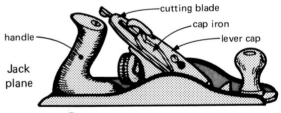

cutting blade

cap iron

handle

lever cap

Jack plane

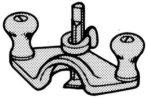

A Router plane is used to clean up 'house joints' that have been sawn and chiselled out first but a machine router would do it all much better.

Planes that cut grooves along the grain
A combination plane (not illustrated) can cut the shapes shown below.

groove · tongue · rebate · moulding

QUESTIONS/EXERCISES

① Draw and label the tools used to (a) Countersink metal (b) cut out a 30 mm plastic or wooden disc (c) cut a 20 mm hole in wood.

② (a) What tool(s) would you use to **carve** out a wooden bowl by hand? (b) Name two kinds of **plane** and give a typical use for each.

Stages in cutting a 6 mm internal and external thread

Cutting an internal thread

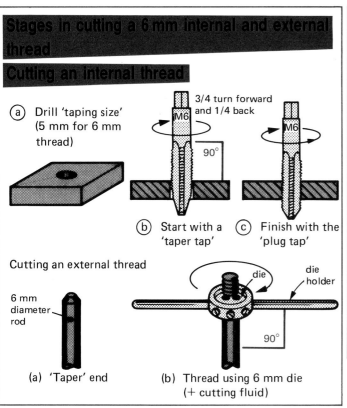

(a) Drill 'taping size' (5 mm for 6 mm thread)

3/4 turn forward and 1/4 back

M6

90°

(b) Start with a 'taper tap'

M6

(c) Finish with the 'plug tap'

Cutting an external thread

6 mm diameter rod

die

die holder

90°

(a) 'Taper' end

(b) Thread using 6 mm die (+ cutting fluid)

Preparation made for a countersink screw

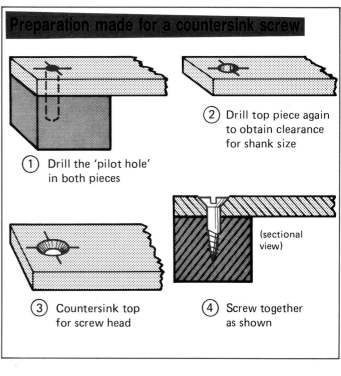

(1) Drill the 'pilot hole' in both pieces

(2) Drill top piece again to obtain clearance for shank size

(3) Countersink top for screw head

(sectional view)

(4) Screw together as shown

LATHEWORK Note – guards omitted

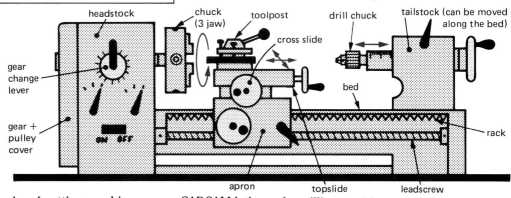

The work to be turned is held in the chuck. When the workpiece turns round, cutting tools are brought into contact with the workpiece and the waste is cut away. The kind of cuts commonly made on a lathe are shown below.

headstock

chuck (3 jaw)

toolpost

drill chuck

tailstock (can be moved along the bed)

cross slide

gear change lever

bed

gear + pulley cover

on off

rack

apron

topslide

leadscrew

Note For two photographs of cutting machines, see a CADCAM lathe and a milling machine on page 34.

CUTS MADE ON A LATHE

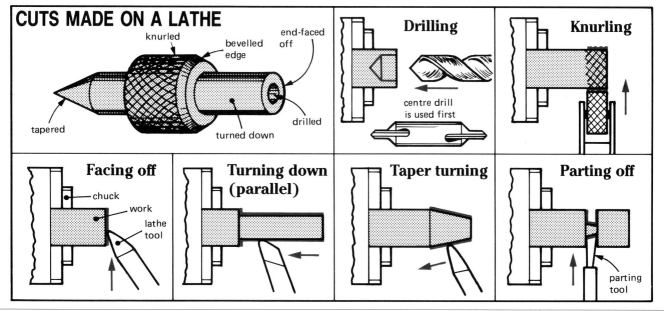

knurled

bevelled edge

end-faced off

tapered

turned down

drilled

Drilling

centre drill is used first

Knurling

Facing off

chuck

work

lathe tool

Turning down (parallel)

Taper turning

Parting off

parting tool

QUESTIONS / EXERCISES

① Explain **step by step** how to cut (a) an **internal thread** and (b) an **external thread**.

② Draw (trace) and label the metal **lathe** above then explain two of the processes that can be carried out on a lathe.

MOULDING MATERIALS

Moulding is a general term to describe the **shaping and forming of materials using force**. The force can be applied using a hammer eg beaten metalwork, fingers (eg pottery) using a machine etc. Some materials require a lot of force to mould them into shape. Steel is easier to mould if it is heated up to red heat first.

Plastics are easy materials to mould because they only require small forces to mould when softened by heating.

MOULDING PLASTICS

Thermoplastics are easily moulded in the workshop when heated to their softening temperature, for acrylic it is about 160°C. **Thermosetting** plastics once set in the factory cannot be moulded using the methods mentioned below. Beware of heating plastics up so that they burn and give off poisonous fumes.

Using a strip heater

The strip heater consists of an electric element that glows hot. It is usually used to blend plastic such as **acrylic polystyrene** and **PVC** sheet. The strips of plastic to be bent is heated, turning it over every so often to prevent the plastic being burnt on one side. Do not bend the plastic before it bends easily or it may crack. Wait until it can be bent with a little hand pressure.

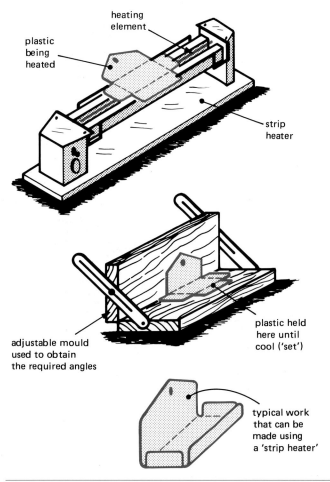

heating element

plastic being heated

strip heater

adjustable mould used to obtain the required angles

plastic held here until cool ('set')

typical work that can be made using a 'strip heater'

Vacuum forming

Sheet plastic is heated until soft then sucked down, using a vacuum pump, onto a mould; which is often made of wood. This technique can be used to make plastic trays, blister packs for displaying things in shops, acrylic sinks and baths etc. The new vacuum forming machines can form plastic sheets up to about 6 mm thick. Polystyrene (very easy to use), PVC and ABS sheet plastic are suitable for use in schools.

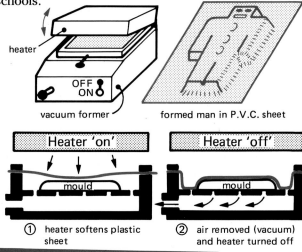

heater

OFF ON

vacuum former

formed man in P.V.C. sheet

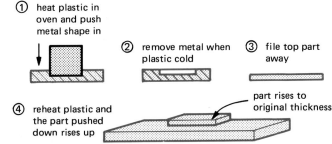

Heater 'on'	Heater 'off'
mould	mould

① heater softens plastic sheet

② air removed (vacuum) and heater turned off

Moulding using plastic memory

This process makes use of '**plastic memory**'. If a thermoplastic such as acrylic is heated and compressed and then reheated it will return to its original manufactured form (ie it can be said to remember the original form). Decorative patterns, in relief, can be made as follows:

① heat plastic in oven and push metal shape in

② remove metal when plastic cold

③ file top part away

④ reheat plastic and the part pushed down rises up

part rises to original thickness

Blow moulding

Thermoplastics can be **blown** up into the air or into a mould. Both methods are shown below and on the next page.

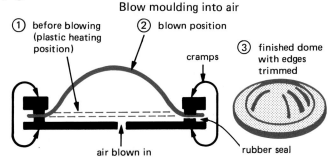

Blow moulding into air

① before blowing (plastic heating position)

② blown position

③ finished dome with edges trimmed

cramps

air blown in

rubber seal

QUESTIONS / EXERCISES

① (a) Explain how a **strip heater** is used to bend a 4 mm acrylic sheet through 90 degrees. (b) Why is the plastic turned over during heating?

② (a) Explain a typical use of **vacuum forming** and the type of plastics used. (b) What do you understand by moulding used **plastic memory**?

Blow moulding into a mould

Mass produced plastic drink bottles are made this way from a tube of plastic which is sealed at the bottom as the mould closes then air is blown into the tube to make the bottle as shown.

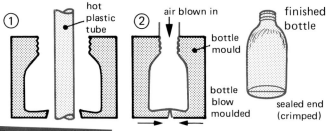

Press moulding

Press moulding or **compression moulding** is a method of moulding plastic into a premade mould. This method of moulding enables thicker thermoplastics to be moulded than when vacuum forming. Note – Work fast so that the plastic keeps hot long enough to mould. The stages in making a container are (a) Heat plastic sheet in an oven (b) Quickly transfer plastic into the mould (c) Add **top ring** and then push **plug** into the mould.

Another version of **compression moulding** is when **thermoset plastic powder** (eg bakelite) is heated and squeezed into a manufactured form.

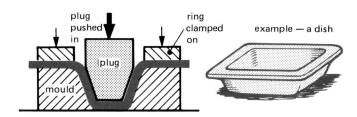

Injection moulding

This is a mass production method used to produce toys, control knobs, buckets etc.

Making a plastic bucket
(a) Plastic pellets (beads) are **heated up**.
(b) The **screw turns** pushing the hot plastic into a two part split mould.
(c) When the plastic has cooled sufficiently the mould is opened – parts A and B – to remove the bowl.
(d) The **sprue** is removed with a knife.

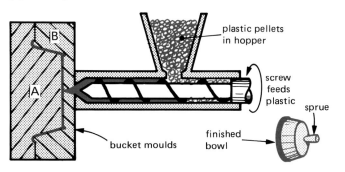

Moulding with GRP

GRP stands for 'Glass Reinforced Plastic'. Glass fibres are very strong when bonded together with a plastic resin such as epoxy or polyester resin. Polyester resin sets in about fifteen minutes after the hardener (catalyst) is added. GRP can be made stronger than mild steel weight for weight. It is used to make car bodies, canoes, decorative panels etc. This work must be carried out in a **well ventilated area**. In school the method used is as follows:
1. **Wax mould** at least three times.
2. Apply **gel coat** (+ colour and hardener).
3. Once **gel coat** layer is 'set' add layers of **lay up resin** and **glass fibre matting** by **stippling.** (up and down motion) with a brush.
4. Add last layer with **surface tissue**.
5. Remove from mould at the **green** (half hard) stage.

Steps in 'laying up' a GRP mould

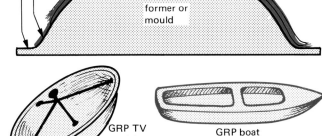

Moulding wood

Wood can be moulded in three basic ways: (1) by **laminating** – This consists of gluing thin pieces of wood together around a former as for the chair below. (2) **Steam moulding** – Wood is steamed to soften it before moulding it. (3) **Moulding wood chippings** mixed with glue into a mould.

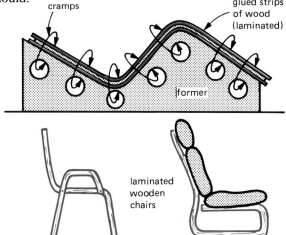

QUESTIONS/EXERCISES

1. What product/s are: (a) **Blow moulded** from a tube (b) **Injection moulded,** (c) Made from **glass reinforced plastics** and (d) **Press moulded?**

2. (a) How can wooden strips be moulded? (b) Explain how to make a tray by **laying up** with **glass reinforced plastics**. Assume the mould is already made.

MOULDING METALS

Ductile metals such as copper, aluminium and silver can be moulded cold. Steel may require heating up to **red heat** so that it can be moulded by forging.

Bending or folding sheet metal

To obtain sharp bends in sheet metal it needs to be held firmly in a vice or in a pair of **folding bars**. Sometimes the metal can be bent by hand but usually it has to be hammered as shown.

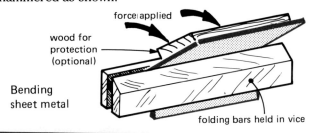

force applied

wood for protection (optional)

Bending sheet metal

folding bars held in vice

Bending rod and tube

Metal rod can be bent while being held in a vice. Tubing is more difficult to bend. **Pipe benders** like the one shown below allow tubes to be bent successfully without collapsing or flattening.

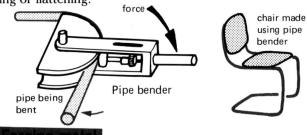

force

chair made using pipe bender

pipe being bent

Pipe bender

Forging metal

Forging traditionally refers to the shaping and forming of steel on an anvil or in a vice after being heated up to **red heat** in a forge.

Four common forging operations are shown below:

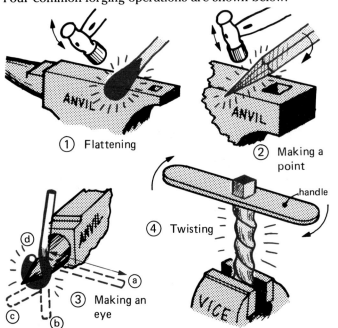

① Flattening

② Making a point

④ Twisting

handle

③ Making an eye

Hollowing

Metals can be **stamped out** to produce hollows such as baking trays, drink cans and stainless sinks etc. This process is now highly automated in industry.

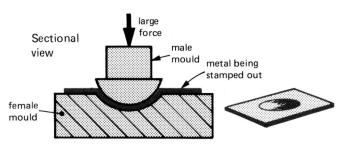

large force

Sectional view

male mould

metal being stamped out

female mould

Beaten metalwork (by hand)

The softer ductile metals can be moulded by hammering them. There are two main ways of doing this.

1 **Hollowing** – The metal is stretched by hammering in the middle as shown below.
2 **Raising** – This method works by hammering the sides in towards the centre. To make a vase the sides would be raised up from the base as shown below.

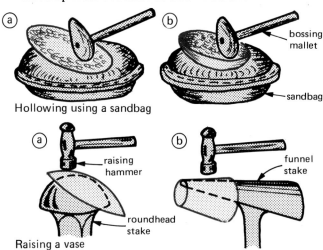

(a) (b)

bossing mallet

sandbag

Hollowing using a sandbag

(a) (b)

raising hammer

funnel stake

roundhead stake

Raising a vase

Notes

1 Metals **workharden** the more they are hammered: to soften them again they are **annealed** (see pages 68/69 for details).
2 **Planishing** – After obtaining the form required the work is finished off by hammering (with planishing hammers). Planishing also provides the right amount of stiffness due to the extra hammering.

Tips when designing moulds

– In GRP work a **female mould** will result in a smooth surface on the outside surface.
– Allow for the thickness of the moulding material when compression moulding etc.
– The surface finish is dependent on the moulds surface finish; if moulding acrylic the moulds surface can be lined with velvet cloth to prevent scratches.
– A **draft angle** is required if the work is to be removed from the mould easily.

QUESTIONS/EXERCISES

① (a) Explain how to **bend** a thin sheet of steel in the middle. (b) How would you **forge** an 'eye' on the end of a 6 mm diameter rod of steel?

② (a) Explain the stages in **making a copper bowl**.
(b) What is the purpose of **planishing**?

SHAPING BY CASTING

Casting in CDT means the pouring of a liquid material into a mould where it **sets** hard. No force is needed to push the liquid into the mould. Castings range from animal forms made out of **jelly** or **plaster of Paris** to cast **aluminium alloy** engine blocks.

Casting with plaster of Paris

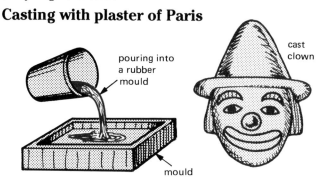

pouring into a rubber mould

mould

cast clown

Plastic resin casting

This is similar to **plaster of Paris** casting except that the end result is much stronger. The plastic resin used in schools is usually **polyester casting resin**. The moulds used can be made from most materials if they are waxed at least three times. **Vinamould** rubber and polythene moulds do not need waxing. The liquid resin sets by chemical reaction. If it sets too quickly it will heat and crack; cool in water if necessary.

How to cast your initials in wax

Using a block of wax for the mould, the following method can be used:

(a) **Carve out the initials** in the wax block.
(b) Mix the **polyester casting resin, hardener** (about 2%) and **colour** if used.
(c) **Pour into the mould** and remove any bubbles with a pin.
(d) Place a sheet of polythene on top. To prevent a tacky surface developing due to a reaction with the air.
(e) When set, about 30 minutes later, **remove from the mould**.

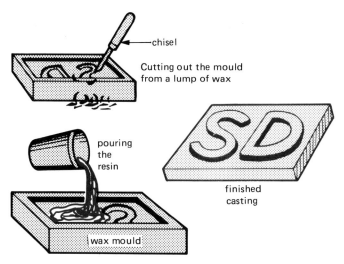

chisel

Cutting out the mould from a lump of wax

pouring the resin

wax mould

finished casting

Embedding/encapsulation

Hard objects such as coins, old watch parts etc. can be embedded, or encapsulated, in **clear casting resins**. This can be used to make decorative items such as paper weights or to protect delicate components.

If polythene or wax moulds are used no release agent (wax) is needed.

Stages in embedding a coin

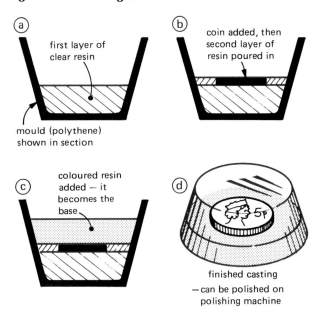

(a) first layer of clear resin

mould (polythene) shown in section

(b) coin added, then second layer of resin poured in

(c) coloured resin added — it becomes the base

(d) finished casting — can be polished on polishing machine

Casting thermoplastics

Plastic powders (eg nylon) can be melted in metal moulds to make castings which are tough.
To make nylon wheels
(a) Fill the metal mould with nylon powder and place in an oven.
(b) When plastic has melted remove it from the oven and let it cool.

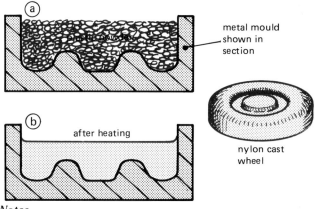

(a) metal mould shown in section

(b) after heating

nylon cast wheel

Notes
– The powder reduces its volume by about half the original volume.
– The mould must have a slight taper.

QUESTIONS/EXERCISES

① (a) Describe what the word **casting** means to a young person. (b) Explain the stages in casting your schools initials in **plastic resin casting**.

② (a) Why is a metal mould required when **casting thermosetting powders** such as nylon? (b) How would you **embed** a small medal in polyester resin?

METAL CASTING

All sorts of metals are cast in industry but in schools casting is usually limited to the casting of the lower melting point metals such as **aluminium**.

The heat involved in casting metals limits the choice of moulding materials. **Casting sand** (eg Petraband) is the most common but other high temperature resistant materials can be used.

Metal casting can be very dangerous and must never be done without teacher supervision. Water is the main danger; it can cause an explosion if trapped when heated (ensure all tools are warm and dry before use).

Patterns can be made from wood, metal or plastic to produce the mould in the sand. If only one casting is needed the pattern can be made from expanded polystyrene; it melts and evaporates as the molten metal is poured into the mould. **Avoid the toxic fumes given off.**

Below is a simple 'one part wooden pattern being used to produce a stand for a soldering iron.

Stages in casting a soldering iron stand

(Most drawings are shown in section)

① section of drag
Place pattern in bottom of 'drag' box then cover with 'parting powder'

② ram — sand
Fill with sand, 'ramming' it in layers as added

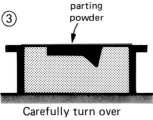

③ parting powder
Carefully turn over 'drag' and cover with 'parting powder'

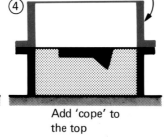

④ cope
Add 'cope' to the top

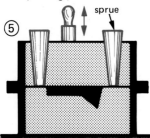

⑤ sprue
Fill cope with sand — holding sprue pins in place

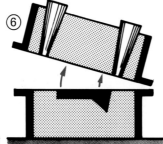

⑥
Very carefully lift top (cope) off — don't allow sand to come out

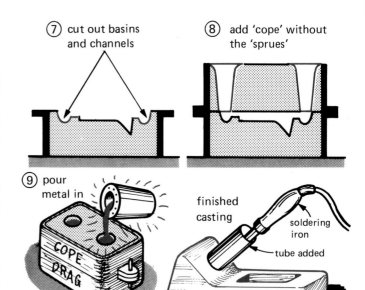

⑦ cut out basins and channels

⑧ add 'cope' without the 'sprues'

⑨ pour metal in

COPE DRAG

finished casting

soldering iron

tube added

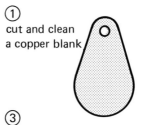

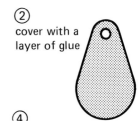

Enamelling

Beautiful colours and patterns can be made with enamels, which are used mainly for decoration.

The two main types of enamelling are:
(1) **Hot Enamelling**, described below, and (2) **Cold enamelling** – This makes use of new **cold setting plastic resins** which can be applied to various surfaces such as card.
Hot enamelling – This is the traditional and most common method, using enamel powders (ground glass powder) which melt and fuses onto the metal blank (usually copper) when heated to a red heat (about 700°C.)
The main disadvantage of hot enamelling is that the enamel cracks if bent.

Making an enamelled pendant

① cut and clean a copper blank

② cover with a layer of glue

③ sieve base colour on

④ add decoration such as threads of glass, beads etc
— thread

⑤ Heat to a dull red heat (about 700 degrees centigrade), it can be heated with a brazing hearth torch or in a special kiln

⑥ The back is cleaned by placing it in acid or using emery cloth, it can then be lacquered

QUESTIONS/EXERCISES

① (a) Why is sand used to make the mould when **casting** aluminium? (b) What materials can the patterns be made from?

all are tapered

JOINING METHODS (+CONTAINERS)

The **three** main ways of joining parts together are by using:
(1) **Permanent joints** eg **glued**.
(2) **Temporary joints** eg **nut and bolt**.
(3) **Movable joints** eg **A hinge**.
This section explains these three methods of joining; at the end various useful container types are shown.

1 PERMANENT JOINTS

Various permanent joints are described starting with:

Glues and adhesives

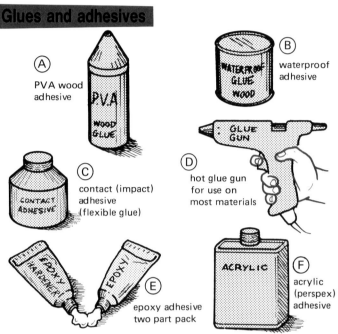

(A) PVA wood adhesive
(B) waterproof adhesive
(C) contact (impact) adhesive (flexible glue)
(D) hot glue gun for use on most materials
(E) epoxy adhesive two part pack
(F) acrylic (perspex) adhesive

(a) PVA (PolyVinyl Acetate) wood adhesive

The common wood glue for indoor woodwork. It is also suitable for absorbent materials such as paper and card. It is a white glue that dries clear in about three hours. It is **not waterproof**. Wash off surplus glue with water before it sets.

(b) Waterproof wood adhesives

There are various waterproof glues such as **Cascamite**; a white powder that is mixed with water to a thick cream. It is heat and waterproof, taking about six hours to set. Some waterproof adhesives come in **two part packs** which need mixing prior to use.

(c) Contact (or impact) adhesives

A flexible rubber-based glue. It can be used on materials such as leather as well as plastics. It is applied to both surfaces then allowed to dry for about ten minutes. The two parts are then pushed together (ie it glues on **contact** or **impact**). Often used to join Formica to wood.

(d) Hot glue gun

Used to join most materials including polypropylene and polythene which are normally difficult materials to glue. The glue emerges hot from the glue gun and sets as soon as it is cold. It will soften if heated again.

(e) Epoxy adhesive

A **two part glue** commonly used for joining metals but it can be used on most rigid materials. It is supplied as an **adhesive** and as a **hardener** which when mixed starts to set due to a **chemical reaction**.

(f) Acrylic (perspex) adhesive

The commonly used adhesive for acrylic (perspex) plastics is **Tensol Cement**. Use a large gluing area.

Other adhesives

There are various specialist adhesives:
Balsa cement – A fast drying balsa wood glue.
PVC adhesive – It is often sold in shops as the glue used to join PVC guttering and tubing.
Polystyrene adhesive – This glue makes very strong joints in solid polystyrene; It **cannot** be used with expanded polystyrene because it dissolves it.

Nails and nailing

The **large round wire nail** is used for general joinery. **Oval wire nails** do not split the wood as easily as the round nails. **Panel pins** are used to hold thin sheets (panels) of wood to a thicker piece of wood (eg for nailing box bases on). **Masonry nails** are specially hardened nails that can be used in bricks or concrete. **Staples** are used to hold wire rods or wire mesh in place.

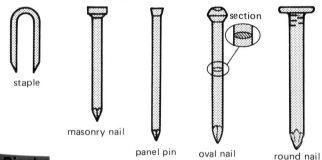

staple
masonry nail
panel pin
oval nail
section
round nail

Rivets

Various rivet types are shown below; the dotted lines indicate the shape before riveting. They are used to join similar or dissimilar materials together.

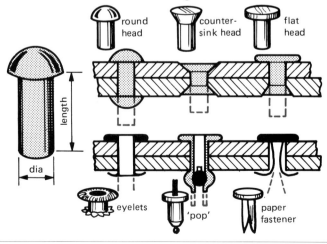

round head
counter-sink head
flat head
length
dia
eyelets
'pop'
paper fastener

QUESTIONS/EXERCISES

① (a) What are the three main ways of **joining parts** together? (b) Name four **adhesives** and indicate what they are used for in the workshop.

② (a) What **nail** types would you use to join: (a) a thin piece of wood to a wooden container, (b) wire netting to a fence post and (c) a piece of plywood to a brick wall?

PERMANENT WOOD JOINTS

The selection of permanent joints depends on:
1 The **strength** and
2 The **appearance** required.
3 The **complexity** in making it.
Below are the joints used in **frame construction** (eg door and panel construction).

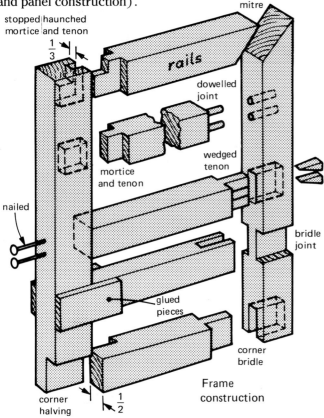

Below are the joints used in **box** or **carcase construction**. Joints marked with a∗ are more suitable for manufactured boards.

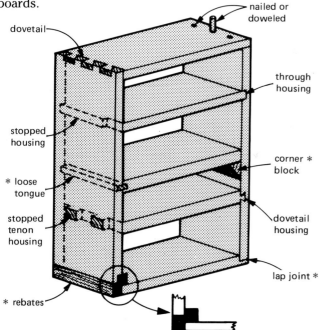

PERMANENT METAL JOINTS

Soldering

The solder melts forming **an alloy** with the metal pieces being joined. **Flux** is used to prevent the joint becoming dirty (oxidised) as the metal is heated up, and aids the flow of solder into the joint.

Soft soldering

Soft soldering is used to join: Electric wires, components on printed circuit boards, tinplate etc. Made from an alloy of **tin** (60%) and **lead** (40%) it melts at about 200°C. **Electrician's solder** has flux in the centre, avoiding the need for separate flux.

Hard soldering

Solders made from **copper**, zinc and **silver alloys** are called the **hard solders**. It includes **brazing** and **silver soldering** described below.

Brazing

Brazed joints are much stronger than **soft soldered** joints. **Brazing rods** are an alloy of **copper** and **zinc** which melts at about 870°C.
To **braze**:
1 **Mix the brazing flux** with water into a thick cream then **apply to the cleaned joint**.
2 Heat metal up quickly to a **bright red heat**.
3 **Apply a fluxed brazing rod** – The solder flows into the joint by **capillary action**.
4 **Cool** slowly.

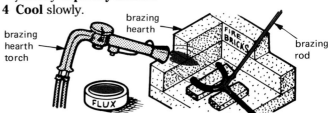

Silver soldering

Silver soldering is very similar to brazing except that the solder melts at a lower temperature and requires a different flux. Used to join copper, brass and jewellery.

Welding

Metals and some plastics can be welded. **Oxy-acetylene welding** uses a gas to produce the intense heat needed to weld metals.
Electric arc welding is faster than gas welding for welding steel. Thin sheet steel is difficult to weld. A method called **spot welding** can sometimes be used on thin steel sheets. **Plastic welders** are used to weld materials such as polythene and polypropylene. Hot air is used rather than a flame.

QUESTIONS/EXERCISES

① Draw two **joints** that could be used on the corners of a wooden frame and two more that could be used elsewhere on a frame. See above for help.

② (a) What is the difference between **soft soldering** and **hard soldering**? (b) Explain the main steps required to **braze** two pieces of metal rod together.

2 TEMPORARY JOINTS

Temporary joints are used if the joint needs to be undone for: repairs, access, maintenance etc. There are hundreds of temporary joints on the market. A few are shown below.

Woodscrew types

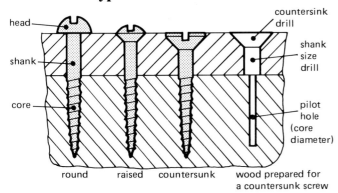

Bolts etc.

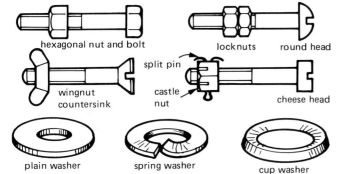

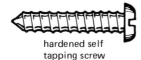

Other joints

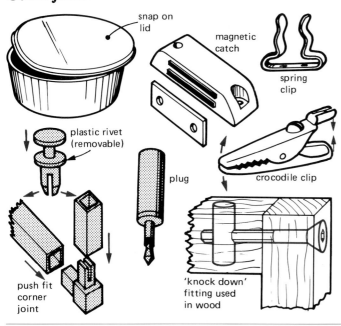

3 MOVABLE JOINTS

Movable joints either move in a **straight line** or **rotate about an axis**. See examples below.

Joints with good **bearings** surfaces are needed if a lot of movement is going to take place.

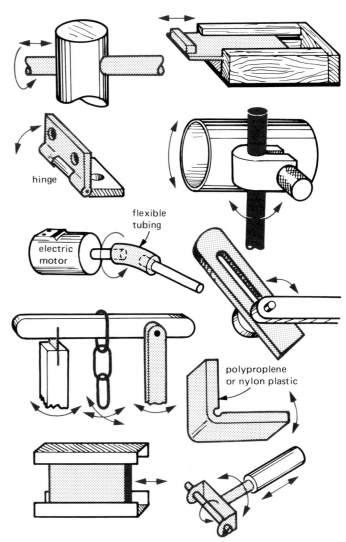

An example of temporary and movable joints - a model bike made from drilled plastic strips. Can you see which parts are fixed, are movable and are temporary?

QUESTIONS / EXERCISES

① Two pieces of wood are to be joined by a countersink screw. Explain how you would prepare the pieces of wood ready for the countersink screw.

② (a) Draw the following: – A wingnut, a self tapping screw, a grubscrew, and a 'knock down' fitting.
(b) Draw three **movable joints** that have more than one movement.

CONTAINERS – IDEAS TO HELP YOU CHOOSE –

The simpler ideas are at the top of the page.

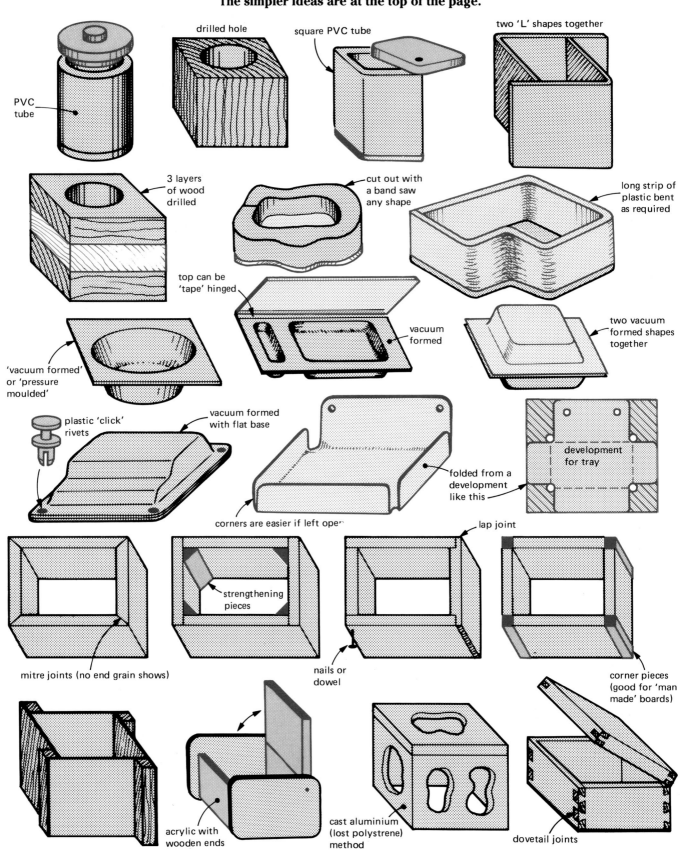

PVC tube

drilled hole

square PVC tube

two 'L' shapes together

3 layers of wood drilled

cut out with a band saw any shape

long strip of plastic bent as required

top can be 'tape' hinged

vacuum formed

two vacuum formed shapes together

'vacuum formed' or 'pressure moulded'

plastic 'click' rivets

vacuum formed with flat base

folded from a development like this

development for tray

corners are easier if left open

lap joint

mitre joints (no end grain shows)

strengthening pieces

nails or dowel

corner pieces (good for 'man made' boards)

acrylic with wooden ends

cast aluminium (lost polystrene) method

dovetail joints

QUESTIONS / EXERCISES

① (a) Draw three container types that are made from plastic (b) Draw two containers that have easy to make lids.

② (a) Draw four container types that would be suitable for a small display box. (b) Explain in some detail how one of them is made.

OBTAINING A GOOD SURFACE FINISH

WOOD

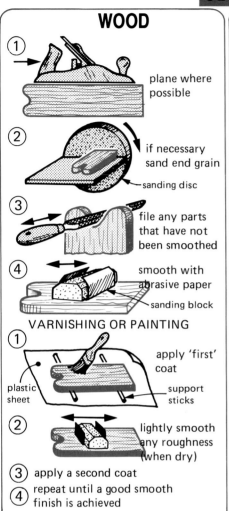

① plane where possible

② if necessary sand end grain — sanding disc

③ file any parts that have not been smoothed

④ smooth with abrasive paper — sanding block

VARNISHING OR PAINTING

① apply 'first' coat — plastic sheet — support sticks

② lightly smooth any roughness (when dry)

③ apply a second coat

④ repeat until a good smooth finish is achieved

PLASTICS

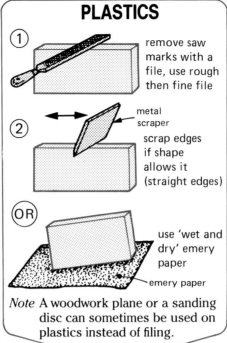

① remove saw marks with a file, use rough then fine file

② scrap edges if shape allows it (straight edges) — metal scraper

OR use 'wet and dry' emery paper — emery paper

Note A woodwork plane or a sanding disc can sometimes be used on plastics instead of filing.

METAL

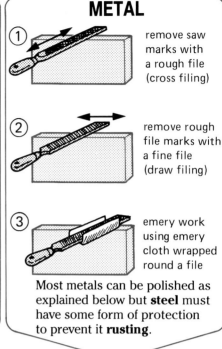

① remove saw marks with a rough file (cross filing)

② remove rough file marks with a fine file (draw filing)

③ emery work using emery cloth wrapped round a file

Most metals can be polished as explained below but **steel** must have some form of protection to prevent it **rusting**.

Polishing metals and plastics

Quite often a polished finish is required on brass, copper, acrylic etc. The polishing machine or a liquid polish can be

<u>Note</u> guards missing

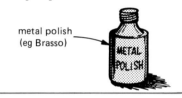

metal polish (eg Brasso)

FINISHES FOR WOOD

① **Varnishes** – There are various varnishes available (a) **Polyurethane varnish** is a modern varnish that can withstand heat and spills from coffee and tea pots etc. (b) **Yacht varnish** is suitable for outdoor use. (c) **French polish** is the traditional varnish and is still used on antiques. (d) **Pre–catalysed lacquer** is a modern fast drying varnish.

② **Paint** – Most paints can be used on wood but remember to **seal** any knots and **fill holes** first. Three or more layers of paint may be needed to obtain a good finish, each layer being smoothed down first.

③ **Stains** – Wood stain can alter its colour and then be varnished if required or use a varnish with a stain already in it.

FINISHES FOR PLASTICS AND METALS

Applied finishes may be needed to:

A Change the colour.
B Prevent deterioration eg rust.
Plastics can be painted but some are naturally slippery (eg polythene) and do not take paint easily.

An applied finish is always needed on steel to stop it rusting, whereas gold is left polished.

Finishes commonly used:

ⓐ **Paint – Cellulose** (car paint) is fast drying and suitable for most situations. **Gloss paint** can be used but takes longer to dry. **Emulsion paint** must never be used on steel because the water in it will cause rust.

ⓑ **Oil** – This provides temporary protection from rust for steel.

ⓒ **Bluing** – Steel is heated up until dark blue and then dipped in oil to cool it.

ⓓ **Lacquering** – Used on trophies etc to prevent tarnishing. It is like a thin colourless varnish.

ⓔ **Plastic dip coating** – A layer of plastic is added about 1 mm thick. Hot metal is dipped into a **fluidised plastic powder** for a few seconds, then removed with a layer of plastic adhering to it.

Other finishes

Electro-plating processes such as chrome plating, nickel plating, or aluminium oxidising can be done for you by local firms.

QUESTIONS/EXERCISES

① (a) Explain the steps needed to produce a good **surface finish** on a piece of wood. (b) Explain the steps needed to produce a good surface finish on metal or plastic. (No applied finishes)

② (a) Why do we need to add an **applied finish** to materials? (b) Explain how the following are carried out: **varnishing, bluing** of steel, and plastic **dip coating**.

SHORT QUESTIONS

Extra to those on each page

(1) Marking out

What are each of the following tools used for when marking out materials: Scriber, try square, marking knife, spring dividers, centre finder, dot punch, and odd leg calipers?

(2) Measuring tools

When would the following measuring tools be used in a workshop: – Steel rule, inside calipers, protractor from a combination set, and a micrometer?

(3) Cutting tools

(a) What materials are the following tools designed to cut: Hacksaw, tenon saw, coping saw, files, rasp, needle files, cold chisel, plane and 'taps and dies'?

(b) What are the following tools used for: Hole saw, machine vice, router plane and a countersink bit?

(c) What is the difference between 'cross filing' and 'draw filing'?

(d) Explain how to cut an 'internal thread' 6 mm in diameter.

(4) Lathework

Draw a decorated drawer knob that could be made on a lathe using the following processes: knurling, drilling, taper turning, and 'facing off'.

(5) Moulding materials

(a) What kind of products could the following processes be used to make: Laminating wood, forging steel, bending on a strip heater, vacuum forming, injection moulding and GRP work?

(b) What kind of work could the following processes be used to make: Forging, beaten metalwork and pipe bending?

(6) Casting

(a) What is casting? (b) Give two examples of products that could be cast. (One example must involve the use of a plastic material.)

(7) Joining methods – wood

(a) List three kinds of adhesive indicating what they are mainly used for. (b) Name three kinds of nail and three kinds of rivet. (c) Name three joints that could be used on a 'frame construction' and three on a 'carcase or box construction'.

(8) Joining methods – metal

(a) Explain the difference between soft soldering, hard soldering and welding.

(9) Containers

(a) Draw two different container types that could be made by assembling pieces of wood together.

(b) Draw a container that could be made by 'vacuum forming' and a container made by folding the sides up (from a development).

LONGER QUESTIONS

When answering the questions below use drawings and provide details of tools used where possible.

Marking out

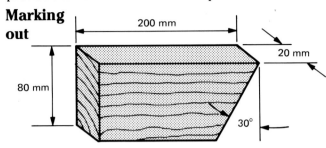

(1) Explain the steps and tools used to accurately mark out the wooden form above.

(2) Explain the steps and tools used to mark out the same form from sheet of 4 mm steel.

(3) Describe two ways of finding the centre of a round bar without using a rule.

Finishing

(1) What kind of protective surface finish would you recommend for the following: A steel gate, a coffee table top, a polished brass mug.

(2) Explain in detail how to produce a good varnished finish on a piece of smooth wood.

(3) Explain the steps necessary to produce a good polished finish on the edge of a piece of acrylic.

Lathe

(1) Draw a metal working lathe and then indicate the following parts on it: Chuck, leadscrew, tailstock, toolpost, topslide, headstock and drill chuck.

(2) Explain how the metal form below could be made on the lathe.

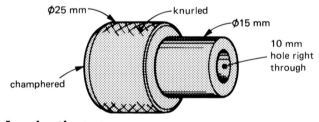

Laminating

Explain the stages in making a laminated chair leg like the one on page 85.

Moulding – Copper and plastic

Explain how to make a brooch form out of (a) copper and then (b) acrylic so that it looks like the drawing below.

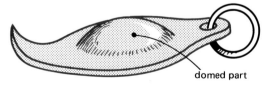

Mass production

Which method of production would you recommend a factory to use if it had to produce (a) 10000 small solid plastic people 50 mm high and (b) 50 plastic food trays 60 mm wide and 20 mm deep. Give your reasons.

SHAPING AND FORMING QUESTIONS

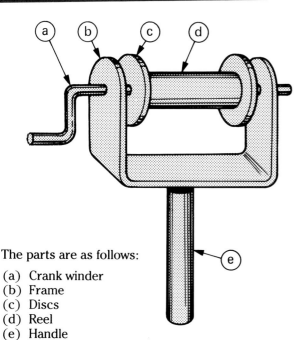

The parts are as follows:

(a) Crank winder
(b) Frame
(c) Discs
(d) Reel
(e) Handle

(**1**) The drawing above shows a **string winder** suitable for kite flying.

(a) What material would you use to make each part from?
(10 marks)
(b) Explain with the aid of a drawing how the handle can be fixed to part D. (10 marks)
(c) Explain in detail how **three** of the parts could be made.
(30 marks)

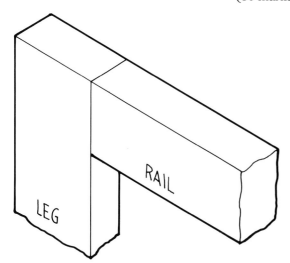

(**2**) The drawing shows a **leg** and **rail** from a small table.

(a) Draw two possible joints that could be used if **leg** and **rail** are made from wood. (20 marks)
(b) Draw a joint suitable if the **leg** *and* **rail** were made from metal. (10 marks)
(c) Draw a joint that could be used if the rail was made from wood and the leg from square metal tube.
(10 marks)
(d) Explain in detail how one of these joints is made and assembled. (20 marks)

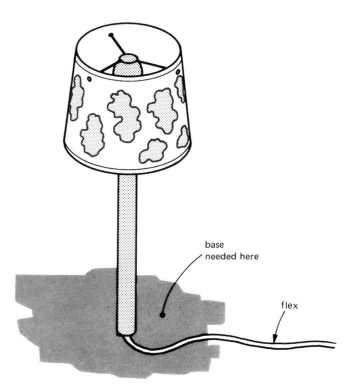

(**3**) A base for the table lamp shown above is needed.

(a) Draw three practical forms that could be used (remember the flex must be neatly hidden and the joint must be strong). (15 marks)
(b) Explain in detail 'step by step' how your best idea could be made in a workshop. (20 marks)

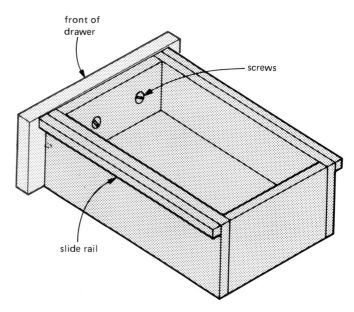

(**4**) The outline of a wooden drawer is shown: It has a separate decorative front which is screwed on after the main part has been made.

(a) Describe fully how this drawer could be made out of wood. (20 marks)
(b) Describe fully how this drawer could be made out of plastics (eg GRP). The form can be altered to make manufacture easier. (20 marks)

SHAPING AND FORMING QUESTIONS

TECHNOLOGY

This section is divided for convenience into the following:

Structures
Mechanisms
Energy
Electrics and electronics
Control and computers
Technology in society

USEFUL DATA

Metric units and conversions

(SI units – **International System**)

Symbol	Prefix	Multiplication factor
G	giga	10^9 or 1 000 000 000
M	mega	10^6 or 1 000 000
k	kilo	10^3 or 1 000
		1 unit (eg gram)
m	milli	10^{-3} or 0.001
μ	micro	10^{-6} or 0.000 001
n	nano	10^{-9} or 0.000 000 001
p	pico	10^{-12} or 0.000 000 000 001

Quantity	Symbol	Unit
length	m	metre
mass	g	gram
	kg	kilogram
temperature	°C	degree Celsius
force, weight	N	newton
moment and torque	Nm	newton metre
velocity	m/s	metre per second
power	W	watt
work and energy	J	joule
stress/pressure	N/m^2 or N/mm^2	newton per square metre
density	kg/m^2	kilogram per cubic metre
frequency	Hz	hertz
potential difference	V	volt
resistance	Ω	ohm
capacitance	F	farad
current	A	ampere

A radio circuit and a 2 watt amplifier (it produces a good sound level), assembled on two EZI-DUN Construction Boards.

A versatile buggy called Trekker from Clwyd Technics, being used as part of a course on control.

A clock radio with pre-select stations, well made by a 15 year old pupil. Case controls also made in school.

A pyramid house designed to be cost effective, very simple to make (DIY) and attractive to a first-time buyer.

STRUCTURES

Structures can be divided up into **two** main types:

1. **Natural** (mostly organic) and
2. **Manmade**.

1. **Natural structures** include things such as trees, animals and caves in mountains etc. Their shapes and forms having evolved over thousands of years. Designers and technologists can learn a great deal about structures by studying natural structures. For example, bird wings and aeroplane wings have many similarities, both have to be light, strong and aerodynamic.

2. **Manmade structures** include things such as bridges, cars, houses, bicycles, aircraft, chairs, tables, tents, cranes, skyscrapers, satellites and artificial joints.

This section of the book deals mainly with the structures that designers, engineers, architects and technologists use.

Structures come in all shapes and sizes, depending on factors such as:

(a) **Width** to be spanned or height to be reached.
(b) Cost.
(c) The expected useful life.
(d) **Materials** and **construction** techniques used to build it.
(e) The **rigidity** or **flexibility** required.
(f) **Safety** factors.
(g) **Maintenance costs**.

Note The materials knowledge needed is covered separately in the **materials** section of this book pages 66 to 74.

A bird skeleton - a structure from nature (Biophoto Associates)

A bridge being tested. The EZI-DUN Construction Board is used to mount the micro switch and buzzer on. The bulb goes off and the buzzer starts at maximum deflection.

A wire rope climbing frame. It is in tension except for the main support in the centre. It is fun and looks good as well.

Oil rig - a structure that has to withstand all the elements including storms and salty water (BP)

A robot arm made from Plawco and other kit parts. The arm is strong and rigid but not bulky. (Commotion)

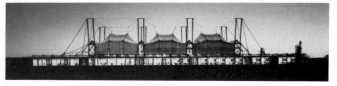

A very attractive building in Cambridge - the Schlumberger Research Centre. (Note the unusual construction.)

FORCES

Forces in structures are either **static** or **dynamic**. **Static** loads (dead) can be resisted easier than the **dynamic** loads (moving) which produce larger forces. The faster an object hits a structure, the greater the force exerted. Structures must be designed to resist these external forces.

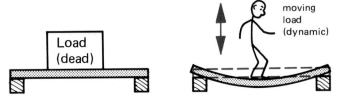

Forces in structures can be classified into one of the following:
(a) **Tension**
(b) **Compression**
(c) **Shear**
(d) **Torsion**
(e) **Bending**

A Tension (pulling forces)

Parts of a structure designed to resist tensile forces are called **ties**.

member in tension

B Compression

Parts or members of a structure designed to resist compressive forces are called **struts**. You will notice that the **strut** shown below is much thicker than the thin cable used for the **tie**. This is due to the fact that **struts** have to resist **buckling**.

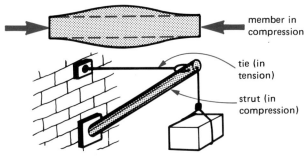

member in compression

tie (in tension)

strut (in compression)

C Shear

The rivets shown below are being sheared due to the pulling forces shown. Scissors also cut using a shearing action.

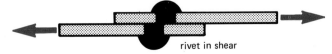

rivet in shear

D Torsion

A **twisting** force. The square shaft shown below is being subjected to torsion by the round rods.

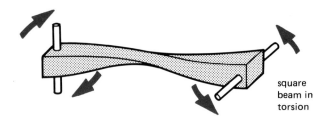

square beam in torsion

E Bending

Parts used to resist bending are called **beams**. The way a beam is placed, its **orientation**, helps determine how large a load it can support. Holding a rule as shown in A, then compare its deflection when held as in B.

The bent foam rubber sponge illustrates how the forces act in a beam. The load acting on the sponge compresses the top half and stretches the bottom half. The **neutral axis** is in the centre. If a '**nick**' is made on the part in tension the beam is considerably weakened.

Orientation of a beam

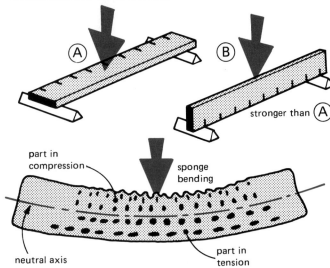

stronger than Ⓐ

part in compression

sponge bending

neutral axis

part in tension

Good shapes to resist bending and buckling

The 'I' **section** beam is one of the most common forms being used in buildings etc. Often referred to as a rolled steel joist (RSJ). **Tee-channel, square sections, round tube** can resist forces economically in most directions. **Corrugated cardboard, fluted plastic** and the **plastic straws** are good for their weight at resisting bending. Concrete beams are often reinforced with steel rods in the parts that are subject to the tensile (pulling) forces.

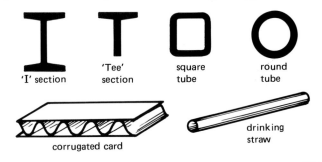

'I' section   'Tee' section   square tube   round tube

corrugated card

drinking straw

QUESTIONS/EXERCISES

① Explain each of the following terms in a sentence giving a practical example for each: (a) dynamic load, (b) tension, (c) compression, (d) shear and (e) bending.

② (a) Why is the **orientation** of a beam important in use? (b) Sketch and name the section of material you would choose for a beam over a large patio door.

RIGIDITY OF STRUCTURES

When designing large structures it is important to keep cost and weight down but still produce a rigid structure. Large bridges, parts of cranes, and other large structures often achieve this by having a hollow form. The **girder bridge** is a typical example; its rigidity is very good. Note the use of triangles in its construction.

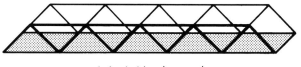

girder bridge (warren)

TRIANGULATION

It is a fact that a **triangle** made up from three strips of steel as shown with 'pin' corner joints produces a rigid form.

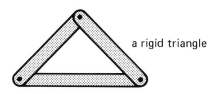

a rigid triangle

A **rectangle** made up from four pieces and 'pin' jointed is not rigid, it can flop about, it needs an extra piece to form a **triangular** shape to make it rigid.

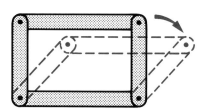

A four 'pin' jointed frame is not rigid

The **gates** shown have been made rigid by various forms of **triangulation**. Gate A uses a **strut** to form two triangles. The force acting on it is in compression. Gate B uses a **tie** (steel wire) to form the two triangles whereas Gate C uses flat plate **gussets** in each corner.

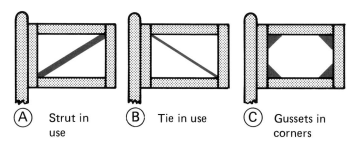

(A) Strut in use   (B) Tie in use   (C) Gussets in corners

The **swing** frame shown is made up from various triangles. Notice the small gussets which prevent the swing falling over sideways.

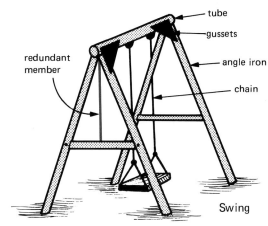

Swing

Redundant members

These are part of a structure that are surplus to requirements and do no useful work. They can be removed without the structure failing. The red metal strip shown added to the swing is not needed. It is **redundant**.

The **roof truss** below may seem to have two redundant members but they are needed to prevent the long beams bending when the roof is covered with snow and to resist strong winds.

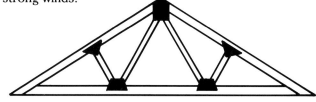

Joints in structures

Many joints can be used, they can conveniently be divided up into three main types:

1 Fixed   2 Movable   3 Temporary

A bicycle makes use of all these types. Various types of joints used in structures are shown below. **Also** see **Joining methods** page 85.

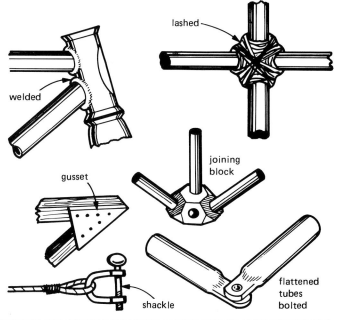

QUESTIONS/EXERCISES

① Sketch in ink a hexagonal shape made up from strips of 'pin' jointed metal. Then add three more strips (in pencil) to make it rigid.

② Sketch a kite or a bicycle, then indicate by labelling where at least one fixed, one movable, and one temporary joint are.

BRIDGES AND OTHER RIGID STRUCTURES

Bridges are used to span large distances. Bridge designers have to consider various factors before deciding on the type of bridge to build. The main considerations are:

1 The **cost**
2 **Life expectancy**
3 **Rigidity**
4 Methods of **assembling** it on site
5 **Maintenance** costs
6 How it will **look**.

The modern **Box girder bridges** are hollow in the middle. They are not used for the largest spans because they are not stiff enough (without extra supports) over long distances. They are often found spanning motorways.

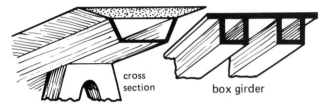

cross section

box girder

Arched bridge

Some stone **arched bridges** still exist from Roman times. The main arch is built first around a wooden form which is then removed when the bridge is complete.

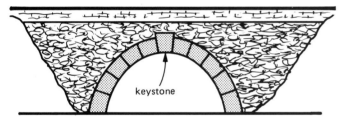

keystone

Modern arched bridges

Many are now made from concrete reinforced with steel rods. They can span large rivers and need very little maintenance if the correct concrete mix is used.

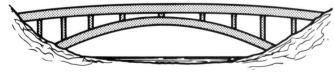

Cantilever bridges

A **cantilever bridge** has a central support with the roadway portion extending outward from the central support.

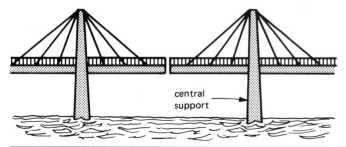

central support

Suspension bridges

Suspension bridges are used for the longest spans. The modern high tensile steels are used for the suspension ropes.

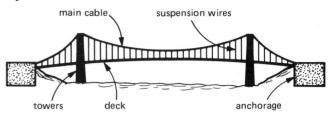

main cable

suspension wires

towers   deck   anchorage

The tower crane is used for helping in the construction of buildings. It is transported to the site and then erected. How do you think it is erected?

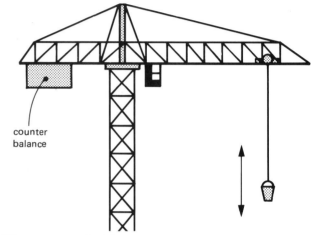

counter balance

The stressed skin wing

Aeroplanes must be as light and as rigid as possible. The wing below shows the ribs which provide the basic shape. The metal skin is riveted to these ribs. The large holes are punched out to lighten the structure where stress is low.

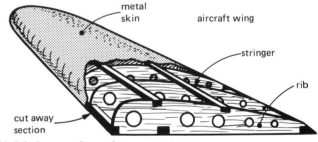

metal skin

aircraft wing

stringer

rib

cut away section

Vehicles – chassis

A chassis is usually considered to be the framework underneath the vehicle that takes the load.

Monocoque body This method uses less material without a separate chassis.

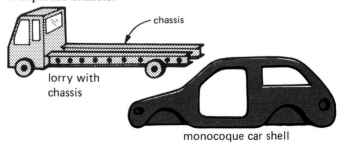

chassis

lorry with chassis

monocoque car shell

QUESTIONS/EXERCISES

① Draw and label one bridge that consists of mainly compressive forces, and a second bridge that makes good use of tensile forces.

② Draw a small old traditional bridge and a modern suspension bridge then say what you think the advantages and disadvantages of each are.

NON DESTRUCTIVE TESTING

There are various ways of testing without destroying the product. Some of the most common ones are described here.

STRAIN GAUGES

They are sensors that enable us to measure the tensile or compressive **strain** by electrical means. If a wire is flexed or stretched a small amount, its electrical resistance is increased or decreased. This very small change is greatly **amplified** enabling us to measure the strain using a **meter** or **graph recorder.** The **strain gauges** used in industry are carefully glued (epoxy) to the material to be tested. They are made from **etched metal foil**, mounted on a thin plastic backing. The pattern on them allows the strain to be measured along the **active axis** but not along the **passive axis**.

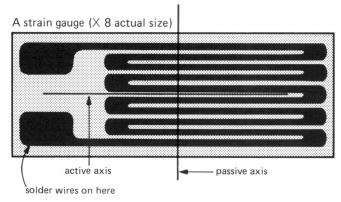

A strain gauge (X 8 actual size)

active axis — passive axis

solder wires on here

To avoid errors due to temperature changes and different wire lengths being used a **Wheatstone bridge** is used consisting of four resistors, one of which is the **strain gauge resistor,** connected as shown. They can also be used as transducers in weighing machines and tensile testers etc.

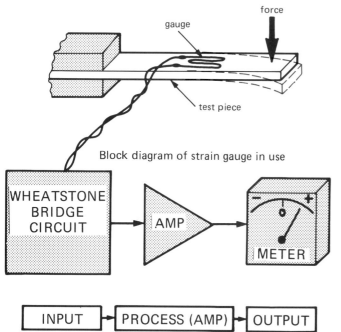

force

gauge

test piece

Block diagram of strain gauge in use

WHEATSTONE BRIDGE CIRCUIT → AMP → METER

INPUT → PROCESS (AMP) → OUTPUT

PHOTOELASTICITY

Can be used to measure **stress** and find out what the stress patterns are. Models are made from transparent epoxy resin (acrylic sheet models can be used) and stressed by applying a load. The load distorts the optical properties of the plastic which when viewed through a **polariscope** can be seen.

A school **polariscope** can be made from two sheets of 100 mm diameter polarised plastic sheet (similar to polaroid sunglasses lens) one sheet is rotated through 90 degrees and light projected through using overhead projector. The test piece being placed in the middle.

If no stress is applied to the model only the outline of the model will show up. When the load is applied lines and colours will show up. Areas of high stress will be indicated by many lines crowded together.

Photoelastic stress analysis

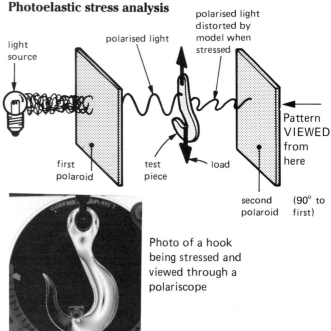

light source

first polaroid

polarised light

test piece

load

polarised light distorted by model when stressed

Pattern VIEWED from here

second polaroid

(90° to first)

Photo of a hook being stressed and viewed through a polariscope

Using a dial gauge or rule

Before structures break there is some deflection or 'give'. This deflection can be used to test how rigid a beam or bridge is as shown. A rule can be used but a dial gauge is more accurate. *Note* the load applied should not have far to fall.

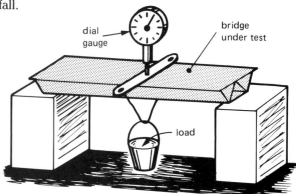

dial gauge

bridge under test

load

QUESTIONS/EXERCISES

① Sketch and describe two situations in which the **strain gauge** method of **testing** could be used.

② Describe one way you would go about **testing** ten

similar balsawood **model bridges**, made by a class of students, for amount of deflection when a **10 N** force is added at the centre.

STRESS IN MATERIALS

The **stress** in materials is dependent on the **cross-sectional area** as well as the **load** applied. **Stress** can be calculated as follows:

$$\frac{\text{Stress}}{(\text{N/m}^2 \text{ or N/mm}^2)} = \frac{\text{Applied load (N)}}{\text{Cross Sectional Area}}$$
$$(\text{m}^2 \text{ or mm}^2)$$

If a 1000 N **load** is applied to a rope with a **cross-sectional area** of 5 mm² the **stress** is 200 N/mm². If the rope is doubled in cross-sectional area the stress is halved giving a **stress** of 100 N/mm².

Example stress calculations

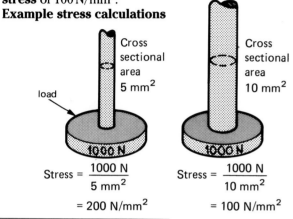

$$\text{Stress} = \frac{1000 \text{ N}}{5 \text{ mm}^2}$$
$$= 200 \text{ N/mm}^2$$

$$\text{Stress} = \frac{1000 \text{ N}}{10 \text{ mm}^2}$$
$$= 100 \text{ N/mm}^2$$

YOUNG'S MODULUS

The **Young's modulus** number indicates the **stiffness** of material. It can be found by dividing the **stress** of a material by the **strain**. The **Young's modulus** for common materials can be found in standard engineering textbooks. **For example** the **Young's modulus (E)** for **mild steel** is about 210 000 000 000 (or 210×10^9) N/m.

$$\text{Young's modulus} = \frac{\text{Stress}}{\text{Strain}}$$

where **Stress** = **Load/area**

and **Strain** = $\dfrac{\text{change in length}}{\text{original length}}$

FACTOR OF SAFETY

The **factor of safety** is the ratio between the **ultimate stress** and the normal **working stress**.

$$\text{Factor of safety} = \frac{\text{Ultimate stress}}{\text{Working stress}}$$

The **factor of safety** will vary according to the work the structure will be used for. The **ratio** varies from 2 to about 18 for structures carrying shock loads.

Example calculation A rod on a swing carries a normal **load** of 600 N but is actually capable of carrying 7200 N (the **cross sectional area** is the same for both). **The factor of safety** is therefore 7200 N/600 N = 12.

RESULTANT AND EQUILIBRANT

When two forces are acting on a point, it is possible to find a single force which could replace them. The single force found is called the **resultant force**. If the two forces cancel each other out they are in **equilibrium**. The first example shows 100 N pulling against 30 N in opposite directions. The resultant force in this case can be found by simple arithmetic:

100 N–30 N = 70 N in the direction of the largest force. Another method is to draw out the vectors 'to scale'. This is known as a **vector diagram** (a vector indicates both magnitude and direction).

Example calculation to find the forces acting on 'P'

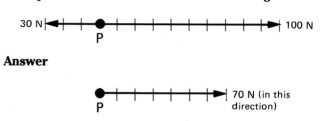

Answer

THE PARALLELOGRAM OF FORCES

This is a method used to find the **resultant** of **two** forces which are **not** in a straight line. The **resultant** can be found if a **vector diagram** (magnitude and direction) is drawn to scale. A **parallelogram** is then drawn to scale as shown below. The **resultant** force and direction is represented by the diagonal of the parallelogram.

Example calculation

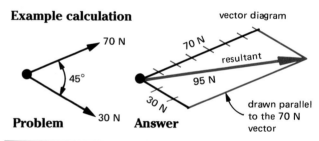

COMPONENTS OF A FORCE

This is the reverse of the **parallelogram of forces**. The example shows how to do this. The **single force** is drawn to **scale** then split up in the directions required. The results are then read off to scale.

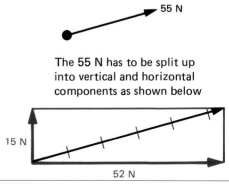

The 55 N has to be split up into vertical and horizontal components as shown below

---

QUESTIONS/EXERCISES

① Calculate the **stress** in a 5 mm diameter rope given that a load of 1500 newtons is applied (convert the diameter to cross-sectional area first).

② Determine resultant force and direction that could replace 100 N and 60 N forces pulling at 45 degrees apart. (Similar to **parallelogram of forces** example calculation above.)

TRIANGLE AND POLYGON OF FORCES
(A PROTRACTOR is needed to do this)

If one force is acting (eg pulling) on a **single** point the two unknown forces resisting it can be found graphically if the angles are know. If three forces are involved it can be solved by what is known as **the 'triangle of forces'**. If more than three forces are involved the same basic method can be used but it is called the '**polygon of forces**' (no example shown). The worked example below shows a 60 kN force acting vertically down being supported by ropes 120 degrees apart. By using the **triangle of forces** the forces in the two supporting ropes can be found.

Triangle of forces First example

1 Obtain the information needed from the **problem** (or **space diagram**) and draw a '**force diagram**' (using a **protractor** to obtain the correct angles). Label it according to '**Bow's notation**'. This states that **capital letters** are placed **between** the lines of force; in a **clockwise direction**. **Small letters** are used next on the **vector diagra**m.

2 (a) The '**vector diagram**' can now be **drawn to scale** starting with the known vector (ie the 60 kN acting vertically down and labelled c–b (small letters). The other vectors are then drawn accurately; **parallel** to the **force diagram**. The **vectors** lines cross at 'a' (*Note*–Arrows follow each other round).
(b) The values of the vectors c–d and a–b can be read by 'scaling off'. The forces in both ropes are 42.5 kN and are in **tension**.

Triangle of forces Second example

This can be answered using the same graphical method as above.

1 Draw the **force diagram** using the information from the **problem** and label according to **Bow's notation**.

2 Draw the **vector diagram** to a suitable scale (the larger the scale the more accurate the results will be). Once drawn, 'scale off' the **vector** a–c (22.5 kN) and b–c (46 kN).

To find out if the parts are in COMPRESSION or in TENSION

Often it is obvious whether the forces are in tension or compression, but if you are not sure you can find out using the following method:
(a) Draw an **answer diagram** like the original problem ready to receive results when found.
(b) Draw a **circle** round the corner (shown in red) and then transfer the arrows from the **vector diagram** drawn when finding forces in second example above to the lines within this circle.
(c) Draw three more arrows the opposite way round at the other end of these lines.
(d) Using the 'key' given at bottom right of page, you can tell whether the member is in **tension 'T'** or **compression 'C'**.

Note The arrows represent the forces in the material resisting the external forces)

Problem

Determine forces in members X and Y and state whether in compression or in tension

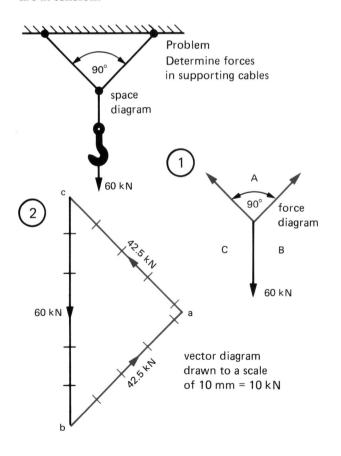

Problem
Determine forces in supporting cables

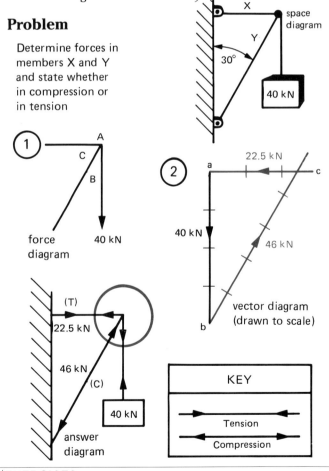

QUESTIONS/EXERCISES

Two structures are shown. For each one find the unknown forces in X and Y using the **triangle of forces** method.

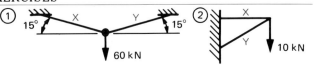

MOMENTS

(also see the turning forces in the mechanisms section)
Moments take into account the **forces** and **distances** involved.

> ie moment (Nm) = force (N) × distance (m)

For example the long spanner tightening a nut exerts more **turning force** than the short one although the same force is being applied to both.

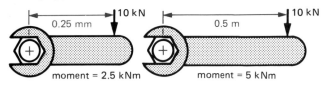

moment = 2.5 kNm   moment = 5 kNm

The principle of moments

The **Principle of moments** for a body in **equilibrium** states that **The total moments tending to turn it clockwise must equal the total moments tending to turn it anti-clockwise.** ie:

> | Anti-Clockwise moments | = | Clockwise Moments |
> | --- | --- | --- |
> | force (N) × distance (m) | | force (N) × distance (m) |

Example calculation – Using principle of moments. The example is of a **see-saw** but it could easily have been a crane or bridge.

Question
How far from the pivot will the girl have to be in order to keep it balanced?

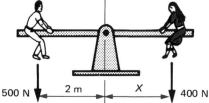

500 N   2 m   X   400 N

Answer

Anti-clockwise moments = Clockwise moments

$$500\,\text{N} \times 2\,\text{m} = 400\,\text{N} \times X$$

$$\therefore \frac{500 \times 2}{400} = X = 2.5\,\text{metres}$$

A question for you
How heavy would the girl have to be if she balanced the boy 3 m away from the pivot point?

BEAM REACTIONS

In beam and bridge design there is sometimes a need to find out what forces are acting on the supports (called **abutments** on bridges) from the downward forces and distances.

To calculate these reactions the **principle of moments** is used. Although there are two supports only **one** is considered to be the pivot, the other is the unknown reaction. In the examples the **moments** are taken about R_1 to find the force acting on R_2, but it would have been just as correct to take moments about R_2 to find the force acting on R_1.

Example – Find the beam reactions

Question
Given the following information, determine the forces acting in R_1 and R_2

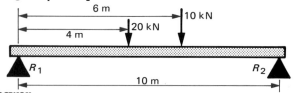

Answer
To find the reaction in R_2 **moments** are taken about R_1

Anti-clockwise moments = Clockwise moments

$$(R_2 \times 10\,\text{m}) = (20\,\text{kN} \times 4\,\text{m}) + (10\,\text{kN} \times 6\,\text{m})$$

$$R_2 \times 10\,\text{m} = 80\,\text{kN m} + 60\,\text{kNm}$$

$$\therefore R_2 = \frac{140\,\text{kNm}}{10\,\text{m}} = 14\,\text{kN}$$

R_1 can now be found by **taking away** the **total downward** forces from R_2 (previously calculated)

$R_1 = $ **Total downward forces** $- R_2$

$R_1 = 30\,\text{kN} - 14\,\text{kN} = 16\,\text{kN}$

FINDING THE SUPPORT REACTION IN FRAMEWORKS

The **Principle of moments** can also be used to find the forces needed to support a **framework** if given the downward forces. The method used is the same as for **beam reactions** once the problem has been simplified as shown below:

Find reactions in R_1 and R_2

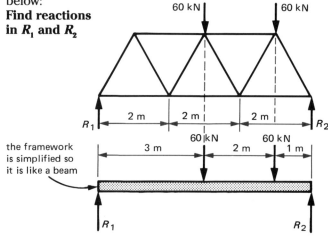

the framework is simplified so it is like a beam

Answer Taking moments about R_1

Anti-clockwise = Clockwise
moments   moments

$$(R_2 \times 6\,\text{m}) = (60\,\text{kN} \times 3\,\text{m}) + (60\,\text{kN} \times 5\,\text{m})$$

$$R_2 \times 6 = 180 + 300$$

$$R_2 = \frac{480}{6}$$

$$R_2 = 80\,\text{kN}$$

$R_1 = $ Total downward force $- 80\,\text{kN}$

$R_1 = 120\,\text{kN} - 80\,\text{kN} = 40\,\text{kN}$

QUESTIONS / EXERCISES

① What is the 'turning force' or moment acting on a lever when a 20 N force is acting at 90 degees to the lever 2 m from the pivot?

② Referring to the **beam reactions** example above, what would the beam reactions R_1 and R_2 be if the 10 kN force in the example was replaced by a 40 kN force?

FRAMEWORKS

Framework problems like the one shown can be solved by mathematical calculations or graphically. The examples illustrate the **graphical method**. (**Protractor** and **rule** needed.)

Frameworks (first example)

1 Sketch a **force diagram** and label it according to **Bow's notation** (described on previous page).

2 Draw the **vector diagram** which represents the **external forces** as follows:

(a) Start with the **external forces**
The 60 kN force a–b acting down, the 22 kN force a–c and 38 kN force c–b are drawn, according to **Bows notation**, on the same line but acting upwards.

(b) **Select a joint** with no more than **two** unknowns. In this case **joint** 1 is drawn out as a **vector** diagram. Once the vector diagram has been accurately drawn to scale, the unknown forces can be found by scaling off.

(c) Select **another joint** (Joint 2) and draw its **vector diagram**.

(d) Shows the last **vectors** added for the **last joint**.

3 Sketch an **answer diagram** and transfer the force values, in newtons, onto it.

To determine whether the forces are in **compression** or **tension** transfer the arrows from the vector diagram on to the answer diagram for each joint in turn. The '**key**' given is used to determine whether members are in **tension (T)** or **compression (C)**.

Note Assumptions made with this method: – Pin joints are used and the forces are in simple compression or tension.

Question

Determine forces and reactions in each member of this framework.

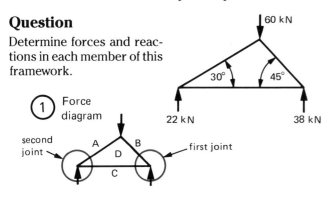

Stages in drawing the vector diagram (drawn to scale)

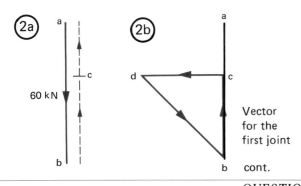

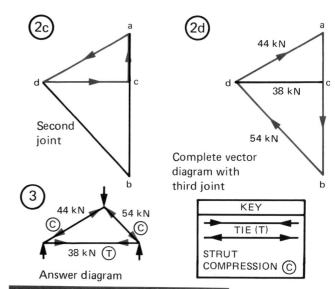

Second joint

Complete vector diagram with third joint

KEY
TIE (T)
STRUT COMPRESSION Ⓒ

Answer diagram

Frameworks (second example)

To solve this the **same procedure is followed as in the first example.** *Note* If some of the external forces are not given they must be found first using the **principle of moments** – see last page.

Only the start and finish of the vector diagram is shown; the **red line** on the completed **vector diagram** shows how joint * was added.

Question

Determine forces and reaction in each member of this framework.

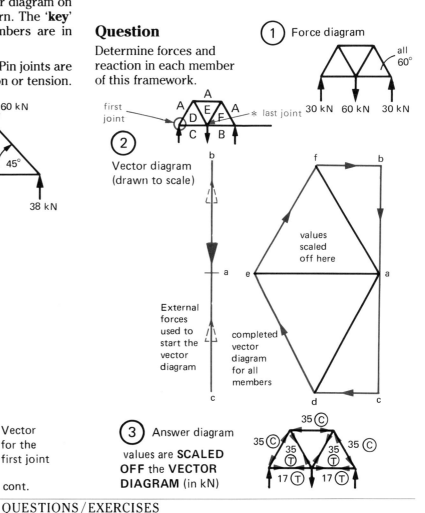

QUESTIONS / EXERCISES

Find **graphically** the force in each member of these **frameworks**. Refer to text above for help.

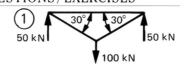

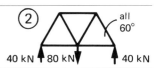

Short questions

1 Explain briefly, with examples, the following terms: Tension, compression, shear, torsion, bending, triangulation and redundant members.
2 Explain briefly what the following are: Strain gauges, dial gauge, polariscope, stress and moments.
3 Sketch the following structures: (a) Box girder bridge, (b) arch bridge, (c) suspension bridge, (d) girder or warren bridge, (e) a lorry with a chassis and (f) a high tower using triangulation.
4 Draw the following beam sections and give a typical use for them: 'I' section, 'T' section and tube.

Longer questions

Moments

How far from the pivot should the record player pick-up be in order to balance the counter weight?

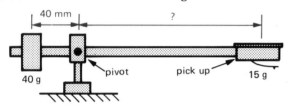

Components of a force – Question

Resolve the following single forces into their horizontal and vertical component forces.

Parallelogram of forces – Question

Find the **resultant** (force and direction) that could replace the other two forces.

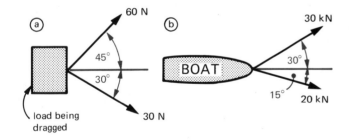

Triangle of forces – Question

Find the forces in the members marked X and Y.

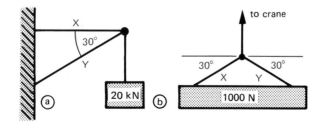

Triangulation – Question

Show how you would make the following shape rigid using the minimum of triangulation, using (a) metal strips, (b) string only.

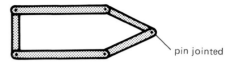

Frameworks – Question

Determine graphically the force in each member of these frameworks.

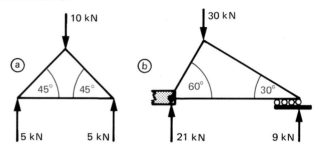

Beam and framework reactions – Questions

Determine the reactions in R_1 and R_2 of the following.

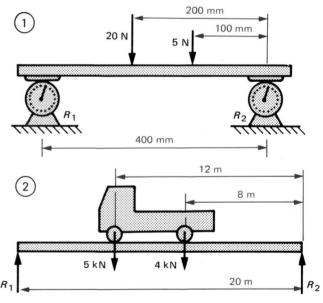

(i) Find the **reactions** in the walls R_1 and R_2 below.
(ii) What **stress** is there in the 10 mm diameter rope used to hold the engine up?

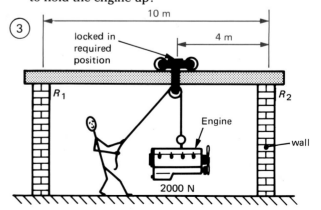

STRUCTURES QUESTIONS

MECHANISMS

Mechanical devices have played a large part in human society; devices such as gears, cams, screwthreads, ratchets etc are used in many everyday products like cars, tin openers, vending machines, cranes, bulldozers etc.

The Industrial Revolution in the nineteenth century made good use of mechanisms to build trains, steam engines etc. Since then the growth of newer technologies such as electric power, electronics, pneumatics and hydraulics has meant the earlier dominance of mechanisms has declined. For example early adding machines were mechanical, but now they have given way to smaller, faster and considerably more powerful electronic calculators.

1 They are usually reasonably efficient if properly designed and made.
2 They can be designed to perform a great variety of tasks, often being the only way to do a particular job.

1 Sliding parts wear unless lubricated.
2 Moving parts sometimes need safety guards.
3 Parts need to be manufactured to high standards of accuracy. This adds to production costs.

A foam-cutting machine that can be controlled by hand or computer. A hot wire cuts the foam. Parts from Vento Solenoids Ltd.

A moving 'action man' mounted on EZI-DUN Construction Boards. The circuit keeps the movement going for five seconds when triggered.

A racing cycle is a very efficient mechanism. Bearings, wheels and gears must be very free running.

A model drive transmission made using a Fischertechnik Construction Kit. Gearbox, clutch and differential are shown.

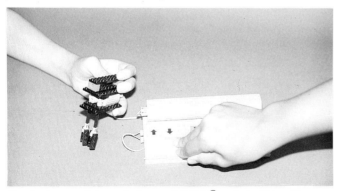

Food mixer model, made from a LEGO® technical kit. The controller being used is the hand controller suitable mainly for more complex systems using more than one motor.

Hovercrafts need to be powered and steered easily. How do you think they are controlled? (ILN Picture Library)

QUESTIONS/EXERCISES

1 What are the main **advantages and disadvantages of mechanisms** compared with other possible alternatives?

2 Give **examples of mechanisms** to be found in: The home, the car, the school workshop and in the kitchen.

Kinds of movement

Linear
(moving in a straight line)

Reciprocating
(moving back and forth)

Rotary (or oscillating)

The six degrees of freedom

It is convenient to think of objects being able to move in one or more of the **six degrees of freedom**. This means an unrestrained object can move in any one of six possible ways (or combinations of these six). For example a 'pillar drill when working moves up and down and turns. *Note* The other four movements not shown are fixed.

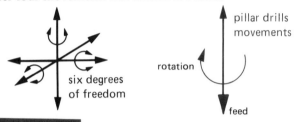

six degrees of freedom

rotation

pillar drills movements

feed

THE LEVER

The lever is one of the earliest machines, often being used to lift heavy weights and/or amplify small movements. There are **three classes**, or **orders** of leverage as shown below (also see page 108 for lever calculations):

First class of lever

This order has the **pivot**, or **fulcrum,** in between the **load** (weight) and **effort** (the force trying to move it). If the **fulcrum** is moved closer to the **load** the **effort** needed to lift the **load** would be less.

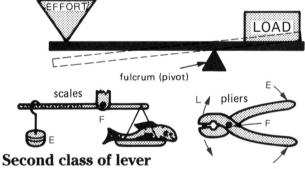

fulcrum (pivot)

scales

pliers

Second class of lever

This time the **Fulcrum** is at **one end** and the **load** between the **effort** and **fulcrum**. The **effort** required to lift the **load** lessens if the **load** is moved towards the **fulcrum**.

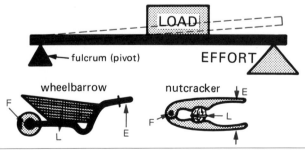

wheelbarrow

nutcracker

Third class of lever

This is similar to the second order of leverage except that the positions of the **load** and **effort** are reversed. *Note* The bend in the pair of tweezers acts like a **fulcrum** (or pivot).

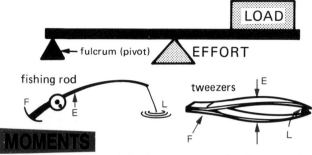

fishing rod

tweezers

MOMENTS

Moments in levers take into account the **force** acting at right angles to the lever and the **distance** of this force from the **fulcrum** (pivot).

Principle of moments

If a lever is **balanced** then the total turning force, or **moment**, tending to turn it **clockwise** must **equal** the total **moment** of forces tending to turn it **anti-clockwise**.

> **Anti-clockwise moments = Clockwise moments**
> (when balanced)

ie $F_1 \times D_1 = F_2 \times D_2$

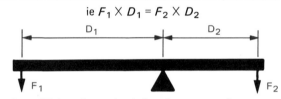

Question (Using the **principle of moments**)

If $D_1 = 4$ m, $D_2 = 2$ m, $F_2 = 10$ N. What would scale F_1 be reading when the beam (or lever) is balanced?

Answer:

$$F_1 \times D_1 = F_2 \times D_2$$
$$\therefore F_1 \times 4\,\text{m} = 10\,\text{N} \times 2$$

$$\therefore F_1 = \frac{10\,\text{N} \times 2\,\text{m}}{4\,\text{m}} = 5\,\text{N}$$

Note These calculations ignore the effect of the weight of the lever.

EXAMPLES OF LINKAGES

Below are a few linkages. Where could you find them being used? Can you think of four more linkage types?

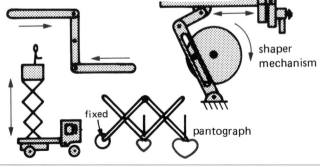

shaper mechanism

fixed

pantograph

QUESTIONS/EXERCISES

① What class or order of **leverage** would you classify: (a) A wheelbarrow, (b) a pair of scissors and (c) a screwdriver being used to remove a lid from a can of paint?

② Referring to the **moments** example question above. What force is needed to balance the lever if $D_1 = 6$ m, $D_2 = 0.5$ m, $F_1 = 100$ N and $F_2 = 500$ N?

ROTARY TO LINEAR MOTION

Examples of mechanisms that convert **rotary** motion into **linear** motion are shown below.

It should be remembered that some **cams** systems require a *spring* to ensure the follower touches the cam as it rotates. Cams are used, in car engines, to control the movements of the inlet and exhaust valves.

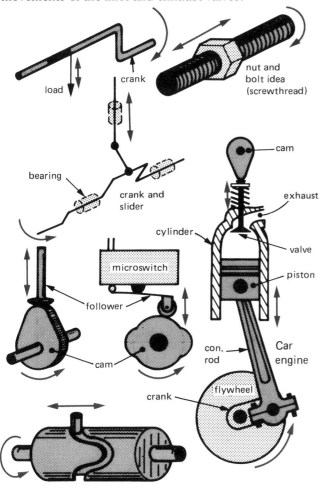

RATCHETS

Rachets usually consists of a wheel with saw like teeth as shown. The part that engages in the ratchet is called the **pawl**. They are used to allow motion in one direction only (eg a bicycle freewheel) or as a means of converting reciprocal motion into intermittent rotary motion (eg ratchet screwdriver).

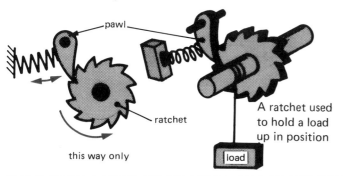

GEARS

Gears are used to transmit **rotary** motion and **forces**. They are efficient if correctly made and mesh (interlock) accurately. Gears can transmit great loads. One reason for using gears is that they cannot slip like a belt drive can. **Spur gears** are the most common type of gear; they have curved sloping sides which form part of an **involute** shape as shown below.

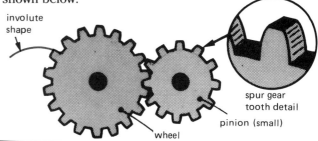

Gear ratio (or velocity ratio)

Gear ratio calculations are based on the number of teeth of each gear. (alternatively the diameter of each gear can be used). If two gears are meshed together the following formula can be used (other formulae are given on the next page):

$$\text{Velocity ratio (or) gear ratio} = \frac{\text{Nos. of teeth on driver gear}}{\text{Nos. of teeth on driven gear}} \left(\frac{\text{input}}{\text{output}}\right)$$

What is the gear ratio (or velocity ratio) of these two gears?

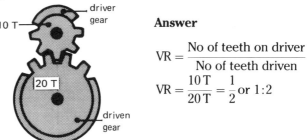

Answer

$$VR = \frac{\text{No of teeth on driver}}{\text{No of teeth driven}}$$
$$VR = \frac{10\,T}{20\,T} = \frac{1}{2} \text{ or } 1:2$$

A three gear train

If three gears are used, as shown below, the **driver and driven** gears rotate in the same direction. The **idler gear** does not alter the ratio between the **driver** and **driven** gears.

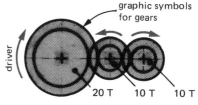

Question If the **driver (input)** rotates at 100 revs/min, how fast will the driven gear turn? (The gear ratio is 2:1)

Answer $\frac{2}{1} \times 100\,\text{rev/min.} = 200\,\text{rev/min.}$

QUESTIONS/EXERCISES

① Name and draw a device or product that (a) makes use of a **ratchet**, (b) **changes rotary motion into linear motion**.

② Explain with a sketch what the following **gear terms** are: (a) a bevel gear, (b) a spur tooth, (c) a worm (d) a rack and (e) an involute shape.

GEAR SELECTION CHART – SUMMARY

drawings INPUT Note the DRIVING GEARS INPUT turn at 100 rev/min (in red)	comments	velocity ratio $= \dfrac{\text{teeth on driven}}{\text{teeth on driver}}$	RPM of driven gear OUTPUT $= \dfrac{\text{RPM of driver}}{\text{velocity ratio}}$
1 100 rev/min. 15 T, 30 T — two meshing gears	Note The change in direction of rotation	$\dfrac{30\,T}{15\,T} \times \dfrac{2}{1}$ or 2:1	$\dfrac{100\ RPM}{2} = 50$ Rev/min.
2 15 T, idler 10 T, 30 T — train drive with idler	Idler makes driver and driven turn in the same direction Ratio stays same as number 1	$\dfrac{10\,T}{15\,T} \times \dfrac{30\,T}{10\,T} = \dfrac{2}{1}$ or 2:1	$\dfrac{100\ RPM}{2} = 50$ Rev/min.
3 15 T, 30 T, 20 T, 10 T — compound gears	Two gears are fixed on the centre shaft	$\dfrac{30\,T}{15\,T} \times \dfrac{20\,T}{10\,T} = \dfrac{4}{1}$ or 4:1	$\dfrac{100\ RPM}{4} = 25$ Rev/min.
4 worm, worm and wheel 40 T	Large speed reduction. The large wheel cannot drive the worm gear. Shafts at right angles to each other	One revolution of the worm moves the wheel gear round one tooth $\therefore$ VR $\dfrac{40}{1}$ or 40:1	$\dfrac{100\ RPM}{40} = 2.5$ Rev/min.
5 12 T, 18 T — bevel gears	Often used to turn through a right angle. Special versions can turn through other angles	$\dfrac{18\,T}{12\,T} = \dfrac{3}{2}$ or 3:2	$\dfrac{100\ RPM}{3/2} = 66.60$ Rev/min.
6 pinion, 12 T, rack — rack and pinion	Changes rotary motion into linear motion (or vice versa)	The rack moves one tooth for every tooth of the pinion	100 Rev/min × 12 teeth = 1200 teeth along the rack in a min.

Black box mechanisms

This is a method of describing what is required without having to decide what gears etc to use. A box is drawn with all the inputs and outputs marked (it need not be black though). The mechanism to be used can be decided later as shown below.

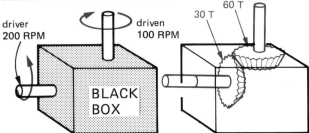

What gear system would you use to solve the following problems? (Red shaft is the driving shaft.)

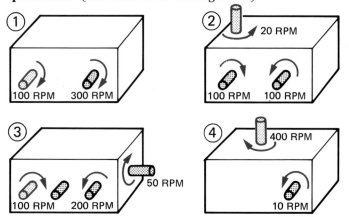

QUESTIONS/EXERCISES

① Answer the four **black box** problems at the end of this page.

② When would you use the following gear types: (a) **worm and wheel**, (b) **bevel gears** and (c) **rack** and **pinion**?

Pulleys

Note The terms **mechanical advantage (MA)** and **velocity ratio (VR)** are described on the next page.

There are **two** main way of using pulleys:

1 The first type, sometimes called **fixed pulley**, allows a change in direction but no MA is achieved.

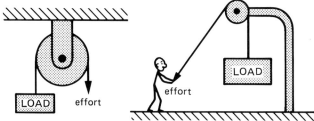

2 The **pulley** and **bearing** moves as shown below. The pulley rises by half the amount the rope moves as shown below; giving a MA and a VR of 2. MA is 2 if the effect of friction is ignored.

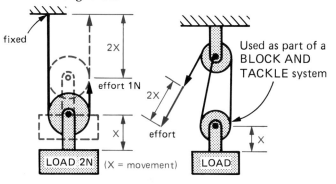

Using two pulleys of different diameter on one shaft (sometimes called WHEEL and AXLE)

This arrangement allows large **mechanical advantages** to be obtained.

The large radii divided by the small radii gives us the ideal Mechanical Advantage and the Velocity Ratio.

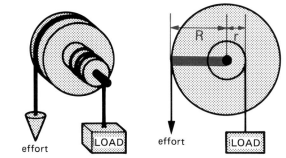

Question
What **load** can be lifted if the **effort** applied to the large diameter is 30 N? Given $R=30$ mm and $r=10$ mm.

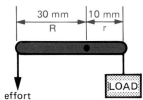

ANSWER
Using PRINCIPLE OF MOMENTS
LOAD × 10 mm = EFFORT
(10N) × 30 mm

∴ LOAD = $\frac{900}{10}$ = 90 N

Belt and chain drives

Belts run on **pulleys** and chains run on **sprockets**. Both can be used to transmit power, increase or decrease speed (**velocity ratio**) or the **mechanical advantage**.

Belts are flexible, do not rust or slip when overloaded. This fact can act as a **safety factor**.

Vee belts can transmit larger loads than flat belts because of the wedging action.

Chains are more efficient than **belts**, do not slip, but need lubrication.

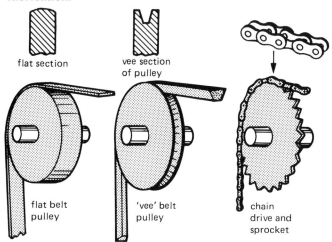

Calculating velocity ratio and speed
The **speed ratio (or velocity ratio) is calculated as follows:**

$$\text{Speed ratio (or velocity ratio)} = \frac{\text{Diameter of driver } (D_1)}{\text{diameter of driven } (D_2)}$$

Find the rev/min. of the 90 mm diameter pulley if the 30 mm diameter pulley turns at 100 rev/min.

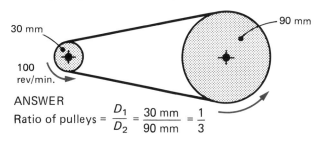

ANSWER
Ratio of pulleys = $\frac{D_1}{D_2} = \frac{30 \text{ mm}}{90 \text{ mm}} = \frac{1}{3}$

Large pulley = 100 rev/min. × $\frac{1}{3}$ = 33.3 rev/min.
(rev/min.)

Crossed belt drive
This enables the direction of rotation to be reversed. (Chains cannot do this.)

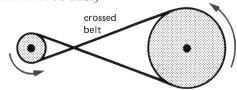

QUESTIONS/EXERCISES

① A 20 mm diameter pulley turns at 900 rev/min. By means of a belt this pulley drives a 70 mm diameter pulley. What is the **rotary velocity** of the driven shaft?

② Explain, giving a practical example, when and under what circumstances you would choose to use (a) a **chain drive instead of belt drive**, (b) a **pulley drive instead of chain drive**.

Velocity ratio (VR) (or distance ratio)

This is a **ratio of effort distance** to **load distance**.

$$\text{Velocity ratio (VR)} = \frac{\text{distance moved by effort}}{\text{distance moved by load}}$$

Example calculation

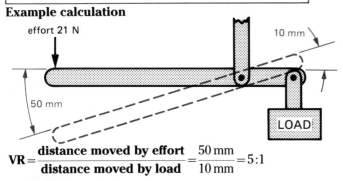

effort 21 N

10 mm

50 mm

LOAD

$$\text{VR} = \frac{\text{distance moved by effort}}{\text{distance moved by load}} = \frac{50\,\text{mm}}{10\,\text{mm}} = 5{:}1$$

Mechanical advantage (MA)

The **mechanical advantage** ratio indicates how much easier a mechanism is to use by comparing the **load** with the **effort** required to move it. Ideally the MA and the VR would be the same but in practice the MA is always smaller due to losses caused by friction etc.

$$\text{MA} = \frac{\text{load}}{\text{effort}}$$

In the case of the lever above the MA

$$\text{MA} = \frac{\text{load}}{\text{effort}} = \frac{200\,\text{N}}{21\,\text{N}} = 4.76{:}1$$

Efficiency of mechanisms

The ratio of **work got out** and **work put in** can be expressed as a percentage.

$$\text{Efficiency}\% = \frac{\text{work out (useful)}}{\text{work in (total)}} \times 100\%$$

NB No mechanism is 100% perfect. Some energy is always lost due to friction etc. The efficiency of a system may vary if different loads are applied to it. Mechanisms usually become more efficient as larger loads are applied. See section on Energy for more details on efficiency, page 115.

Another way of finding the **efficiency** of a system is to use the following formula which can be used if the **mechanical advantage** and **velocity ratio** are already known.

$$\text{Efficiency}\% = \frac{\text{MA}}{\text{VR}} \times 100\%$$

The efficiency of the lever above is therefore:

$$\text{Efficiency}\% = \frac{\text{MA}}{\text{VR}} = \frac{4.75}{5.00} \times 100\% = 95\%$$

(*Note* The 5% lost is due mainly to friction)

Example problem and solutions
(VR, MA and efficiency%)

Find the velocity ratio, the mechanical advantage and efficiency of the following mechanism.

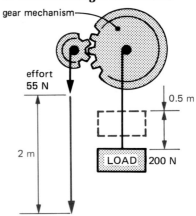

gear mechanism

effort 55 N

0.5 m

2 m

LOAD 200 N

$$\text{VR} = \frac{\text{distance moved by effort}}{\text{distance moved by load}} = \frac{2\,\text{m}}{0.5\,\text{m}} = 4{:}1$$

$$\text{MA} = \frac{\text{load}}{\text{effort}} = \frac{1200\,\text{N}}{55\,\text{N}} = 3.63{:}1$$

$$\text{Efficiency}\% = \frac{\text{MA}}{\text{VR}} \times 100\% = \frac{3.63}{4} \times 100\% = 90\%$$

Friction

Friction is the name given to the force which tends to prevent surfaces sliding relative to each other.

Friction is needed in brakes and clutches but sometimes we want to reduce it as much as possible so that wheels run freely etc. **Friction** is dependent on:

A The materials being used.
B The roughness of the surfaces.
C The forces pushing the surfaces together.

Lubrication

We **lubricate** mechanisms to reduce the level of friction. A good lubricant: separates the surfaces, is as slippery as possible (thin) and does not fail due to temperature or pressure changes.

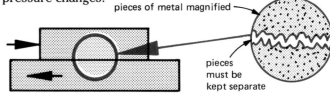

pieces of metal magnified

pieces must be kept separate

Viscosity

This is the resistance to flow. Thin oils have a low viscosity. To measure this we use the Society of Automotive Engineers of America's code (SAE).
eg SAE 10 is a very thin oil.
  SAE 30 is used for car engines.
  SAE 80 is thick oil (heavy duty work).
Greases are made by adding thickeners, such as wax, to the oil.

QUESTIONS/EXERCISES

① Using the example problem about two gears on this page, find the **velocity ratio**, the **mechanical advantage** and the **efficiency** of the mechanism if the **load** is 400 N and **effort** is 110 N.

② What is the purpose of a **lubricant**? What does SAE 10 refer to?

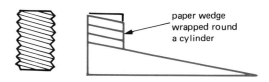

paper wedge wrapped round a cylinder

Bearing types

The type of bearing used depends on various factors such as cost, speed of shaft rotation, whether it is to be lubricated, the forces involved etc. The following bearings are commonly used.

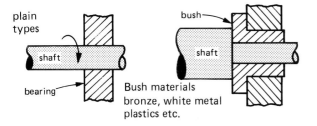

plain types — shaft — bearing

bush — shaft — Bush materials bronze, white metal plastics etc.

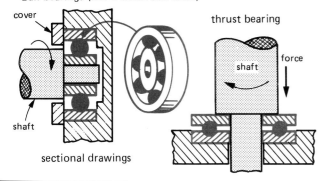

Ball bearings (less friction and wear)

cover — shaft — shaft

thrust bearing — shaft — force

sectional drawings

Fixing onto shafts

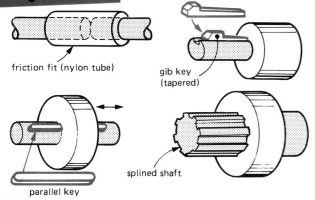

friction fit (nylon tube)

gib key (tapered)

parallel key

splined shaft

Wedges

Wedges can be used to exert a sideways force, eg when splitting wood with an axe or to hold something in place due to the friction on the wedging surfaces, eg a door wedge. Small angled wedges exert a greater sideways force than large angled wedges.

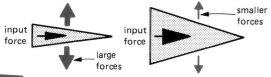

input force — large forces

input force — smaller forces

Screws

Screws can be thought of as long wedges wrapped round a cylinder. Every turn of a screw advances the thread one **pitch**. Fine threads are less likely to work loose than coarse ones but take longer to screw up.

Screwthreads in use

'V' – threads – Used on nuts and bolts.

Square thread – Used on car lifting jacks and 'G' clamps. They are easier to turn than V – threads.

Buttress thread – Used on woodwork vices with a quick acting mechanism.

Acme thread – Similar to a square thread but it allows for adjustment of wear – on lathes leadscrews etc.

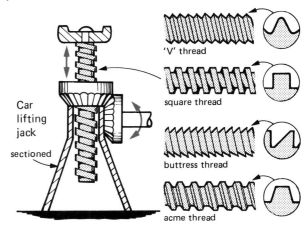

Car lifting jack — sectioned

'V' thread
square thread
buttress thread
acme thread

The 'four stroke' petrol engine

The **four strokes** are briefly explained below.

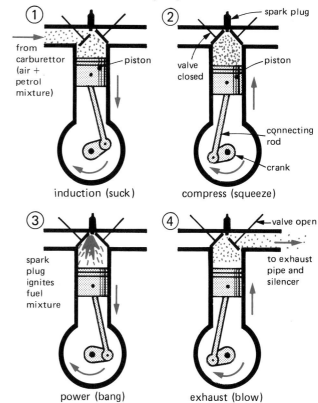

① from carburettor (air + petrol mixture) — piston — induction (suck)

② spark plug — valve closed — piston — connecting rod — crank — compress (squeeze)

③ spark plug ignites fuel mixture — power (bang)

④ valve open — to exhaust pipe and silencer — exhaust (blow)

QUESTIONS/EXERCISES

① Explain with diagrams the following **bearings types:** A plain bearing, a ball bearing, and a thrust bearing.

② Why are '**square threads**' used for car lifting jacks? Give one other kind of thread and a typical use for it.

VEHICLE MECHANISMS

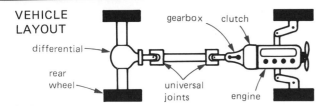

VEHICLE LAYOUT

gearbox   clutch
differential
rear wheel
universal joints
engine

STEERING

The steering geometry of a three-wheeled vehicle is fairly straightforward, but a four-wheeled vehicle can create problems because the inside wheel must automatically turn sharper than the outside wheel.

The **Ackerman Principle** allows the front wheels to be aligned correctly at all times.

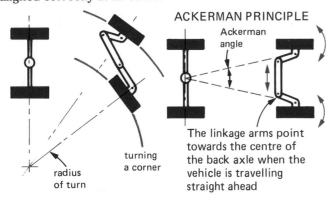

ACKERMAN PRINCIPLE

Ackerman angle

turning a corner

radius of turn

The linkage arms point towards the centre of the back axle when the vehicle is travelling straight ahead

THE REAR WHEELS

When turning a corner the outside wheel has to travel further than the inside wheel. Fixed axles do not allow this to happen, but a **differential gearing** system will allow this.

Most vehicles use a differential. It allows both wheels to be driven at the same time, allowing one wheel to rotate faster as needed. Simple karts can achieve a similar effect by driving only one rear wheel, the other freewheels.

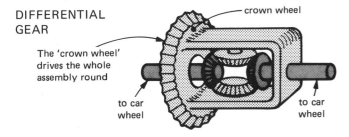

DIFFERENTIAL GEAR

crown wheel

The 'crown wheel' drives the whole assembly round

to car wheel

to car wheel

Universal joints

Universal joints (UJ) are used to transmit the power to the rear wheels. Two UJ's are used on rear wheel drive vehicles as shown above with the vehicle layout.

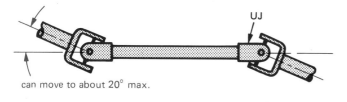

UJ

can move to about 20° max.

CLUTCHES

The **clutch** enables the engine to be disconnected from the driving wheels so that the gearbox can be used. Automatic vehicles do not need a clutch.

Sometimes **multiple plate clutches** are used to save space. (not shown)

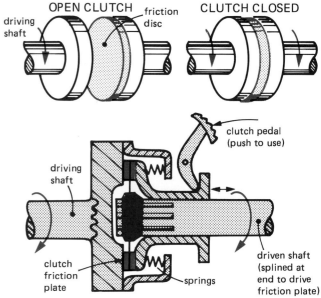

OPEN CLUTCH   friction disc   CLUTCH CLOSED
driving shaft

clutch pedal (push to use)
driving shaft
clutch friction plate
springs
driven shaft (splined at end to drive friction plate)

A SINGLE PLATE CLUTCH (part sectioned for clarity)

BRAKES

Vehicles when moving possess a lot of energy which has to be dissipated as heat when the brakes are applied. The brake pads (made mainly from asbestos substitute) rub on a steel drum or disc. A common arrangement is to have drum brakes, mechanically operated for parking, on the rear wheels and hydraulically operated disc brakes on the front.

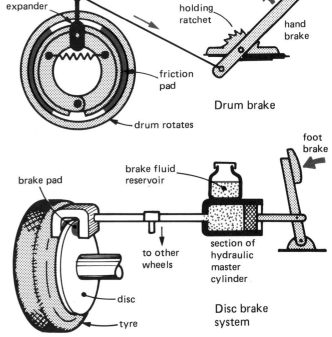

cam expander
brake on
holding ratchet
hand brake
friction pad
drum rotates

Drum brake

foot brake
brake pad
brake fluid reservoir
to other wheels
section of hydraulic master cylinder
disc
tyre

Disc brake system

QUESTIONS/EXERCISES

① Why is it necessary to have 'Ackerman steering' on most vehicles?
② What is the purpose of a 'differential gearbox'?
③ Explain with a sketch how a clutch works.
④ Why do you think vehicles have a mechanical linkage between handbrake and wheels for parking?

Radio controlled vehicles can provide a good source of ideas for transmission, steering and other vehicle technologies.

Shorter questions

(1) Sketch four **kitchen utensils** that make use of leverage or gears.

(2) Draw a **bicycle** then indicate where examples of the following can be found: Leverage, chain drive, friction, ball bearings.

(3) Explain with drawings the following terms (a) **linear motion**, (b) **reciprocating motion** and (c) **rotary motion**.

(4) What effect does crossing a belt drive, on a two **pulley drive**, have on the direction of rotation of a pulley system?

(5) Sketch a mechanism that makes use of a **pawl** and **ratchet** and say why it is needed.

(6) Give an example of **bevel gears** in use in the kitchen or in the workshop.

(7) Why can **'V' belts** transmit a larger force than flat belts?

(8) How can the end of two shafts be **coupled** (joined) together to make: (a) A rigid joint, (b) A flexible joint?

(9) How can **pulleys** be fixed onto a round shaft to provide: – (a) a fixed joint that can be removed if need be, (b) a movable joint that allows the pulley to be moved along the shaft's axis while in use?

(10) Name and sketch three **types of thread** then indicate on one of them what is meant by the 'pitch'.

(11) (a) What are the four strokes of a **four stroke petrol engine**? (b) Why is it difficult to start a car off in top gear on level ground?

(12) What is the difference between disc and drum brakes?

(13) A **driving gear** with 30 teeth turns at 400 rev/min. What would the **rotary velocity** be, of the driven gear, if the meshing **driven gear** had 120 teeth?

(14) Write in full the **formula** for: **Mechanical Advantage**, **Velocity Ratio** and **Efficiency**.

Longer questions

(1) Explain how **two** of the following mechanisms work: A **car jack**, the **quick return mechanism** on a shaping machine, or a **food whisk**.

(2) An electric motor fitted with a 75 mm diameter pulley which revolves at 2000 rev/min. Calculate the size pulley that is needed to turn a polishing machine pulley at 3000 rev/min.

(3) The drive mechanism suitable for a small vehicle is shown below.
(a) How fast will the driving wheel turn?
(b) How far will the vehicle go in a minute?

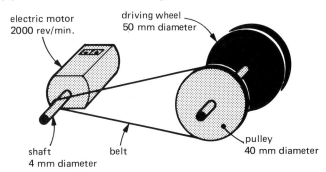

(4) (a) Find the **velocity ratio** of the compound gears shown below. (The shaft sizes are the same therefore they cancel each other out.)
(b) Find the **mechanical advantage**.
(c) Find the **efficiency**.

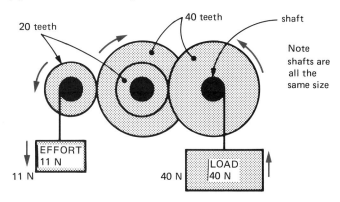

(5) Redraw the diagram below and then decide what mechanisms and bearings should be used for the parts marked A to H. The mechanism will be heavily used.

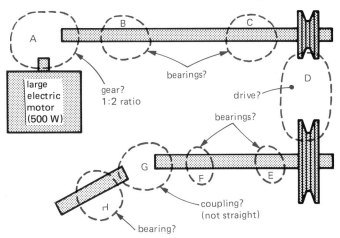

MECHANISMS QUESTIONS

ENERGY

This section provides the basic energy theory needed when solving problems in CDT. Everything we 'make or use' requires energy at some stage to make it work. In some problems the efficient use of energy can be the most important factor to consider (eg solar panels and aircraft). Most terms used in this section have precise technical meanings.

ENERGY SOURCES

Nearly all the energy we use came originally from the **sun** (exceptions being **nuclear power** and the **heat from the earth's crust**).

Green plants use the sun's energy to make their own food by a process called **photosynthesis**. The **plants** are then eaten by **animals** or **humans** or left to **decay**. After thousands of years some of the dead matter will have been converted into **coal** and **oil** which we can use to **power** our **industries** and **homes**.

It is important to realise that some forms of energy are convenient to use such as **oil** and **petrol**, which can be stored cheaply until required. **Solar power** can be trapped and converted into useful energy (eg greenhouses, solar panels for heating water and solar panels which provide small quantities of electricity). **Wind** varies, making it difficult to store and match power requirements. **Water power** is reasonably easy to store (in a reservoir), but a lot of water is needed for a given amount of power. Two promising methods are: using the heat from below the earth's crust (geothermal) and harnessing sea waves.

> **Energy cannot be created or destroyed, but it can change its form.**

This statement is fundamental to the understanding of energy. It is called the principle or law of **conservation of energy**. An example to illustrate how energy changes its form: **Water** which provides **kinetic energy** can turn a **turbine** and produce **electrical energy** which in turn can be converted into **heat energy** by an **electric heater**; this heat could **bake** a loaf of bread, a person can **eat** the bread and use the **chemical** energy provided to ride a bike using **mechanical energy** etc, etc.

TYPES OF ENERGY

Chemical energy
This is energy stored in a chemical form such as **food, coal, oil, petrol** and **electric batteries**.

Energy is released from food when it combines with **oxygen** in the body. **Coal** and **oil** are sometimes referred to as **fossil fuels.**

Electrical energy
Electrical energy can be described as the movement of electrons through an electrical conductor. It is a very convenient form of energy.

Electromagnetic energy
Electromagnetic energy examples include light, radiowaves, microwaves, X-rays etc. Light is especially important to plants. Frequency distinguishes each of the examples.

QUESTIONS / EXERCISES

① Collect at least two **advertisements** that claim to save energy (eg double glazing, wall insulation, roof insulation etc.) Then make an advert of your own for **cavity wall insulation.**

② Write down the **Law of conservation of energy** and then explain, with examples, a typical **energy chain.**

Heat energy

When substances are burned or heated the **molecules** move faster and expand. Petrol when burnt can be used to power vehicles using the **internal combustion engine**.

Sound energy

Sound energy is carried through the air by vibrating the air. You can feel this if you stand in front of a powerful loudspeaker.

Nuclear energy

By splitting the **atom** of **uranium 235** or **plutonium** by **nuclear fission**. The energy produced by 1 kg of **uranium** is equivalent to about 1 million times the amount produced by the same weight of coal. In order to prevent all this power being produced at once (as in a nuclear bomb) **control rods** are inserted to control the reaction speed. The **sun's** power comes largely from joining hydrogen atoms. This is called **nuclear fusion**. There are three main dangers: (a) **Radiation** which is invisible, (b) The possibility of a large **explosion** and (c) Its use for **nuclear weapons** by more countries.

Electric power from nuclear power

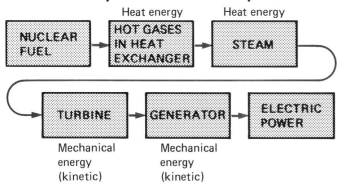

MECHANICAL ENERGY

There are basically two types of **mechanical energy** – (a) **Potential energy** and (b) **Kinetic energy**.

A Potential energy

Potential energy has the **capacity** to do **work**. For example a rock on the edge of a high cliff has the **potential** to knock a house wall down. The higher the cliff the more **potential energy** the rock is said to have. **Hydroelectric** electric power schemes rely on the **potential energy** of the water above the dam to work. **Elastic bands** possess **potential energy** when they are stretched; when released they have no **potential energy**.

B Kinetic energy (moving energy)

When an object moves it is said to have **kinetic energy** or **moving energy**. A car moving has **kinetic energy**. If it hits a large wall the **kinetic energy** is used in the damage caused. The **kinetic energy** is **zero** when everything is **stationary**. Other examples include a **bullet** and a **ball** moving through the air.

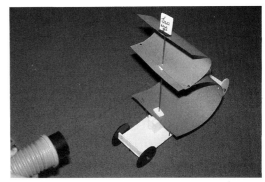

School energy mini project: wind-driven vehicle being tested. The problem was to see how far a wheeled vehicle could go using a blower. (A vacuum cleaner was set up to blow.)

A model of a low energy use house called 'House of the Future'. It faces south to catch the sun, has a thermal store, wind generator etc.

The first non-stop flight without refuelling round the world. The craft is the 'Voyager' and it carried two people. (Associates Press)

Alternative energy sources

The energy sources that we use at present rely largely on **non renewable** resources such as: coal, oil and nuclear. There are many alternative energy sources being tried that harness the **renewable energy sources** such as the wind, the sun, plants, the tide etc. but they usually have some disadvantages that make them unsuitable for large scale use.

Some problems that have to be considered:

- Transport or distribution costs (if bulky materials).
- Converting the energy type (eg heat to electricity).
- The varying nature of the energy source (eg wind).
- Storage of any surplus energy.
- Be able to cope with peak demands.
- Maintenance and repair costs.
- The skills needed to operate it all year.

QUESTIONS / EXERCISES

1. List three types of energy with examples of each type then explain what you know about **nuclear energy**.
2. What is **kinetic** and **potential energy**. Explain with practical examples.
3. What do you think the following terms commonly refer to: **alternative, non-renewable** and **renewable energy** sources?

ENERGY CALCULATIONS

Below are a few energy calculations that may be needed in CDT work.

Force

Force is measured in **newtons (N)** named after **Sir Isaac Newton**. *Note* – To convert kg into **newtons** use the following conversion:

> 1 kg = 9.81 N (use 10 N for rough approximations)

This conversion is only true on earth.

Work done (mechanical)

In technology the **work done** (or **work**) equals **force × distance**.

> **Work Done (WD)** = force × distance

The unit of **work** is the **newton metre (or joule)**. **Force** is measured in **newtons** and **distance** is measured in **metres**. **Example** – A person lifts a **load** of 50 newtons up through 2 metres. What **work** is done?

Answer   Work done = 50 N × 2 m
                            = 100 Nm (or 100 joules)

Power

This is the **rate** (speed) **or working** and is measured in **watts (W)** and expressed as follows. *Note* 1 watt (W) = 1 joule/sec.

> $$\text{Power (W)} = \frac{\text{work done (in newton metres or joules)}}{\text{time taken (in seconds)}}$$

Example calculation

How much power does the mobile crane need to lift 1000 newtons up through 6 metres in 5 seconds?

Answer

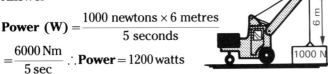

$$\text{Power (W)} = \frac{1000 \text{ newtons} \times 6 \text{ metres}}{5 \text{ seconds}}$$

$$= \frac{6000 \text{ Nm}}{5 \text{ sec}} \quad \therefore \textbf{Power} = 1200 \text{ watts}$$

Measuring electrical power

Electrical power can be measured directly using a **voltmeter** and an **ammeter**. The readings are recorded and used in the following formula.

> **Power (W)** = **Voltage (V)** × **Current (A)**

Example calculation

How much **power** does an electric motor use, given that the **ammeter** reading is 0.6 amps, and the **voltmeter** reading is 12 volts?

Answer
Power = V × A
Power = 12 volts × 0.6 amps
        = 7.2 watts

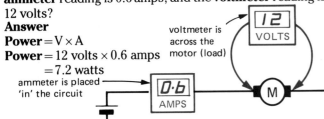

voltmeter is across the motor (load)

ammeter is placed 'in' the circuit

Paying for electricity

Mains electricity is paid for by the **unit**.

> **One unit** = 1000 watts for **one hour**.

If a 2 kW heater is turned on for 4 hours it will have consumed 8 kW hrs or 8 units.

HOW ENERGY ESCAPES FROM HOUSES

When heating your house what you are really doing is **replacing** the heat already lost through the wall, windows, the floor and the roof. Below are two houses, one has extra insulation, the other has none. The uninsulated house owners need to pay **twice** as much for their heating to maintain the same temperature.

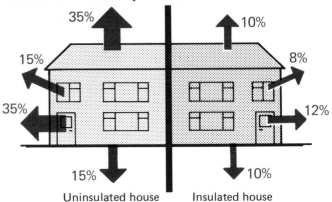

Uninsulated house   Insulated house

Heat escapes in three main ways:
- by **conduction** (heat travels through the materials).
- by **convection** (heat carried away by the movement of the air).
- by **radiation** (like the sun's rays).

Note **Vacuum flasks** have been designed to reduce these three heat losses to a minimum by silvering the lining and having a **vacuum** between the inner and outer lining.

Heat loss through materials (eg walls)

In order to find the heat loss through a wall or roof the following method can be used but first the 'U' values must be known; they can be found in technical building books. Typical 'U' values being for **double glazed windows** 2.5, **solid brick wall** 3.0 and **cavity walls with insulation** 0.5. The following formula can then be used:

> **Heat loss (W)** = A × t × 'U'

where A = surface area in metres
    t = temperature difference (inside − outside temp.)
    'U' = watts/square metre/degree C

Question – What is the heat loss through a solid brick wall, with a 'U' value of 3? The wall is 6 m × 3 m high, the inside temperature = 22°C, outside = 2°C.

Answer
Heat loss (W) = (6 m × 3 m) × 20 deg C × 3 ('U' value)
              = 1080 watts is lost through the wall

QUESTIONS / EXERCISES

① Define the formulae for the following: **Work, power** and then explain how **electrical power** is measured.

② (a) What are three main ways **heat energy** can be lost? (b) How can **insulation values** of the walls, windows and roof loft of a house be improved?

Efficiency

No machine is 100% efficient. If it were it would have achieved **perpetual motion** which is impossible; there are always unwanted losses, eg an electric fire is about 98% efficient, an electric motor 85% and an early steam train engine about 6%.

Efficiency is expressed as a **percentage** and is calculated as follows:

$$\text{Efficiency (\%)} = \frac{\text{work out (useful)} \times 100\%}{\text{work in}}$$

Example calculation
A small 6 volt electric motor consumes 2 watts of electrical power. The output power of the shaft is only 1.6 watts. What is the electric motor's efficiency?

Answer:

$$\text{Efficiency (\%)} = \frac{\text{work out} \times 100\%}{\text{work in}}$$
$$= \frac{1.6 \text{ watts} \times 100\%}{2 \text{ watts}}$$
$$\therefore \textbf{efficiency} = 80\%$$

20% is lost as heat and noise.

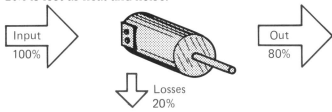

Input 100% → Out 80%

Losses 20%

Note Electric fires and motors are efficient at converting electrical energy but the electricity has first to be produced in a power station which is not very efficient. The overall efficiency is therefore not as good as it first seems.

Making your project more efficient

Below are a few tips to help you make your projects reasonably efficient:

(a) **Bearings** A good simple **plain bearing** will be made from as small a diameter shaft as is practically possible and runs in a good bearing material such as bronze. Lubrication such as oil can also help.

(b) **Gearing** Gearing 'up' or 'down' can cause a large loss of energy. It is best to select, if possible, a power source that avoids the need for a lot of gearing. If gearing is unavoidable use a method with the least number of moving parts (ie only use two gears if it can achieve the same effect as four).

(c) **Wheels** Large wheels roll along easier than small wheels. Large wheels also have the effect of gearing up a powered model. This also alters its speed and efficiency. Soft tyres are sometimes needed to obtain grip; they do not make the model roll easier. To compare the effect of different wheels and shafts, test vehicles can be rolled down a standard slope to see how far they go; the best going the furthest.

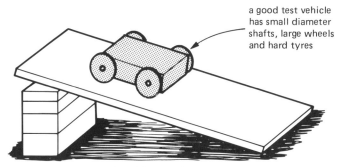

a good test vehicle has small diameter shafts, large wheels and hard tyres

Vehicle test slope

---

1 (a) Define the formulae for the following: **Work, power, efficiency**.

(b) Explain what the following terms refer to: **Fossil fuels, potential energy** and **kinetic energy**.

2 A boy makes a model of an electrically driven vehicle but it hardly works.

Suggest at least three steps he could have taken to improve the vehicles **efficiency**.

3 How much power in **watts** is used by the following products in your home: electric kettle, the largest light bulb, a television or radio? The answers will be found printed on the products.

4 A girl lifts a sack of mass 10 kg, using a pulley system, up through a distance of 10 metres. How much **work** did she do on the sack? (*Note* – First convert kg into newtons.)

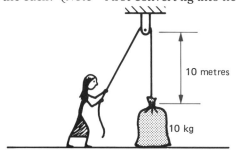

10 metres

10 kg

5 How much **power** in **watts** did Tom produce when he lifted a 20 kg box a distance of 2 metres upwards in 2 seconds? (Convert kg into newtons.)

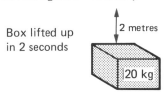

Box lifted up in 2 seconds

2 metres

20 kg

6 How much **power** did an electric motor consume when connected to a 12 volt supply and the ammeter reading was 0.8 amps?

7 What do you think are the advantages and disadvantages of using the sun, wind and plants as **alternative energy sources**? Give a practical example of how each could be used in this country if the government were backing new energy projects.

8 Make a good case out for the **nuclear energy** industry and then against the **nuclear energy** industry. (At least eight reasons for each)

9 A block and tackle pulley system is used to lift an engine weighing 5000 newtons up through 1 metre. The operator uses an effort of 2000 newtons through 10 metres to do this work. What is its **efficiency**?

ENERGY QUESTIONS

ELECTRONICS

This section on electronics covers **basic electricity**, **electronics** using Transistors and Integrated Circuits (IC's or chips).

The electricity and electronics industries have transformed many peoples lives. In the 1950's it was rare to see a television or a transistor radio. Today we have computers, videos and games that are made by the electronics industries. The trend in electronics is towards smaller, cheaper and more reliable products. The container they come in can now cost more than the electronic parts inside.

A practical electronics course

All the circuits used have been tried and tested by pupils in schools.

The circuits marked with a red circle ● could form the basis of a practical course in electronics. The circuits selected will depend on the examination course being undertaken. A **systems approach** is used to explain how circuits work. The systems approach describes a system as having three main stages which are 〈**Input**〉 〈**Process**〉 and 〈**Output**〉.

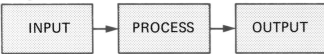

THE SYSTEMS APPROACH

By the end of a **CDT Electronics course** you should be able to understand and make (using kits if available) for this section; at least one **printed circuit board** to ensure the necessary practical making skills are known.

Hardware notes

Only 4.5 and 9 volts batteries are used. (Two 4.5 volt batteries can be joined together to make a 9 volts supply). The bulbs used are 6 volts 0.06 A, resistors 1/4 watt, relay 6–12 volt eg the continental series (185 ohm) from RS Components. Transistors and diodes (eg IN4001) are general purpose types.

Light Dependent Resistor type ORP12 is used. Specialist components are detailed where necessary.

Electrical safety

See page 3 for electrical safety rules in detail. Remember **mains electricity can kill**.

BASIC THEORY

Some basic electric/electronic terms and theory are **given** at the start of this section, then more complex electronic circuits follow.

Voltage (measured in volts) (symbol V)

Voltage (V) can be considered to be the pressure pushing the electricity along. Voltage is sometimes referred to as the **potential difference** (pd). The voltage between two points is measured by a **voltmeter**. If a 4.5 V battery is connected up to a 6 V bulb it will glow dimly but if two 4.5 V batteries are connected up in **series**, giving 9 volts, the bulb glows brightly due to the pressure increase.

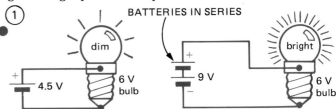

The voltage is not increased if two or more batteries are connected up in **parallel** as shown below. This can easily be seen in practice or checked with a **voltmeter** (or multimeter) by placing the probes either side of the **load** (in this case the bulb).

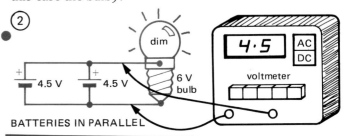

Electric current (symbol I)

Current is the flow of electric charge. It is measured in **amperes (A)** with an **ammeter**. A water analogy is water flowing through a pipe, the larger the pipe diameter the greater the flow of water. A thick wire must be used if a high current is used or else it will heat up and may melt. To measure current the **ammeter** is placed **in circuit** as shown below. To avoid damaging the ammeter start with the higher ranges and move down as needed.

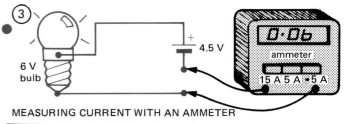

MEASURING CURRENT WITH AN AMMETER

Electric power measured in watts (W)

Electric power is the **rate of doing work**. The power being used at any one instant is found by multiplying the **voltage** with the **current**.

Power (watts) = Voltage (V) × Current (I)

Example calculation

Find the power consumed by a 12 V car headlight bulb if it consumes 5 amps.

Answer Power = 12 V × 5 A = 60 watts.

QUESTIONS/EXERCISES

① (a) Explain what **voltage** and **current** are.
　(b) How are voltage and current measured? Explain with a practical example.

② (a) What **power** is consumed by a 12 V car battery powering two spotlights rated at 4 amp?
　(b) A calculator consumes 0.002 amps and runs off a 3 V battery. What is the power consumed?

Resistors

Resistors provide **resistance** to the flow of electrons, rather like a tap can in a water system. **Resistance** is measured in **ohms** (Ω). All electrical components have some electrical resistance, for example bulbs are really resistors that glow. Resistors can be bought separately as either **fixed resistors** or as **variable resistors** also called **pots** (which is short for potentiometer).

Resistors are colour coded. The chart below explains what the colours mean.

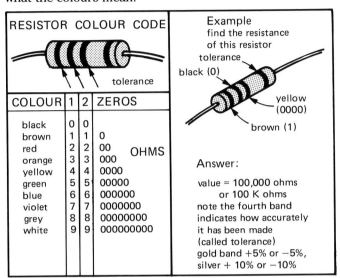

RESISTOR COLOUR CODE				Example
COLOUR	1	2	ZEROS	
black	0	0		
brown	1	1	0	
red	2	2	00	OHMS
orange	3	3	000	
yellow	4	4	0000	
green	5	5	00000	
blue	6	6	000000	
violet	7	7	0000000	
grey	8	8	00000000	
white	9	9	000000000	

Example
find the resistance of this resistor
tolerance
black (0)
yellow (0000)
brown (1)

Answer:

value = 100,000 ohms or 100 K ohms
note the fourth band indicates how accurately it has been made (called tolerance) gold band +5% or −5%, silver + 10% or −10%

Note Use preferred values if possible – multiples of 1.0, 1.2, 1.5, 1.8, 2.2, 2.7, 3.3, 3.9, 4.7, 5.6, 6.8 or 8.2.

Question What colour bands will a 560 ohm resistor have?

Altering resistance – A special resistor known as a **variable resistor** can control the flow of electricity and brightness of bulbs as shown below.

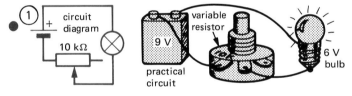

circuit diagram
10 kΩ
variable resistor
9 V
practical circuit
6 V bulb

Resistors in series

If a 100 ohm resistor and a 200 ohm resistor are connected in **series** their values are added to make 300 ohm. The formula is:

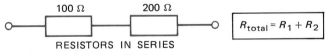

$$R_{total} = R_1 + R_2$$

RESISTORS IN SERIES

Resistors in parallel

If resistors are connected up in **parallel** the resistance does **not** increase but decreases. The formula is as follows.

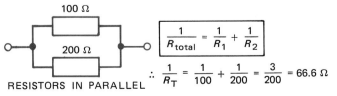

RESISTORS IN PARALLEL

$$\frac{1}{R_{total}} = \frac{1}{R_1} + \frac{1}{R_2}$$

$$\therefore \frac{1}{R_T} = \frac{1}{100} + \frac{1}{200} = \frac{3}{200} = 66.6\,\Omega$$

Ohm's law

George Ohm discovered a relationship between **voltage, current** and **resistance**. The relationship can be written down as a 'memory aid' triangle as follows:
If you cover the quantity you want with your finger the formula required is shown. Try to get the following formulae

ie $V = I \times R$ $I = \frac{V}{R}$ $R = \frac{V}{I}$

Question 1 What resistance does a 6 V bulb have if it is rated at 0.06 A?

Answer $R = \frac{V}{I} = \frac{6}{0.06} = 100$ ohms

Question 2 What current is flowing if 12 V is placed across a 200 Ω resistor.

Answer $I = \frac{V}{R} = \frac{12}{200} = 0.06$ amps

Capacitors (measured in farads (F))

Capacitors can store small amounts of electricity and release it as required rather like a water cistern which stores and releases water as required. Capacitors consist of metal plates separated by an insulator. Capacitors are used in three main ways:
1 In **time delay** circuits.
2 In **sound amplifiers**.
  They allow **alternating current** (AC) to pass but block the **direct current** (DC) (see page 118 for AC and DC).
3 To **filter out unwanted frequencies**.

Capacitor types

1 Non-electrolytic capacitors (the lower values).
2 **Electrolytic capacitors**. Connect the correct way round (used for larger values of capacitance).
3 Variable capacitors (eg radio tuners).

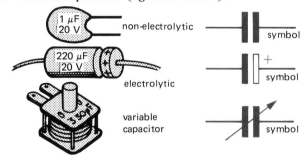

1 μF 20 V
non-electrolytic
symbol
220 μF 20 V
electrolytic
symbol
variable capacitor
symbol

Formulae for series and parallel connection of capacitors (note they are the reciprocal of the parallel formulae).

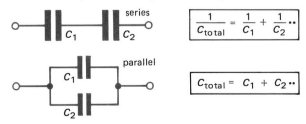

series
C_1 C_2

$$\frac{1}{C_{total}} = \frac{1}{C_1} + \frac{1}{C_2} \cdots$$

parallel
C_1
C_2

$$C_{total} = C_1 + C_2 \cdots$$

QUESTIONS / EXERCISES

① Read the value of the resistors given the following resistor colours: (a) brown, black, red, (b) yellow, violet, orange and (c) red, red, red.

② What is the total resistance of a 200 Ω and a 1 kΩ resistor connected in (a) **series** and (b) **parallel**?
③ What **resistance** does a 12 volt bulb have if it is rated at 0.5 A?

Measuring instruments

The most useful instruments in electronics are: The **multimeter** (shown), the **oscilloscope** (or CRO) which enables voltage to be seen and measured on a screen. It is very useful for audio circuit work. Another useful instrument for audio work is the **signal generator** which produces square or sinusiodal wave forms.

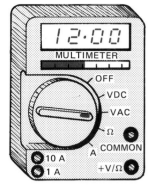

The **multimeter** is the most useful general purpose instrument because it can measure **voltage, current, resistance** and test **transistors** etc. The digital multimeter shown has a digital output as well as a bar graph readout which is analogue.

Switch types

Common switches and their symbols are shown below.

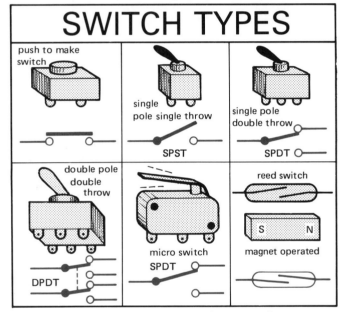

Switches in use – Three useful circuits

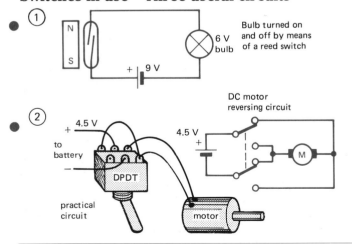

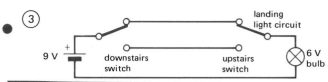

Alternating and direct current

Alternating current (AC)

Alternating current constantly changes direction; cars and power stations use **alternators** which produce the **sine** wave AC shown below.

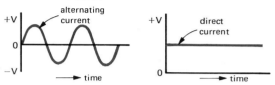

Power stations produce alternating current which is then transformed up, via **transformers**, to 400,000 V so that it can travel with little power loss over long distances. Local **substations** with transformers, reduce the voltage to 250 V for use in the home.

Direct current (DC)

Direct current travels in one direction only. Batteries provide us with direct current. Electronic circuits use direct current. Transformers cannot be used with DC to change the voltage.

Power supply unit (PSU) (or battery eliminator)

To operate the electronic circuits in televisions or powerful radios etc from batteries would be expensive so they have a circuit that converts the **mains voltage** into **low voltage** DC. A fairly simple circuit that can be used to do this is shown below:

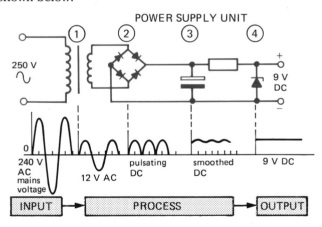

1 The 'mains' 250 V AC is transformed into 12 V AC, with a **transformer**.
2 The 12 V AC is then converted into a pulsating DC by the **four diodes** connected up in a 'bridge' configuration.
3 The **capacitor** and **resistor** smooths out the pulsating DC.
4 A **zener diode** allows a maximum of 9 V to pass through.
PS **Buy 'double insulated' PSU's – don't make them.**

QUESTIONS/EXERCISES

① (a) Name three **electrical measuring instruments.**
(b) What can a **multimeter** measure?
② (a) Draw the **switch symbols** for the following types: SPST DPDT (b) Draw the switches.
③ How would you connect up a DPDT switch to make it reverse a motor?
④ (a) What is the difference between AC and DC current? (b) How is **mains current** converted to 9 volts **direct current**?

CIRCUIT CONSTRUCTION

General comments

Choose a construction method that suits your own situation. In schools this usually means a method that can be easily altered and tested. Some methods are more difficult than others. The most difficult circuit construction methods for the experimenter are those that do not look like the circuit diagram and have some parts above the circuit boards surface and some below it.

Planning a circuit

The **flashing light circuit** example below uses a 555 timer chip and is **surface mounted**. The circuit diagram can be found on page 123.

1 Decide which components are to be fixed to the board and which are not.
2 **Plan** a **full size drawing** (on graph paper) using actual components rather than using symbols. Add dots where joints are needed.

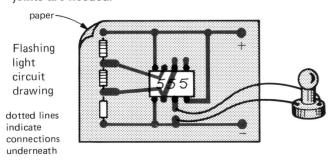

paper

Flashing
light
circuit
drawing

dotted lines
indicate
connections
underneath

3 Transfer the drawings onto the circuit board to be used, in this case a **PCB board** is used but other methods described below could be used. For help with actually making a PCB see page 58.

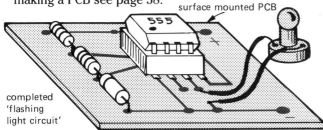

surface mounted PCB

completed
'flashing
light circuit'

Other board types

Matrix boards are easy to use and check because the layout is the same as the circuit diagram. Pins are pushed into the matrix holes as required. It can look reasonably neat if care is taken.

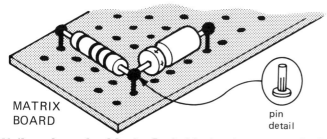

MATRIX
BOARD

pin
detail

Nails and wooden block – Probably the cheapest method. Nails are hammered, where required, into a block of plywood. It is not a good enough method for examination purposes but may be useful for trying out ideas.

Strip board (or Veroboard)

Strips of copper are attached on the underneath side. Components are mounted on the top with the wires coming through the holes to be soldered on the underneath side. Breaks in the copper strips are made as required by drilling. A fast method if pre-planned carefully but difficult to check.

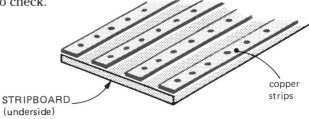

STRIPBOARD
(underside)

copper
strips

Tips on components and their use

Integrated circuits (IC's) – Use an IC holder if possible.

Variable resistors – The thread limits the thickness of material it can pass through as marked ⌶ below.

Resistors – Can be mounted upright to save space.

Switches – Avoid difficult to fit ones.

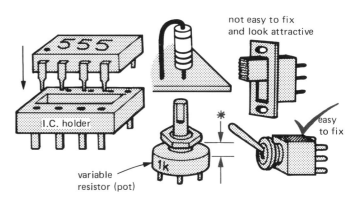

I.C. holder

not easy to fix
and look attractive

easy
to fix

variable
resistor (pot)

Printed circuit boards (PCB)

This is a **mass production method** enabling small compact circuit boards that are automatically soldered in one pass. The PCB copper tracks are made by etching the unwanted parts away using a corrosive chemical such as **ferric chloride**.
See page 58 for steps in making a PCB in school.

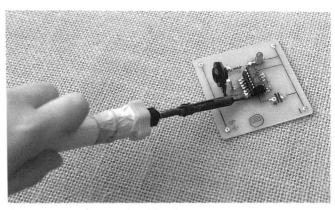

A timer circuit being soft-soldered together with a soldering iron.

QUESTIONS/EXERCISES

① Name and describe **three methods of circuit construction** giving their advantages and disadvantages.
② Explain the stages in **planning a circuit**.

③ Explain how a **printed circuit board** is made (refer to page 58 for help).

SEMICONDUCTORS (Diodes, transistors etc)

Semiconductors are made from materials whose electrical conductivity can vary between that of a good **insulator** like plastic and good electrical **conductor** like copper. **Silicon** and **germanium** are examples of semiconducting materials. In electronics they are **doped** with, for example, phosphorus, to make an 'N' **type** and boron to make P **type** semiconductors during manufacture.

Diodes

Diodes behave like a 'one way' gate or valve; they only allow electricity to flow in one direction. A variation known as a **light emitting diode** (LED) glows and is used for indicators. LED's work on low voltage of about 1.5 V so resistors are connected in **series** to protect them if higher voltages are used. **Diodes** are made up from a 'P' type and an 'N' type semiconductor joined together. Electricity flows through the diode easily if the positive of a battery supply is connected to the 'P' side of the diode as shown. If connected the other way round the diode blocks the flow of electricity.

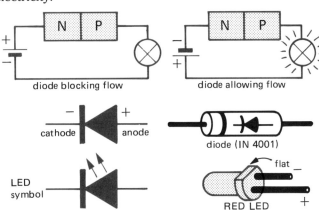

diode blocking flow   diode allowing flow

cathode   anode   diode (IN 4001)

LED symbol   flat   RED LED

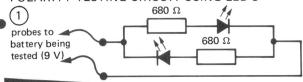

POLARITY TESTING CIRCUIT USING LED'S

① probes to battery being tested (9 V)
680 Ω
680 Ω

Transistors

Transistors can be used as: (1) a sensitive switch or **(2)** An **amplifier**. They are made from **three layers of semiconductor material** either as NPN or PNP types. The central layer is the **base** (b) connection and acts like a trigger. The other connections are called the **collector** (c) and **emitter** (e). NPN transistors are connected differently to the PNP types. Can you spot the difference? Clue – The arrow direction on the symbol at the top of next column.

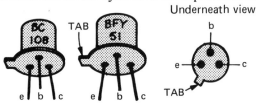

Underneath view

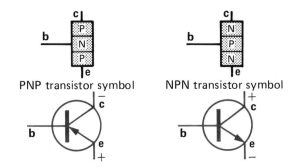

PNP transistor symbol   NPN transistor symbol

Integrated circuits (chips)

Integrated circuits (IC's) contain all the transistors, resistors, diodes, etc needed to make up a particular integrated circuit. **Microprocessors** are very large IC circuits containing hundreds of components. The actual working part is very small as can be seen below.
There are two main categories of IC:
1 **Analogue** IC's eg Amplifier types for radios etc.
2 **Digital** IC's switching circuits – 'on' or 'off'

IC Symbols and drawings

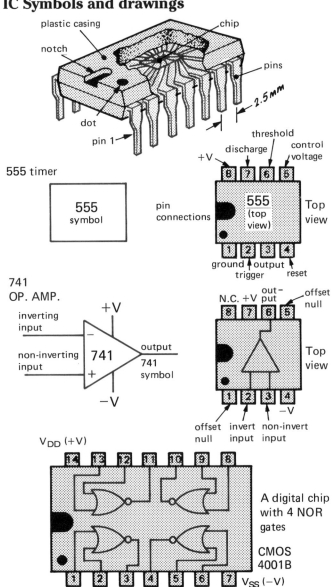

555 timer

555 symbol   pin connections   555 (top view)   Top view

741 OP. AMP.

inverting input
non-inverting input
+V
741
output
741 symbol
−V

V_{DD} (+V)

A digital chip with 4 NOR gates

CMOS 4001B

V_{SS} (−V)

QUESTIONS / EXERCISES

① (a) What is a **semiconductor**?
(b) Explain, using drawings, the construction of a **diode** and a **PNP transistor**.

② (a) Draw the symbols used for: A **diode**, **transistor**, and **operational amplifier**, (b) What are the two main categories of **transistors** and **integrated circuits**?

Transistor switching

The advantages of using transistors to switch on circuits is that they are **sensitive**, can **switch fast**, and are **reliable**. More sensitive circuits can be made if two transistors are used. If an even more sensitive circuit is needed an **operational amplifier** (OP AMP) can be used as described on the next page.

Switching a transistor

A transistor is rather like a watertap which needs a certain amount of force before it can be turned but once **on** can easily vary the flow of water as required. A general purpose transistor such as the BC108 (an NPN type) requires a **trigger voltage** of 0.6 volts to turn the transistor on.

Transistors provide a **current gain** or amplification. The **current gain** (hFE) varies with different transistors. It is a ratio which is calculated as follows:

$$\text{current gain (hFE)} = \frac{\text{collector current (Ic)}}{\text{base current \quad (Ib)}}$$

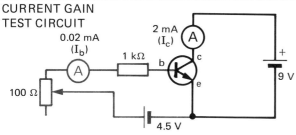

CURRENT GAIN TEST CIRCUIT

The current gain shown on the diagram above is.

$$\text{hFE (current gain)} = \frac{\text{Ic}}{\text{Ib}} = \frac{2\,\text{mA}}{0.02\,\text{mA}} = 100$$

Potential dividers (One battery or two?)

The circuit above uses two batteries which is rather wasteful. Two resistors connected up to form a **potential divider** can be used to divide the battery voltage up as required.

If two identical resistors (eg 10 k ohms) are used; the voltage at the centre will be half the supply voltage. ie 4.5 V if a 9 V battery used.

The formula to calculate the output voltage across R_2 is

$$\text{Voltage across } R_2 = \frac{R_2}{R_1 + R_2} \times \text{Supply voltage}$$

Example calculation

Voltage across R_2

$$= \frac{R_2}{R_1 + R_2}$$

$$= \frac{20\,\text{k}\Omega}{80\,\text{k}\Omega + 20\,\text{k}\Omega} \times 9V = 1.8\,V$$

To find voltage across R_1

Take 1.8 V from supply voltage

$\therefore$ 9 volts $- 1.8\,V = 7.2$ volts

Useful circuits using potential dividers

By having one of the potential divider resistors changing in response to the light (via the LDR) the bulb is turned **on** or **off**. If the second potential divider resistor is also adjustable (with a variable resistor) the light level can be **preset**.

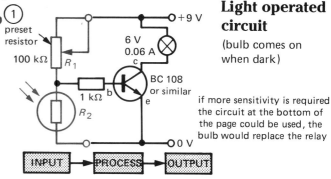

Light operated circuit

(bulb comes on when dark)

if more sensitivity is required the circuit at the bottom of the page could be used, the bulb would replace the relay

The **potential divider** part of the circuit above (in red) can be changed for other sensors that change resistance. If the effect required is opposite to that needed R_1 and R_2 are switched round. For example the **fire alarm** below becomes an **ice alarm** when the **thermistor** and **variable resistor** are swapped over (The variable resistors value may need changing).

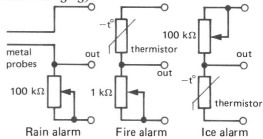

Rain alarm   Fire alarm   Ice alarm

Relay outputs (to control motors etc)

Instead of using a bulb in the above circuit a **relay** can be used. This allows large motors, bells etc to be controlled. A relay **isolates** the electronic circuit. For example a motor can be run off 20 volts while the main circuit is run off 9 volts. Relays require a protection **diode** to protect the transistor from the **back EMF** (electromotive force) produced when the relay coil is turned off. (For more about relays see page 125.)

Motor controlled by light

Note – Two of these circuits can control a light seeking vehicle.

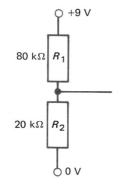
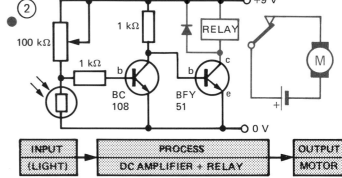

QUESTIONS/EXERCISES

① What is the hFE of a power transistor with a base current of 0.02 amp and a collector current of 3.6 amps?

② (a) Why are **potential dividers** used in transistor circuits? (b) What is the **voltage across** R_1 and R_2 if the potential divider calculation above had $R_1 = 10\,\text{k}\Omega$ and $R_2 = 2\,\text{k}\Omega$?

Other outputs to try

Replace the motor in the last circuit with the following (symbols shown in red).

Note – You may need to alter the voltage required to operate different motors, bells, counters etc, but the 9 V electronic circuit stays the same.

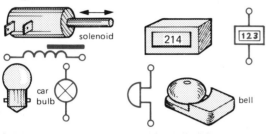

OPERATIONAL AMPLIFIERS (OP-AMPS)

OP AMPS were originally developed to solve mathematical problems such as addition and division, hence their name. They are very sensitive, having a high **voltage gain** (or amplification) and are versatile **analogue AC** and **DC** amplifiers with a **linear** output. An OP AMP has **two** inputs called the **inverting** and **non inverting** inputs, indicated with a small + and − sign which **must not** be confused with the battery supply voltage.

The **difference between the two inputs** is amplified.

Voltage gain calculation example

If **inverting input** is 5 V and the **non inverting input** is 5.0001 V, what is the output voltage? Assume a maximum gain of 10,000.

Answer Output $= 0.0001$ V $\times$ gain of $10000 = 1$ V.

Some circuits only vary one OP AMP input, the other input being **fixed** with resistors as in the example below. (Resistor R_1 and R_2). Some OP AMP circuits require the use of **two** batteries as shown on this page.

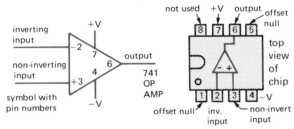

Sensitive light operated switch

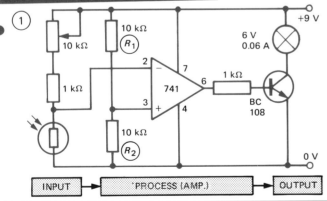

The OP AMP circuit above is very sensitive. It turns **on when dark**. If the LDR and **variable resistor** are swapped round the light comes **on when light**. If a **relay** (and protection diode) is used instead of the bulb, counters and motors etc can be controlled.

White line follower/light following vehicle

By using the high current OP AMP shown below two small motors can be driven directly. If one LDR is covered one motor turns **on** if the other LDR is covered the other motor turns **on**. The variable resistor adjusts the **sensitivity** by altering the **gain**.

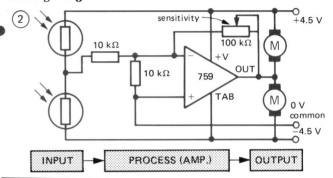

Negative feedback

Sometimes the **voltage gain** is too high and needs to be reduced to make the circuit more stable and less sensitive. This is done by adding a **feedback** resistor (R_f). The formula is (if using the **inverting input**):

$$\text{Voltage gain} = \frac{R_f}{R_1}$$

The voltage gain would be 100 if R_f is 100 kΩ and R_1 is 1 kΩ. Without a **feedback resistor** the **gain** can be up to 10000.

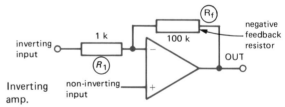

Electronic thermometer (voltmeter used for readings)

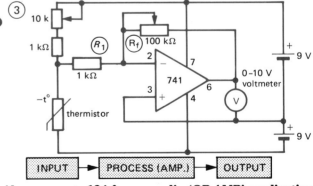

Also see page 124 for an audio 'OP AMP' application.

QUESTIONS / EXERCISES

① Draw a **two transistor light sensitive circuit** that controls a large **bell**, needing the use of a relay.

② (a) What were OP AMPS originally developed for?
   (b) What are the main properties of an OP AMP?

③ (a) What **gain** does a OP AMP have if R_f is 100 kΩ and R_1 was 1 kΩ? (b) Draw the OP AMP symbol and label it.

MULTIVIBRATORS – ASTABLE AND MONOSTABLE –

Astable multivibrators (clock)

Sometimes **called freerunning** or **clock** circuits. Once turned on these circuits produce a continuous **on/off** digital output. There are transistor and integrated circuit variations. The 555 IC **timer chip** is used here, pin details on page 120.

The **frequency** of the **time on** and **time off ratio** can be altered by changing the values of resistors R_1, R_2 and capacitor C_1. The **on/off ratio** is sometimes referred to as the **mark space ratio**.

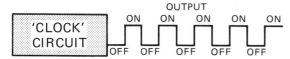

(1) Flashing light circuit

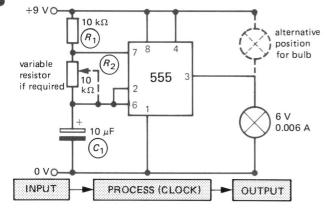

alternative position for bulb

6 V
0.006 A

INPUT → PROCESS (CLOCK) → OUTPUT

(2) Organ or siren

A **siren** is made by using only one **resistor** across X – X. An organ (as shown) requires at least **eight preset resistors** which will need tuning.

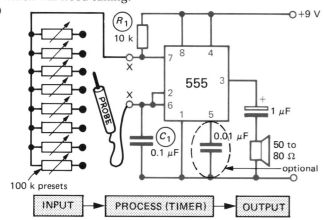

100 k presets

INPUT → PROCESS (TIMER) → OUTPUT

Astable multivibrator calculations

Time ON (T_1) $= 0.7(R_1 + R_2) \times C_1$

Time OFF (T_2) $= 0.7 \times R_2 \times C_1$

Total period $(T) = T_1 + T_2$

Frequency (f) $= \dfrac{1}{T}$ Hz

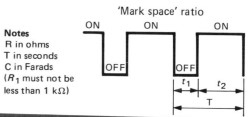

'Mark space' ratio

Notes
R in ohms
T in seconds
C in Farads
(R_1 must not be less than 1 kΩ)

Monostable multivibrators (timers)

Once **triggered 'on'** it will stay **'on'** for a preset time. It only operates once unless reset providing a **time delay** and can be used to: make chess timers, egg timers, photographic timers etc. The 555 timer can be used for delays up to 1 hour.

The **variable resistor** R_1 allows the time set to be varied.

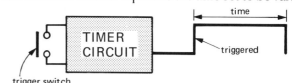

trigger switch

(3) Time delay – LED output (10 seconds)

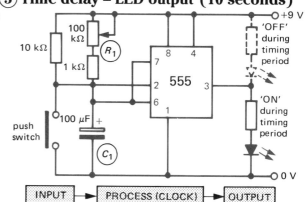

'OFF' during timing period

'ON' during timing period

push switch

INPUT → PROCESS (CLOCK) → OUTPUT

(4) 'Finger touch' time delay

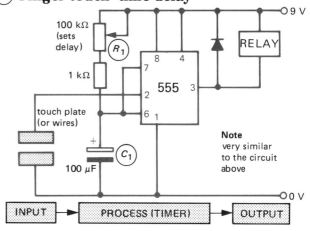

touch plate (or wires)

Note
very similar
to the circuit
above

INPUT → PROCESS (TIMER) → OUTPUT

Monostable (timers) calculation

Time delay (T) $= 1.1 R_1 \times C_1$ (or $R_1 \times C_1$ approx).

Note C in farads and R in ohms.

Example What is the approximate time delay if R_1 is 200 kohm and C_1 is 100 microfarads?

Answer $200\,000$ ohms $\times 100 \times 10^{-6} = 20$ seconds

---

QUESTIONS/EXERCISES

(1) (a) What is the difference between **astable** and **monostable multivibrators?** (b) What is meant by the **mark space ratio**? (c) How can the **mark space ratio** be altered?

(2) Calculate the **frequency** of an **astable circuit** using a 555 timer given the following: $R_1 = 10$ kΩ $R_2 = 22$ kΩ and $C_1 = 100$ microfarads ($= 0.0001$ farad).

AC AMPLIFICATION (of sound and other signals)

Radios, record players and intercoms need to amplify weak **alternating current** (AC) signals so that they can be heard easily. The block diagram shows this in outline. It should be noted that the voltage is amplified but the **wavelength** or **cycle** stays the same. **Frequency** is the number of cycles a second.

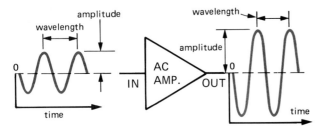

To check the performance of an AC circuit an **oscilloscope** (or CRO) is needed so that the signal can be seen. In order to get a good input signal a **signal generator** can be used, or a person can whistle into a microphone. If a **clipped output**, see drawing, is produced it may be due to **overloading** the input or too much **voltage gain**.

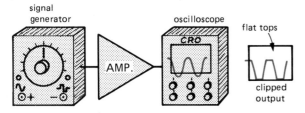

One transistor AC amplifier

In order for a transistor to amplify **alternating current** using a DC battery the resistors and capacitors are connected up as follows: Capacitors C_1 and C_2 allow the AC signal to pass as shown, in red, while preventing the DC current leaving this amplifier stage.

The **potential divider resistors** R_1 and R_2 are selected so that the transistor is always 'on', or **biased** at about 1.6 V across R_2. The **output voltage** is produced across the **load resistor** R_1.

This circuit is not very powerful so more transistor stages could be added or a specialist audio amp chip used such as the 2 amp LM 380 illustrated next.

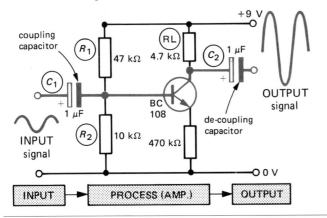

2 Watt audio amplifier

An **audio** AMP which can be made into a useful **intercom**.

When choosing a practical amplifier the following should be considered:

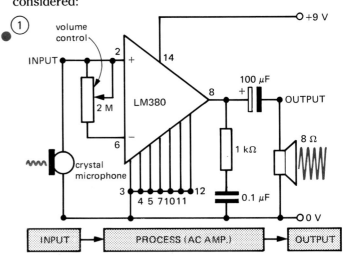

1 The **power output** required: 1 watt or more is recommended for a useful intercom.
2 The **speakers impedance** (AC resistance). If using old radio speakers they are usually 4 or 8 ohms.
3 The **power supply** needed. Voltage and current.
4 **Input impedance** of microphone (high or low).
5 Any extra needed such as **volume** and **bass control**.

Radios

Radios **tune** into the broadcast **modulated signal**, using the **coil** and **variable capacitor**. The signal is then **demodulated**, the **carrier wave** removed before being amplified and fed to a **loudspeaker**.

Below is a simple radio circuit to make a radio that uses the ZN414Z chip made by Ferranti Electronics; it does **not** need a separate aerial like very simple radios.

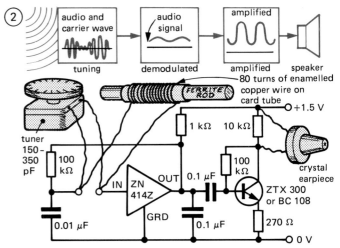

The coil and tuner shown are set for use on mediumwave (MW). The coil would need changing for longwave (LW). To make it drive a speaker further amplification would be needed such as the LM380 amplifier above. Using old radio coils and tuning capacitors will keep costs down.

QUESTIONS / EXERCISES

(1) Explain why an **oscilloscope** and a **signal generator** are used in audio construction work.

(2) (a) Draw the **one transistor AC amplifier** circuit then explain what C_1 and C_2 are used for.
(b) What factors should be considered when buying an audio amplifier?

CONTROLLING MOTORS and large bulbs etc.

Motors and devices that consume a lot of **current** (amps) will 'blow' sensitive low power electronic circuits so devices that can safely cope are needed.

Check in electronic catalogues to determine the maximum power requirement your motor needs.

Possible power devices

If using a transistor circuit a **power transistor** could be used. If using OP AMPS a **power** OP AMP could be used.

A **relay** may be needed if a separate (isolated) power supply is required or if high currents are involved.

Mains current can be controlled by a device called a **thyristor** (as used in house light dimmers).

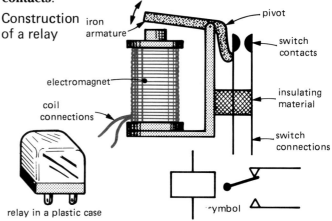

Motor speed controllers

A simple variable resistor would seem to be the obvious way to do this but in practice this is unsatisfactory because slow speed control is difficult and the variable resistor could burn out. There are two practical ways of doing this as shown below:

1 Analogue – By altering the power supplied as required via a **power transistor**.

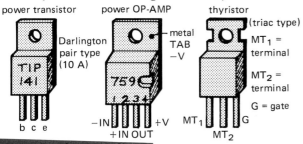

2 Digital – By turning the device **on** and **off** fast and varying **mark space ratios** to alter the speed.

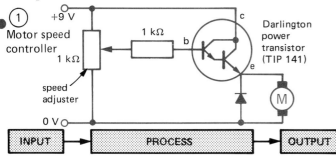

Relays

A relay consists of a **Switch**(s) that is turned ON or OFF with an **electromagnet**. The outline of a **relay** is shown below. When a small current flows through the **coil** in the **electromagnet** the **iron armature** moves and operates the **contacts**.

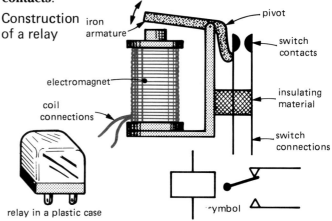

Relay used to 'latch' a circuit 'ON'

Once triggered the circuit **latches** (stays ON). It is important that a **protection diode** (IN4001) is used as shown in the circuit below to protect sensitive electronic circuits.

Light operated latching circuit

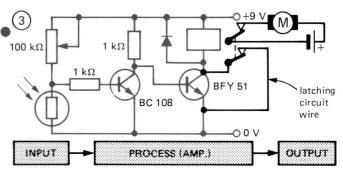

Vehicle reversing circuit

This uses one **double pole double throw relay**. It can be controlled by a light beam if an LDR is used as shown or reed switches etc. A large capacitor 47000 microfarads plus can provide a time delaying action.

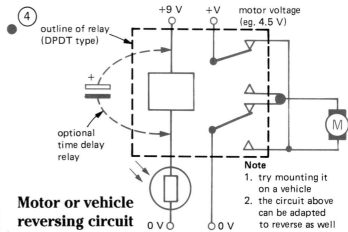

Motor or vehicle reversing circuit

QUESTIONS/EXERCISES

① (a) Explain **two** ways of **controlling a large motor** (with diagrams).
(b) Explain how a **relay** works.

② (a) Explain, with a diagram, how a relay can be made to **latch**, stay on, once triggered.
(b) Draw a **motor reversing circuit** using a relay.

DIGITAL ELECTRONICS

Digital electronics are very important because they are used in digital computers, telephones and the new information technology systems. Digital 'chips' are reasonably cheap, reliable, efficient, and may be used to solve complex problems. Digital electronics are replacing other systems of control and information work. The present **information technology** explosion is partly the result of cheap, complex digital electronics systems becoming available such as wordprocessors and facsimile machines.

What is digital electronics?

Digital electronics is concerned with electronic switching circuits. They are either ON or OFF; their output voltage levels being either **high** (logic 1) or **low** (logic 0). *Note* – If ordinary switches are used with digital electronic circuits they may need an extra **debouncing** circuit to prevent the switch contacts bouncing and producing more than one signal when switched.

logic 1 (ON)   Digital pulses

(OFF) logic 0

LOGIC GATES

Digital, or **binary**, electronic logic gates come in **three** basic sorts: they are AND, OR and NOT gates. By combining an AND and a NOT gate a NAND gate is produced. A NOR gate is made up from a NOT gate and an OR gate. The output possibilities of each gate is given in the form of a **truth table** (O means OFF and 1 means ON). **American logic symbols** are used in this book; being the most commonly used.

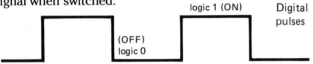

Electrical equivalent circuit   symbol

TRUTH TABLE		
A	B	OUTPUT
0	0	0
0	1	0
1	0	0
1	1	1

practical circuit

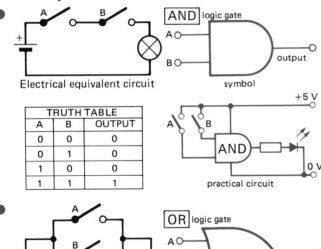

Electrical equivalent circuit   symbol

TRUTH TABLE		
A	B	OUTPUT
0	0	0
0	1	1
1	0	1
1	1	1

practical circuit

TRUTH TABLE		
IN	OUT	output is
0	1	**opposite**
1	0	the input

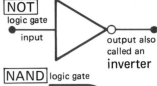
NOT logic gate   input   output also called an **inverter**

A	B	OUTPUT
0	0	1
0	1	1
1	0	1
1	1	0

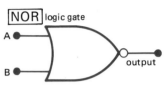
NAND logic gate   A   B   output

A	B	OUTPUT
0	0	1
0	1	0
1	0	0
1	1	0

NOR logic gate   A   B   output

Using digital chips to solve problems

If you look in an electronic catalogue you will see a wide selection of digital chips. The main types used in schools being the 7400 TTL (Transistor Transistor Logic) series and 4000 CMOS (Complementary Metal Oxide Semiconductor) series. They often have a few circuits on one chip sharing the same + and − rails.

Advantages of CMOS

Can be used on 3 to 15 volts (TTL requires a 5 volt supply). Uses less power than TTL types but it does not switch as fast as TTL. They can survive short circuits for a while if using 3 to 9 volt batteries.

Advantages of TTL

It is a well established family of chips that can be handled (CMOS types need careful handling during construction to avoid static build up – use 'sockets'). Unused TTL inputs naturally 'float high' unless connected to 0V, but unused CMOS inputs **must** always be connected either to the +V rail or 0V rail via a 10 kΩ resistor to prevent them behaving unpredictably.

BURGLAR ALARM PROBLEM

Make an alarm which will indicate when either a door OR a window is opened.

Answer (shown in two stages **A** and **B**).
An OR gate could solve this if connected up as shown.

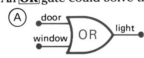
(A) door   window   OR   light

WINDOW	DOOR	INDICATOR
0	0	0
0	1	1
1	0	1
1	1	1

B Practical circuit diagram – The battery connections are missed out for reasons of clarity.

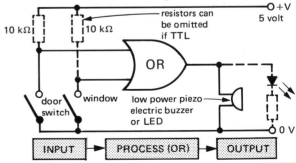

| INPUT | PROCESS (OR) | OUTPUT |

QUESTIONS / EXERCISES

① (a) What is meant by **digital electronics**? (b) Draw out the five main **logic gate** types using American symbols. (c) Make a **truth table** for an AND gate.

② What differences and advantages do TTL chips and CMOS chips have compared to each other?

An improved burglar alarm

If the burglar shut the door or window after entering the alarm would be turned off. A **latching circuit** (**S–R flip flop** [Set and Reset]) shown below will keep the alarm circuit **on** until **reset**.

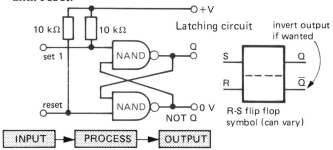

INPUT → PROCESS → OUTPUT

Burglar alarm with 'latched circuit'

Alarm sounds if either switch is closed.

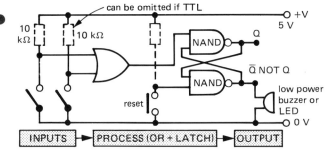

INPUTS → PROCESS (OR + LATCH) → OUTPUT

Real alarms drive a large siren or bell which means a **power transistor** or a **relay** to **interface** the low power circuit with the high current requirements of a large bell. The following circuit could be used (see page 125 for more ideas).

Drive interface for digital work

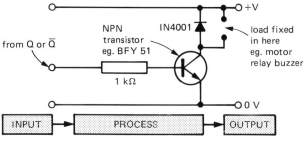

INPUT → PROCESS → OUTPUT

Changing gate types

There are specialist chips but it is often more convenient to connect up the required gates from **NAND** gates (or **NOR**) as shown below to make other logic gates.

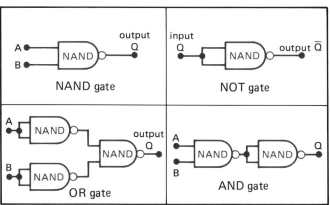

A sensitive switch – electronic latching

The circuit below shows how two (out of four) **NOR** gates on one cheap C-MOS chip (4093) are used to produce a **latching circuit** (two **NOR** gates are connected to produce two **NOT** gates). The high value resistor (about 10 M ohm) makes it sensitive enough to operate by touch.

Touch sensitive switch (on-off)

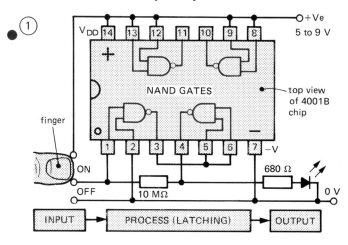

INPUT → PROCESS (LATCHING) → OUTPUT

Counting in binary (with flip flops)

By connecting T type **flip flops** (Toggling) in series as shown below, the input pulses are **divided** by **two** at each stage. Three **flip flops** will divide by eight. The first stage divides by 2, the second divides it again making 4 and the third one divides again making 8. A fourth stage would divide by 16 etc....

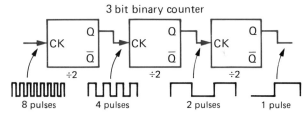

Counting in tens (decimal)

A **decade up/down counter** can be used. It contains **four flip flops** connected internally to count 0–9. (0000 to 0101 in **binary**) It also has a **reset** facility. This chip is shown connected to a **seven segment display** via a **driver chip**.

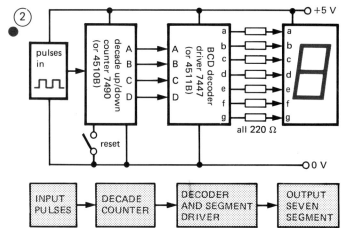

INPUT PULSES → DECADE COUNTER → DECODER AND SEGMENT DRIVER → OUTPUT SEVEN SEGMENT

QUESTIONS/EXERCISES

① (a) Design a **burglar alarm** (digital) that indicates if the front door **or** the safe is opened. It must stay on once 'triggered' and operate a **mains** siren.

② (a) How could two **NAND** gates be used to make an **AND** gate. (b) How could a train of input pulses be divided up into 16s using **flip flops**?

Questions involving logic

Example Design a system which makes sure A **or** B **and** C safety devices are in place before a machine can be started.

Possible answer with **truth table.**

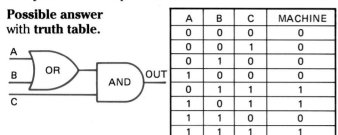

A	B	C	MACHINE
0	0	0	0
0	0	1	0
0	1	0	0
1	0	0	0
0	1	1	1
1	0	1	1
1	1	0	0
1	1	1	1

Problem 1 Design a greenhouse watering system that must only come **on** when the soil is dry **and** it is night time to make use of cheap 'off peak' electricity.

Problem 2 Design a fire alarm that must sound when either a fire occurs or a check is needed on whether the system is working properly.

Problem 3 Design a **washing machine** that can only work if the machines water is hot **and** the door is closed but **not** if the water supply pressure is low. Two **AND** gates and a **NOT** gate could be used.

Alternative inputs

In a **real digital electronic** circuit various types of **input** are required. For example the switches on the alarm circuit (page 126) could be replaced with any of the following sensors. The **variable resistor** allows adjustment. If the **variable resistor** and the **sensor** are changed round the effect is **opposite** (inverted).

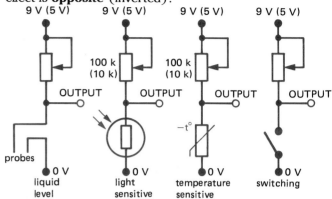

The circuits are correct for CMOS. TTL variations are shown in brackets but TTL circuits will work without the variable resistors.

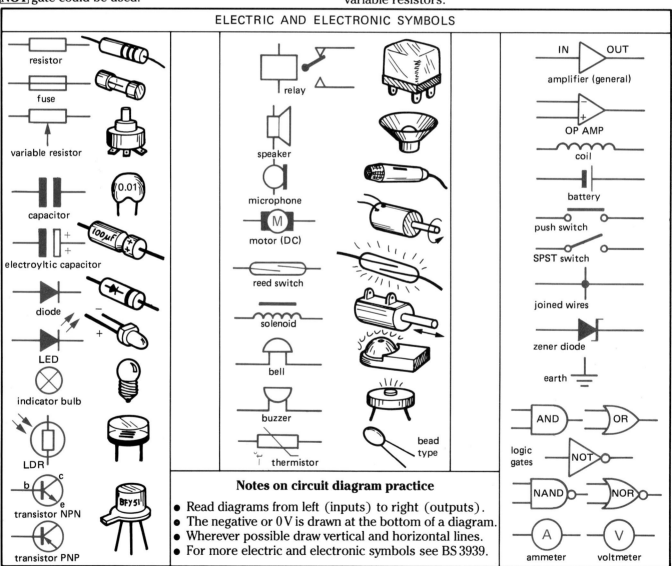

ELECTRIC AND ELECTRONIC SYMBOLS

resistor, fuse, variable resistor, capacitor, electroyltic capacitor, diode, LED, indicator bulb, LDR, transistor NPN, transistor PNP

relay, speaker, microphone, motor (DC), reed switch, solenoid, bell, buzzer, thermistor, bead type

amplifier (general), OP AMP, coil, battery, push switch, SPST switch, joined wires, zener diode, earth

logic gates: AND, OR, NOT, NAND, NOR, ammeter, voltmeter

Notes on circuit diagram practice

- Read diagrams from left (inputs) to right (outputs).
- The negative or 0 V is drawn at the bottom of a diagram.
- Wherever possible draw vertical and horizontal lines.
- For more electric and electronic symbols see BS 3939.

QUESTIONS / EXERCISES

① Draw the following symbols: **Resistor, variable resistor, capacitor, diode, LED, bulb, LDR, transistor, relay, thermistor, battery** and **bell.**

② Draw the following symbols: **Motor, reed switch, buzzer, OP AMP, zener diode,** and **and, nor, not, nand, or,** gates.

Short questions

(1) List ten products that make use of electronics.

(2) Name four **measuring instruments** used in electronics or electrical work.

(3) Name two electrically **conducting** materials, two **insulators** and a **semiconductor** material.

(4) What do the following symbols mean M, p, μ, n when used with resistors or capacitors? Write out in full (using numbers) the following: 1.2 kohm and 0.1 μF.

(5) Explain with examples the difference between **analogue** and **digital** displays.

(6) Name the parts A, B, C, D, E, F, G and H in the circuit below. What could this circuit be used for?

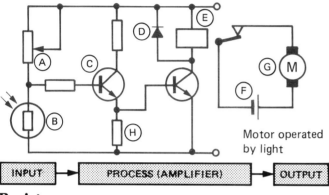

Motor operated by light

Resistors

(7) What resistance values do the following resistors have: (a) yellow, violet, and orange? (b) brown, red and black? If the last resistor had a tolerance of 5% what would its maximum and minimum value be?

(8) A 6 ohm resistor is connected across a 12 volt power supply. What is the power dissipated (in watts) by the resistor?

(9) What is the total resistance of two resistors, 100 kΩ and 500 kΩ, connected in (a) **series** and (b) **parallel**?

(10) Why is a **voltage divider** used in transistor circuits?

(11) Why is a resistor connected in **series** with an LED when connected to a 5 volt power supply?

Other

(12) Draw the symbols for a **non electrolytic capacitor** and an **electrolytic capacitor.** (b) Name two properties of a capacitor.

(13) Draw a NPN **transistor** and explain what the letters c, b and e stand for.

(14) Draw a **plan** view of a 8 pin DIL package such as the 555 timer and indicate how it is **numbered**.

(15) Draw a **truth table** for a |NOT| an |OR| and an |AND| gate.

(16) Draw **truth tables** for the following circuits:

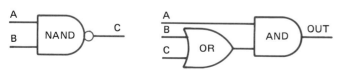

(17) Draw a **power supply** circuit that could be used to convert 250 volt **mains voltage** (alternating current) into 9 volt DC suitable for use in a tape recorder.

Longer questions

(1) Sketch a **light operated** electronic circuit that operates a relay, then using a coloured pen draw the extra wires needed to **latch** it on.

(2) (a) Draw a **flashing light** circuit (astable multivibrator) of your choice, then indicate which **two** components could be varied to alter the flashing rate. (b) What does a **mark space ratio** of 2 to 1 mean? Explain with the use of a diagram.

(3) (a) What main property does a **flip flop** circuit have? (b) Name two applications for a circuit with 'flip flops' in. (c) What do the letters Q and $\bar{Q}$ refer to on the 'flip flop' symbol?

(4) Draw a practical **burglar alarm circuit** using **digital electronics** that **latches** 'on' if either a **window** or the **safe door** is opened.

(5) The **light sensitive circuit** below operates a counter that requires 16 volts. (a) Redraw the transistor symbol and label the connections. (b) What do the + and − mean on the op amp? (c) What are parts labelled A B C D E called?

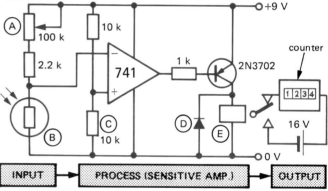

(6) (a) Name the components A, B, C and D of the **thermometer** circuit below. (b) How can the **gain** (sensitivity) be adjusted. (c) How would you **calibrate** the meter? (d) What would the **gain** be if the R_f resistor is set to 60 kΩ?

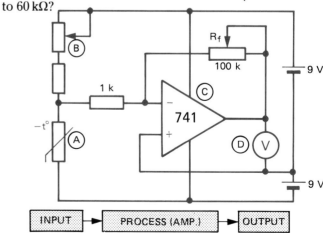

(7) Draw electronic circuits that could be used to:
(a) Make a bulb **flash on** and **off** at various frequencies.
(b) **Count people** entering a museum with the aid of a light beam across the door.

ELECTRONICS QUESTIONS

COMPUTERS IN CDT

Introduction

Computers can help us in CDT in many ways. This section of the book concentrates mainly on controlling devices which have motors or bulbs etc, such as buggies. This introductory page shows various uses that computers can be used for in CDT.

Note – In order to control motors and other devices that use more than a few milliwatts of electricity a suitable **control interface** is needed (such as that shown below) in order to protect the computer from damage and to allow an external power supply to be used to power the motors.

A video camera and a digitiser from Commotion used to capture images which can then be manipulated as required.

Controlling a mobile crane using a Barnet Box interface from Commotion. Based on an EZI-DUN Construction Board.

Computers can be linked up to machines such as the Denford Orac lathe shown.

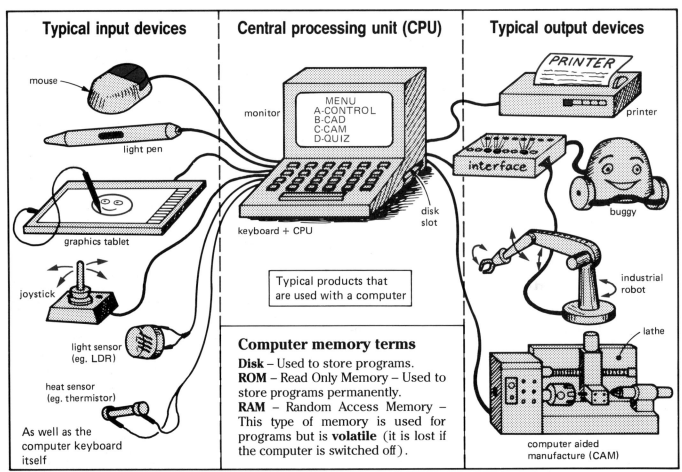

Typical input devices

- mouse
- light pen
- graphics tablet
- joystick
- light sensor (eg. LDR)
- heat sensor (eg. thermistor)

As well as the computer keyboard itself

Central processing unit (CPU)

monitor

MENU
A-CONTROL
B-CAD
C-CAM
D-QUIZ

keyboard + CPU

disk slot

Typical products that are used with a computer

Computer memory terms

Disk – Used to store programs.
ROM – Read Only Memory – Used to store programs permanently.
RAM – Random Access Memory – This type of memory is used for programs but is **volatile** (it is lost if the computer is switched off).

Typical output devices

- printer
- interface
- buggy
- industrial robot
- lathe
- computer aided manufacture (CAM)

QUESTIONS / EXERCISES

① Name four uses a computer can be put to in schools.
② Copy the diagram above but only connect the **input** and **output devices** you would like to use most to the computer (at least two **inputs** and two **output devices**).
③ What do the following abbreviations stand for? **CPU, ROM** and **RAM**.

DIGITAL COMPUTERS

Most modern computers are **digital computers** and work using **binary** numbers. A binary number is made up of either a '0' or a '1' (ie 'ON' or 'OFF'). The values are dependent on which binary columns the number is in (the 0, 1, 2, 4, 8, 16, 32 or 64 value columns etc.) When writing simple control programs it is essential that the **binary system** is understood. Examples below.

Decimal to binary examples

	8	4	2	1	value of columns
1 in binary is	0	0	0	1	
3 in binary is	0	0	1	1	(one 2 and one 1 = 3)
12 in binary is	1	1	0	0	(one 8 and one 4 = 12)

A number system similar to **binary** is the **hexadecimal** system. It divides **binary** numbers up into blocks of 16, counting 0 to 15. **Hexadecimal** numbers are often used in **machine code**. Below is a chart showing how to write numbers in **decimal**, **hexadecimal** and **binary**.

Some decimal, hexadecimal and binary conversions									
decimal		hex. decimal		binary					
10's	1's	16's	1's	32	16	8	4	2	1
	0		0	0	0	0	0	0	0
	1		1	0	0	0	0	0	1
	2		2	0	0	0	0	1	0
	4		4	0	0	0	1	0	0
	9		9	0	0	1	0	0	1
1	0		A	0	0	1	0	1	0
1	2		C	0	0	1	1	0	0
1	5		F	0	0	1	1	1	1
1	6	1	0	0	1	0	0	0	0
4	4	2	C	1	0	1	1	0	0
5	0	3	2	1	1	0	0	1	0
6	3	3	F	1	1	1	1	1	1

Control through the input/output port

In this book the **user port** on the **BBC Computer** is used as the **input/output port** and can be used to control devices such as motors and robots if connected up via a suitable **control interface**. The **input/output port** has **eight** channels or ports which can be used to control eight separate devices 'ON' and 'OFF' or when used in combinations produce effects such as the reversing of electric motors. The **ports** can be arranged as **output** ports, **input** ports or a **mixture** of both. The ports are turned 'ON' or 'OFF' using **binary** or **hexadecimal control code numbers**. The computer code used to turn 'ON' port 1 within a program is ?65120 = 1. *Note* – It is different for other computers eg OUT 63,1 for the **Sinclair**.

A **practical computer course** could be based on the programs marked with a red square: ☐

1 **Type in the following** (with interface connected)

?65122 = 255   This **sets up** the **user port** so they can be used for output control,

?65120 = 1   This turns 'ON' port 1,

?65120 = 3   This turns 'ON' ports 1 and 2 (ie 1 + 2 in binary code),

?65120 = 9   This turns 'ON' ports 1 and 4 (ie 1 + 8 in binary).

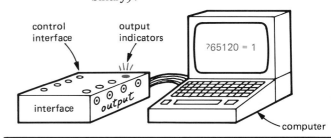

Control interfaces

The **Input/output** port by itself is only capable of driving very small loads (such as LED's). In order to control more powerful devices a **control interface** is needed to protect the computer and provide the power needed for the devices to be controlled. A simple one port interface is shown below (Eight needed for an eight port interface).

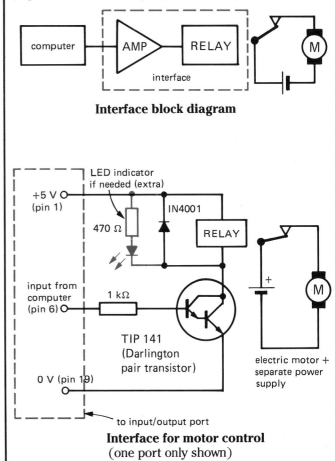

Interface block diagram

Interface for motor control
(one port only shown)

---

① What **base numbers** do the **decimal**, **hexadecimal** and **binary** systems use?

② What two purposes does a **control interface** serve when used to turn 'ON' and 'OFF' large 20 volt electric motors?

③ How would the following numbers be written in the **binary** and **hexadecimal** system? 3, 5, 8, 13, 16, 34, and 52.

2 Program with time delay

Programs with more than one line require a method of **ordering**. In the computer language called BASIC it is done with **line numbers** (usually in steps of **ten**). Below is an example you can try typing into the computer, it will turn 'ON' and 'OFF' devices for a **time** determined by the number in the 'FOR...NEXT' **loop in lines** 20 and 50.

`10  ?65122=255`	'set up' the user port
`20  ?65120=3`	Turns port 1 and 2 'on'
`30  FOR D=1 TO 5000:NEXT D`	5 seconds delay
`40  ?65120=4`	Turns port 3 'on' (4 in binary)
`50  FOR D=1 TO 6000:NEXT D`	6 seconds delay
`60  ?65120=0`	Turns all ports off

When copied out type RUN then press **return** to 'RUN' the program. Add line 100 GOTO 20 to make the program endlessly **repeat**.

3 A versatile control program

This program **can be loaded** from a **disk** if already saved, then RUN it. It can be used to control up to eight outputs in any order or sequence. To alter the sequence the DATA **statements** only are altered, lines 310 onwards. The **first** number after the word DATA is the port that will be turned 'on', as a **decimal** equivalent, the **second** number is the **time** the port stays 'on'. Try changing line 310 to '310 DATA1,900'. Port 1 will then be 'on' for 9 seconds. Your final program can be **saved on disk** for later use.

```
 10 REM *CALLED  "CONTROL"*
 20 ?65122=255
 30 READ port
 40 IFport=-1 THEN 270
 50 IFport=0  PRINT"0000 ALL PORTS OFF"
 60 IFport=1  PRINT"0001 PORTS ON"
 70 IFport=2  PRINT"0010 PORTS ON"
 80 IFport=3  PRINT"0011 PORTS ON"
 90 IFport=4  PRINT"0100 PORTS ON"
100 IFport=5  PRINT"0101 PORTS ON"
110 IFport=6  PRINT"0110 PORTS ON"
120 IFport=7  PRINT"0111 PORTS ON"
130 IFport=8  PRINT"1000 PORTS ON"
140 IFport=9  PRINT"1001 PORTS ON"
150 IFport=10 PRINT"1010 PORTS ON"
160 IFport=11 PRINT"1011 PORTS ON"
170 IFport=12 PRINT"1100 PORTS ON"
180 IFport=13 PRINT"1101 PORTS ON"
190 IFport=14 PRINT"1110 PORTS ON"
200 IFport=15 PRINT"1111 PORTS ON"
210 READ time
220 PRINT"        FOR ";time/100" SECONDS"
230 ?65120=port
240 D=TIME+time
250 REPEAT UNTIL TIME=D
260 GOTO 30
270 ?65120=0
290 PRINT "TO REPEAT TYPE 'RUN' AND PRESS 'RETURN'"
310 DATA9,200
320 DATA3,200
330 DATA6,200
340 DATA12,100
1000 DATA-1
```

If the following lines are added the program will **repeat itself.**

```
270 RESTORE 310: GOTO 30: DATA-1,-1
```

Controlling buggies

A **buggy** can turn in one of two ways as shown below:

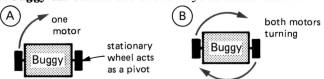

A Only one motor turns – the buggy turns in a large circle pivoting on the stationary wheel.

B Both motors turn but in **opposite directions** thus allowing the buggy to **turn on the spot.**

In order to have maximum control both driving motors need to be able to **reverse** as well as go **forwards**. When a **buggy** is connected up to a **computer interface** for the first time the control codes may need to be found as follows:

Type ?65122 = 255 ⟨ +RETURN⟩ then on a new line ?65120 = 1 to ?65120 = 15 ⟨ +RETURN each time⟩ recording the code numbers that make the buggy go FORWARD, BACKWARD, LEFT, RIGHT and PAUSE.

If help is needed in changing **binary** to **decimal** numbers look at lines 50 to 200 of **program 3.** A different **turning time** is needed for each **buggy** type to **turn** through 90 degrees, time how long it takes to turn through a 90 degree angle then see if you can program your **buggy** to move in a **square** pattern on the floor by amending the following program, **if needed**. The **program lines** and numbers (in brackets) that may need altering are:

```
10 line 40 (=3)    -MOVING FORWARD CODE
20 line 50 (2000)  -TIME MOVING FORWARD
30 line 60 (=5)    -TURN RIGHT CODE
40 line 70 (2000)  -TIME FOR TURNING
```

Note – It is a good idea to make a record of the codes needed eg on the underside of the buggy itself.

4 Buggy moving in a square

```
10 REM CALLED "SQUARE"
20 ?65122=255       :REM SETS UP USER PORT
30 FOR X=1 TO 4
40 ?65120=3:PRINT "FORWARD"
50 FOR D=1 TO 2000:NEXT D
60 ?65120=5:PRINT "RIGHT"
70 FOR D=1 TO 2000:NEXT D
80 NEXT X
90 ?65120=0         :REM STOPS BUGGY
```

The program works as follows: **Buggy** moved **forward** and then **turns** 90 **degrees**, this is then **repeated four** more times. To turn 8 times type 25 FOR X = 1 to 8.

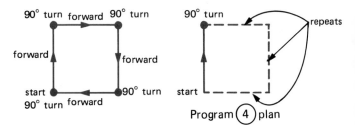

QUESTIONS/EXERCISES

① What **line** of BASIC programming could be used to obtain a 12 second delay (approx)?

② Buggies can be made to **turn on the spot**. Explain what is happening to the two driving wheels to achieve this.

③ What alterations are needed to program **4** above in order to make the **buggy** move in an **octagonal** (eight sided) pattern? Draw the **octagonal** shape first and explain your thinking.

Programing using PROCEDURES

As **programs** get longer and more complicated a programing method using **procedures** is sometimes used. **Procedures** are usually placed at the end of a program. **Program 5** below uses a **procedure** (PROC in Basic) called PROC motion ('motion' must be in small letters as in **lines** 1000 to 1040 below). The program controls a **Buggy** in any **polygon** pattern (eg a hexagon).

A **procedure** starts with **DEFPROC** (DEFine PROcedure) and **ends** with **ENDPROC**.

LOAD and RUN program **5** then alter **line** 60 from 2000 to 6000 and observe the effect it has. (*Note* – **Lines** 20 and 30 may need altering to suit your **buggy**).

5 Buggy control using procedures

```
   1 REM CALLED "POLYGON"
   2 REM BUGGY CONTROL USING A PROCEDURE
  10 ?65122 =255
  20 forward=3 :right=5
  30 turnTIME=9000 :REM ALTER turnTIME IF NEEDED
  40 INPUT "NUMBER OF SIDES ",sides
  50 FOR number=1 TO sides
  60 PROCmotion(forward,2000)
  70 PROCmotion(right,turnTIME/sides)
  80 NEXT number
  90 REM TYPE '90 GOTO 50' TO LOOP
 100 END
1000 DEFPROCmotion(direction,time)
1010 ?65120=direction
1020 FOR D=1 TO time:NEXT          PROCEDURE
1030 ?65120=0
1040 ENDPROC
```

Problem Make the **buggy** move in a square pattern (300 mm square).

Using the input ports

So far we have only used the **output ports** to control devices with no **input** into the computer via the **input/output** port. The **user port** on **BBC** computers can have any combination of **input** or **outputs** (eight ports maximum) by using the correct **control code**.

Below are two examples of **control codes**.
?65122 = 255 –Sets all ports for output
(**ie 225** = 128 + 64 + 32 + 16 + 8 + 4 + 2 + 1)
?65120 = 15 –Set 4 ports **input** and 4 **output**
(ie 15 = 8 + 4 + 2 + 1)
Your **control interface** probably has its **ports** marked as shown below. Sometimes the **ports** are referred to by BIT (short for **binary digits**) **numbers** as shown below.

Input/output connections
(Called 'user port' on BBC)

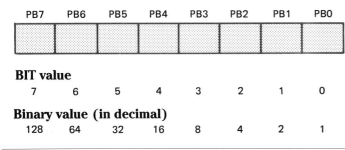

PB7	PB6	PB5	PB4	PB3	PB2	PB1	PB0

BIT value

7	6	5	4	3	2	1	0

Binary value (in decimal)

128	64	32	16	8	4	2	1

In program **6** below **four outputs** can be used to control devices such as electric motors, bulbs etc and the other **four ports** used for **sensors**, such as reed switches sensors, which are connected to the **input ports**.

6 Using input/output ports

```
 1 REM CALLED "IN/OUT"
 2 REM OUTPUTS TRIGGERED IF PB4 INPUT 'ON'
10 ?65122=15
20 ?65120=0:PRINT"NOT YET TRIGGERED"
30 IF?65120=16 THEN ?65120=15:GOTO 80
40 IF?65120=32 THEN ?65120=15:GOTO 80
50 IF?65120=64 THEN ?65120=15:GOTO 80
60 IF?65120=128THEN ?65120=15:GOTO 80
70 GOTO 20
80 CLS:PRINT" INPUT TRIGGERED "
```

Problem – LOAD and RUN program **6** then alter **line** 30 so that only ports PB0 and PB3 are switched '**ON**' when the switch is triggered.

Note 1 – connect bulbs to ports PB0, PB1, PB2, PB3 and a sensor switch to PB4 or PB4 or PB5 or PB5.
Note 2 – **Control interfaces** without any **input** facilities are not suitable.

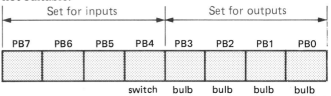

	Set for inputs				Set for outputs		
PB7	PB6	PB5	PB4	PB3	PB2	PB1	PB0
		switch			bulb	bulb	bulb	bulb

Input/output connections set when ?65120 = 15

Motor speed control

When using a digital computer the speed of a motor cannot be controlled by changing the voltage so the method used is to turn the *electric power* 'ON' and 'OFF'. The **time** ON to the **time** OFF ratio is also called the **mark space ratio**.

LOAD and RUN program **7**. When TIME ON? appears on the screen type 60 and then press **return**. When TIME OFF? appears on the screen type 20 and then press **return**.

Problem Get the motor to rotate at about half the previous speed.

7 Controlling a motor's speed

```
 1 REM CALLED "SPEED"
10 ?65122=255
20 INPUT"TIME ON",Y:INPUT"TIME OFF"Z
30 ?65120=3          :REM FORWARD
40 FOR D=1 TO Y:NEXT :REM TIME ON
50 ?65120=0          :REM MOTOR
60 FOR D=1 TO Z:NEXT :REM TIME OFF
70 GOTO 30           :REM LOOP
```

Mark space ratios

Fast speed (**ON** more **time** than **OFF**)

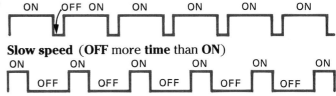

Slow speed (**OFF** more **time** than **ON**)

QUESTIONS/EXERCISES

① Draw the **input/output** connections to the computer with the **BIT** and **binary** values (ignore battery connections).

② What would be the **decimal** value and **hexadecimal** value of the following binary numbers? 10101010, 11111110 and 11000011.

THE ANALOGUE PORT

The previous examples have used **digital inputs** or **outputs** (ie '**ON**' or '**OFF**' controls) but sometimes it is better to use **analogue input** signals so that varying analogue voltage inputs coming from **temperature** or **light sensors** etc can be measured. To do this the **analogue port** (sometimes called the **joystick port**) is used. Because the computer is a digital device an **analogue** to **digital converter** (ADC) chip is used, within the BBC computer. To make life simple the **analogue port** has a 1.8 volt supply so that resistive components such as a **variable resistor** or **thermistor** can be connected directly to **inputs** 1, 2, 3 or 4; any change in the resistance is sensed by the computer as a changing voltage (**maximum** of 1.8 volts). The **call up** code for the **analogue port** is **ADVAL** (1) for **channel** 1 and **ADVAL** (2) for **channel** 2. Program 8 opposite shows a typical application. A **graph of movement** is drawn on the screen when the 100 k ohm **variable resistor** is turned. LOAD and RUN program 8 after connecting the **variable resistor** up as indicated below. (It can be connected up directly, as shown below, but is best connected up via an analogue plug and cable).

Note – No separate **interface** is needed.

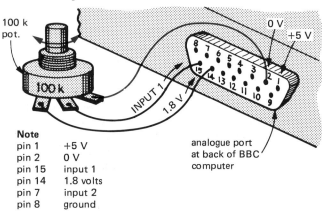

```
Note
pin 1    +5 V
pin 2    0 V
pin 15   input 1
pin 14   1.8 volts
pin 7    input 2
pin 8    ground
```

8 Analogue graphs

```
1REM CALLED "GRAPH"
2REM ANALOGUE PORT INPUT GRAPH DRAWN
10 MODE 0
20 FOR N=0 TO 1279 :REM SCREEN WIDTH
30 DRAW N, ADVAL(1)/16 : REM INPUT ON
40 NEXT
50 GOTO 10
```

Exercise Add a **light dependent resistor** (LDR) in **series** with the **red wire, light levels** can **then** be recorded as a graph. (Adjust **sensitivity** – 16 in **line** 30).

A note on stepper motors

A **stepper motor** is a special type of motor that moves in small steps, of 7.5 degrees for one type, as it rotates. If the motor is pulsed 4 times the motor moves $4 \times 7.5 = 30$ degrees. As you can imagine they are used for accurate work. Computer printers and plotters used stepper motors to ensure the printout is correct. Consult a specialist book for more details.

A LEGO® robot being used to pick up a white rubber and place it as required. It has three motors. The robot's position at any time is recorded by the LEGO Opto sensors and discs.

1 Give the full meaning of the following abbreviations: ROM, RAM, ADC (or A to D) and EPROM.

2 What **decimal code number** would be needed to turn the **lamp** and **motor** '**ON**' using the **BIT** information provided below.

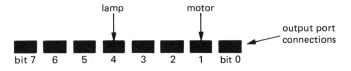

3 The following **BIT** numbers were fed out from the **output ports** of a computer.

00000111 00011111 **and** 10010110.

What **hexadecimal** numbers do these **binary** numbers represent?

4 (a) What purpose does an **output control interface** serve if used for electric motor control work?

(b) Draw a **one port interface circuit** diagram suitable for operating a large lamp or a motor.

5 What devices would you use to sense the following when used with a computer:

Heat, light and **angular movement**?

6 A teacher requires one demonstration set of **traffic lights** that is operated by a computer. The lamps to be used are car head light bulbs (36 watt) operated from a car battery via an **interface**.

(a) Write down the **traffic light sequence** then,

(b) Write a **computer program** that turns the lights on and off in sequence, with appropriate time delays, refer to program **2** for help.

7 **A burglar alarm** for a house makes use of **four sensors**, a **siren** and a mains operated flashing **lamp** which are linked to a **computer** via the **input/output** port.

(a) Write a **computer program** that will respond to any of the **sensors** (eg reed switches) being activated. The **siren** and **lamp** are then turned **ON** for about two minutes.

(b) Describe **two additional features** a more sophisticated alarm system could include.

COMPUTER CONTROL QUESTIONS

TECHNOLOGY IN SOCIETY

Technology is neither **good** or **bad**; it is **neutral** but can be used by people in better or worse ways. It is up to us, the human race, to decide what is actually allowed to happen. This can be affected through the way we choose to live, our work, through pressure groups and the kind of policies adopted by political parties.

Technology has enabled us to:

- Have a **high standard of living**.
- **Fly in aeroplanes** to hot countries for holidays.
- Have 'clean' **central heating systems** in the home.
- Own **cars** and **video** recorders.
- **Communicate** with people in other parts of the world.
- Make special **aids for handicapped people**, etc.

There are **side effects** that accompany **technological** change. Some of these effects become a problem when the **environment** and **ecosystem** cannot cope. If the world's **population** continues to increase and the demand for an even higher **standard of living** continues the problems will become even more acute. Below are some of the problems we are presently facing:

Carbon monoxide and **Carbon dioxide** levels are building up in the atmosphere due to exhaust emissions from cars, lorries and from industry. Some scientists believe it could effect the worlds weather. In Los Angeles (USA) there is often a smog cloud covering the city.

Sulphur dioxide is emitted in quite large quantities from **coal burning power station** chimneys. It combines with the air and rain forming a dilute **sulphuric acid** which is killing trees in some parts of the world and dissolving the limestone of some ancient monuments.

Nitrogen fertilizers in the form of **nitrates of ammonia** is used by farmers to increase yields. Some of it is finding its way into the water supplies giving a high **nitrate** count. Baby foods must now use **low nitrate** water in their manufacture.

Radioactive waste products from **nuclear power stations**, comes in various forms some of which have a '**half life**' of over a thousand years. This means the waste products must be kept away from people for thousands of years in concrete or glass containers. Too much **radioactivity** can cause **genetic defects** and in severe cases death.

A famous nuclear power plant fire at **Chernobyl**, Russia, in 1986, caused a major rethink about nuclear power. Some local people died and in the United Kingdom it led to a ban on the sale of home produced sheep meat products.

One of the main problems with any new technology is that the bad side effects are not always obvious so exhaustive testing is very important before it is applied on a large scale.

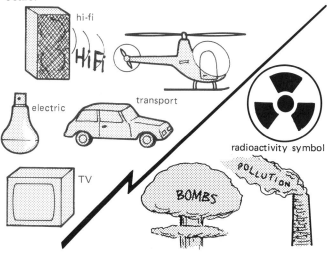

Standard of living

As our material **standard of living** and **income** has increased, so has the amount of **energy consumed**. It has been estimated that the average American family, with their cars, large houses, heating bills, lawn mowers, dish washers, doctors fees, holidays, consume energy that would be equal to employing 300 slaves. In the poorest countries most people have few if any luxuries, they have to make or find everything from food to the clothes they wear.

The developed countries consume most of the world's oil and resources.

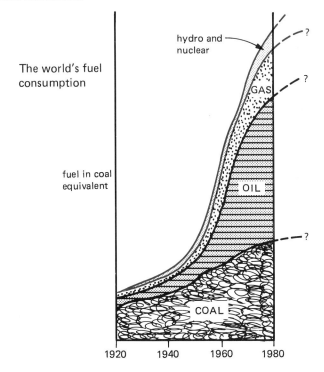

QUESTIONS/EXERCISES

① Give four good uses technology has been put to to benefit the human race and then four bad side effects.

② What is **oil, coal, and gas** used for in an industrialised country?

③ In what way is **the emission of sulphur dioxide** from chimneys causing problems?

The graph at the bottom of the last page showing the **world's fuel consumption** illustrates how important **oil** has become to industrial countries. The **world's population** growth follows a similar graph shape.

Energy saving

A vast amount of energy is wasted in heating houses and in industrial processes. Much of this could be saved by better **insulation** and careful **design of new buildings**. If this was done there would not need to be as many power stations.

Below are a few other ways of saving energy. Can you think of a few more?

- **Recycling materials** such as glass and plastics.

- **Energy management** using timers or computer control.

- Alter our life styles – become more self sufficient and less wasteful.

- **Use the waste heat from power stations** to heat homes etc (60% of the energy is wasted).

- Making **products last longer** (eg clothes and cars).

- **Taxing** the high energy users more (eg large car owners).

- Trapping the so called '**free energy**' such as the sun and wind.

A low energy house

There are some houses designed to use very little energy from the 'mains'; below is an example of such a house.

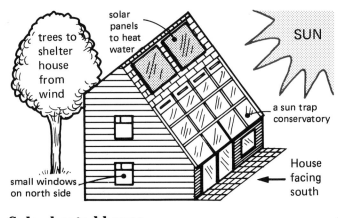

trees to shelter house from wind

solar panels to heat water

SUN

a sun trap conservatory

House facing south

small windows on north side

Solar heated house

It will also have very good **insulation** and perhaps a **heat pump** to recover low grade heat from inside the building.

A change of life style

Many people's **life styles** have been affected by the way life is now organised. The **values** needed to cope with this technological society may be different to those of your parents.

Below are changes that have occurred in recent times.

- Some people **commute** long distances to work.
- **Hypermarket** shopping.
- More **reliance on professional people** such as dentists, engineers, solicitors etc.
- People **live a lot longer**.
- Obtaining information from **television**.
- **Noise** due to air and road transport.
- **Entertainment** in fun parks and amusement arcades.
- **Cleaner working environments** for most workers.
- **Mass production** giving cheaper, more reliable products.
- **More competition** from overseas countries.
- **Package deal holidays**.
- Need for a more **technological education** for all, and its effects on society.
- A **cashless society** (plastic money).
- Some people feel **dehumanised**.
- More **bureaucracy**.
- **The centralisation of information** (eg police files).
- Becoming **unemployed** due to new technology.
- **Women** entering traditionally men only jobs.
- Whether to have more than **one or two children**.
- **More** families **break up**.
- Whether to keep up with **high fashion**.
- The pressures to **conform** and buy more products, even if not needed.
- Some people are in danger of living in a world of 'make believe' as provided by the media.

Possible growth industries

Below is a list of possible growth industries:

**Transport,
Information technology (IT),
Tourism and leisure,
Security,
Education,
Social services,
Service industries,
Micro electronics and computing.**

---

1 What do you understand by **recycling products** and **materials, hi-technology, waste products, insulation** and **our environment**?

2 Give the **benefits** and the bad **side effects** of the following: – Aeroplanes, videos, computers and convenience foods.

3 Is it practical to share the worlds material wealth more evenly if it means that the rich countries become poorer? Discuss.

4 Do you think the following question should be asked by designers about a new project such as a factory or a new perfume? 'Is the project really necessary and what effects will it have on the environment?''

5 (a) What typical things would a rich family, in this country, use and consume and use each day at home and going to work or college?
(b) What things would a very poor person use each day in a 'third world' country to stay alive?

6 Discuss the following quote, giving reasons. 'No family should have more than two children'.

TECHNOLOGY IN SOCIETY QUESTIONS

TECHNOLOGICAL PROJECT IDEAS

Over 250 ideas here

General

A person sensor/counter
Air powered vehicle
Aquarium feeder
Automatic food dispenser
Automatic plant feeder
Baby alarm
Bike security device
Circle compass
Coin sorter
Distance measuring – eg map roller
Doorbell for a deaf person
Electric powered bike
Engine testbed
Hero's slot machine
Liquid level indicator
Mist propagator for plants
Model fork lift truck
Model garage door opener
Moving toy
Obstacle race
People counter
Photoelastic analyser
Photograph holder
Plastic moulding machines
Play centre
Polythene sheet sealer
Projectile device
Rainfall recorder
Reaction timer
Scales
Seismograph
Slot machine
Strength tester
Vehicle up a slope
Wake a deaf person
Water level indicator
Weather station
Weighing machine
Wind direction indicator

Electrics/electronics and computers

Advertisement display with lights
Aerial direction controller
Ammeter
Amplifier
Bar strip reader
Bike lamp or lock
Bleeper
Burglar alarm
Camping light
Car alarm
Combination lock
Communication system
Computer aided design
Computer control of vehicle etc
Computer oscilloscope
Continuity tester
Counter–People/objects
Digitiser
Disco effects
Disco music mixer
Distance detector
Doorbell
Drama show
Electro-plating
Electronic dice
Electronic jewellery
Electronic organ
Fire or cold alarm
Flashing light
Fruit type machine
Fuse tester
Game for school fair
Graphics tablet
Hotwire cutter for expanded
  polystyrene
Illuminated display
Intercom
Joystick
Joystick–Control of vehicle
Light display
Light meter
Light pen
Lighthouse
Lighting level controller
Live wire detector
Logic probe

Metal detector
Metronome
Moisture detector
Music device or instrument
Noise meter
Optical communication
Personal slide viewer
Piped light sign
Plant propagator
Plotter
Porch lamp
Powered vehicle
Quiz
Race timer
Radio
Rain alarm
Reaction timer
Remote ON and OFF controller
Robot
Scoring system
Signal generator
Signal generator
Smoke detector
Sound activated device
Sound meter
Sound to light system
Speed controller
Stage lighting control
Steady hand game
Stepper motor interface
Tachometer
Tape recorder control of devices
Teaching aid for handicapped
Teaching machine
Television planner/timer
Theatre effects
Time delay
Timing device eg for photography
Traffic lights
Train controller
Train set controller
Using a circuit to make a ?
Washing line — (wet/dry indicator)
White line follower
Windspeed indicator
X–Y machine tool control

Also see page 43 for mainly craft projects

QUESTIONS/EXERCISES

① Which **ten technological project ideas** would you like to make? Use the lists above to help you.

② Select then sketch **two project ideas** you would like, given 6 hours to make it.

③ Make a **list of the technological project work** you have completed at school and at at home.

Structures

Air supported support
Bridges
Car layout in a monocoque shell
Geodesic domes
High free standing structure
Joint tester
Kites
Ladder steady
Lifting bridge
Marble jump game
Model futuristic house
Model town
Polaroid stress analysis
Ski lift towers
Spaceframe structure (no joints)
Strain gauges
Strength tester
Towers
Workbench

Energy

Boat (elastic powered)
Calorie counter
Competition – Fastest vehicle
Competition – Furthest
Competition – Pull the largest load
Competition – Up the steepest slope
Dynamometer
Electricity from the sun
Engine tester (for power)
Heat pump
House heating/lighting etc
Human energy tester/exerciser
Insulation
Insulated house testing
Model house/power station
Plant growth recorder
Projectile
Rubber band powered vehicle
Solar panel/heater
Steam engine
Temperature measurement
Turbine powered device
Wind powered vehicle
Yacht

Aerodynamics

Aerial photography – From a kite
Aerodynamics
Aerofoil
Aeroplane – Round the pole
Air track
Anemometer
Boat hull testing
Boomerang
Drag tester
Glider
Hot air balloon
Hovercraft
Jet engine
Kites
Landyacht
Lift a heavy load
Paint sprayer
Parachute
Round the pole hovercraft
Storing wind energy
Streamlining a vehicle
Vacuum or blowing pump
Wind speed measurement

Hydraulics, pneumatics and fluidics

Airbrush
Automatic vice
Badge maker/stamp
Boat hull shape testing
Car park barrier
Dome maker
Drill control
Drink dispenser
Food slicer
Fun rocking horses
Garage door opener
Hero's fountain
Hydraulic tensile tester
Joint tester
Lathe tool control
Linear air Track
Model – Crane, forklift, arm etc
Model braking systems
Printing press
Punching or stamping machine
Tensile testing
Using syringes as cylinders
Vacuum former
Vehicle that tips/moves
Walking machine

Mechanisms

Brake system
Catapult
Clock, eg water clock
Compass
Crank shaft then add fun things
Drilling machine
Drink dispenser
Engraver copier (pantograph idea)
Fair ground
Folding chair
Fork lift truck
Harmonograph
Kart
Map reader (distance)
Mini lathe
Model of a man riding bike
Model vehicles
Moving face
Moving model insect
Moving (kinetic) sculpture
Music operated by cams and levers
Musical instrument
Nodding toys
Pantograph
Pedal car
Piano
Portable workbench
Proportional dividers
Puppets
Ski lift
Steering system
Teaching machine
Theodolite
Using a crankshaft make a ?
Vehicle to climb up a steep slope
Walking robot
Weighing machines
Weight powered vehicle
Wind powered generator

QUESTIONS/EXERCISES

1. (a) How can **surveys be carried out** that give as true a result as possible?
(b) Carry out a **survey on behalf of your teacher** to find out which projects individuals in the class would like to undertake.
2. List and sketch **three projects** that you could undertake for your major technological project.

INDEX